Remaking Foreign Policy

Remaking Foreign Policy:

The Organizational Connection

JX
1706
.A86
West

GRAHAM ALLISON

&

PETER SZANTON

Basic Books, Inc., Publishers

NEW YORK

The Council on Foreign Relations, Inc., is a non-profit and non-partisan organization devoted to promoting improved understanding of international affairs through the free exchange of ideas. Its membership of about 1,700 persons throughout the United States is made up of individuals with special interest and experience in international affairs. The Council has no affiliation with, and receives no funding from, the United States government. The Council does not take any position on questions of foreign policy.

The Council publishes the quarterly journal, *Foreign Affairs*. In addition, from time to time, books and monographs written by members of the Council's research staff or visiting fellows, or commissioned by the Council, or (like this book) written by independent authors with critical review contributed by a Council study group, are published with the designation "Council on Foreign Relations Book" or "Council Paper on International Affairs." Any book or monograph bearing that designation is, in the judgment of the Committee on Studies of the Council's board of directors, a responsible treatment of a significant international topic worthy of presentation to the public. All statements of fact and expressions of opinion contained in Council books, monographs, and *Foreign Affairs* articles are, however, the sole responsibility of their authors.

The authors gratefully acknowledge permission to reprint Chapter 9, in somewhat altered form, from *Foreign Policy* 22 (Spring 1976).

For E. K. M. A. and J. G. S.

Contents

Preface

FOR a decade and a half, the major participants in American foreign policy have found the organization of the U.S. government profoundly frustrating. As James Reston put it recently:

> There have been so many puzzles here over the conduct of American foreign policy in the last couple of years that the notion is getting around that the President and Congress can't agree on anything, but this is not precisely true. On at least one thing they are in total agreement: that the present decision-making "system," if that's the right word, is an incoherent mess, excessively irritating to both branches of the government and dangerous to the national interest.[1]

The deepest source of this frustration is that the power necessary to the conduct of foreign policy is fragmented—diffused among executive agencies and departments, congressional committees and subcommittees, industries, labor unions, ethnic associations. That circumstance is not new in kind, but it is quite new in degree, and it is compounded by a constraining organizational legacy. The present structure of the U.S. government for the conduct of foreign policy dates largely from the late 1940s, especially from 1947, when the National Security Act at one stroke unified the Department of Defense, created the CIA, and established the National Security Council as the principal forum for presidential deliberation and decision in foreign affairs. That structure was appropriate to its time—a time when foreign relations were dominated by an overriding military threat, when the U.S. economy was relatively autonomous, when "politics stopped at the water's edge," and when Congress deferred to presidential judgment in matters of foreign policy.

Times have changed. "Foreign" policy has almost disappeared as a distinct and specialized realm. The tightening economic and physical interdependence of nations causes actions in one country to affect the daily lives and therefore the domestic politics of others. Responsibilities for policies that concern foreign governments are now held not only by the departments of State, Treasury, and Defense but by Agriculture, Labor, Commerce, Transportation, the Energy Administration—virtually every major agency except HUD. Authority is now divided between the Executive and Congress not only in constitutional theory but in fact, a result partially of the reaction to Vietnam and Watergate, but more importantly because interdependence has thrust foreign policy into domestic politics. And congressional authority is itself broadly dispersed, partly because foreign policy issues cut across committee jurisdictions, partly because recent congressional leadership has been weak. Moreover, influence important to the conduct of foreign policy is now also divided between the government and the private sector, a result of the multinationalization of key industries and of the growing importance of economic factors—food production, inflation, the growth of the nuclear power industry—on the foreign policy agenda. Finally, power is more widely spread among nations. It is held not solely by two super states, or a "Big Five," but by six or eight nations of great size or productive strength, and a dozen others of middling population, ambition, technical accomplishment, or important natural resources. Yet the organizational framework of the late 1940s—the filter that largely determines the problems our government attends to, the information it is provided, the choices it is presented, the decisions it makes and the actions it takes—that framework remains largely unchanged.

The resulting mismatch between the work at hand and the means available for dealing with it is not simply inefficient; it is dangerous. It largely accounts for fifteen years of intermittent White House efforts to govern without the government—

a circumvention of the cabinet departments and the Congress that has deepened the isolation of the President, demoralized able bureaucracies and embittered executive-congressional relations. It partially accounts for the tendency of Congress to focus on details of policy, neglecting its harder and more important role of policy review. It accounts for doubt at home and abroad about U.S. purposes and capacities. And its consequences are likely to grow steadily worse. Change, we believe, is imperative.

Organizational reform is difficult. Yet a time of change now seems at hand. The last two elected Presidents were driven from office. Popular discontent with both the scale and the performance of the American government has reached historic highs. Demoralized by a decade of disuse, especially in the foreign affairs agencies, the elements of a system of government intended to function through interaction await repair, refurbishing, and a new infusion of energy. The Bicentennial encourages reassessment and reminds us of ambitious standards. The Presidential campaign highlights promises of change. In short, the period just ahead offers the best opportunity since the late 1940s for important organizational reform.

To cope with the great domestic problems of health, housing, employment, welfare, inflation, and economic growth, radical reconstruction of both policy and machinery will be required. Effective management of those problems will necessitate terminating programs, disbanding some government agencies and merging others, and reassigning responsibility among the federal, state, and local levels of government. Only a determined President working effectively with strong Congressional leadership over many years, and doing so on the basis of a shared vision of desired change, will be able to accomplish such far-reaching changes.

Equally radical reforms in the organization of the government for the conduct of foreign affairs might also be proposed. In this book, such reforms are suggested only in passing, since—as we shall try to demonstrate—most of the gains *most of the* to be had from organizational reform in foreign affairs can be achieved through less formal, more subtle and far more feasible changes. Indeed, many of these reforms might be substantially accomplished by a determined President operating alone.

The purpose of this book is to propose such reforms. As a basis for those proposals we suggest a perspective on the nature and function of government organization that, we hope, may prove useful more broadly in understanding American government. But our intention has been to produce neither a scholarly treatise nor a detailed blueprint for action. Rather, it has been to trace the organizational sources of failure in our international relations, to anticipate some major characteristics of the near future, to identify reform likely to improve foreign policymaking in such a future, and to present our evidence and conclusions throughout as simply and non-technically as we can.

The book has three main parts. Chapters 1 to 3 establish a base. Chapter 1 suggests how organization matters and what it does; Chapter 2 identifies important and characteristic failings of recent U.S. foreign relations and suggests their organizational connections; Chapter 3 shows how, if left untended, such failings are likely to prove even more damaging in the next decade than they were in the last. Chapters 4 to 6 discuss in order the central institutions in the management of our foreign relations: the Presidency, the Congress and the Department of State. These chapters assess the recent performance of each, reassess the roles appropriate to each, and suggest the organizational reforms those roles require. The next three chapters review more specifically how the government's performance in foreign economics, defense, and intelligence might be improved.

Only the authors, of course, are responsible for what follows. But our debts are deep and numerous. We have drawn heavily on the studies performed for the Murphy Commission (the Commission on the Organization of the Government for the Conduct of Foreign Policy), of which Peter Szanton was research director and Graham Allison was principal researcher for defense and arms control studies. In Washington, Les Aspin, William I. Bacchus, John Bross, William J. Barnds, C. Fred Bergsten, David Cohen, Fisher Howe, John Huizenga, Robert G. Livingston, Joseph Kirsheimer, Robert Komer, Andrew W. Marshall, Clark McFadden, Benjamin H. Read, Allen Schick, Gregory Treverton, Harrison Wellford, and R. James Woolsey read portions of the book in draft; each offered useful comments. In Cambridge, William M. Capron, Franklin Lindsay, Ernest R. May, Ed McGaffigan, Richard E. Neustadt, Don K. Price, John Steinbruner did the same. We are grateful to the members of a Survey Discussion Group of the Council on Foreign Relations, who in six meetings in the fall and winter of 1975–76 reviewed initial drafts, challenging data, theory and conclusions; they were Morton I. Abramowitz, William E. Brock III, Dean Brown, Ray S. Cline, I. M. Destler, Lawrence S. Eagleburger, Peter M. Flanigan, Alton Frye, David C. Gompert, Gen. Andrew J. Goodpaster, Morton H. Halperin, Thomas L. Hughes, John N. Irwin II, Nicholas DeB. Katzenbach, Franklin A. Long, Abraham F. Lowenthal, A. L. McDonald, Edwin M. Martin, Joseph S. Nye, John R. Petty, Walter B. Slocombe, Theodore C. Sorensen, John Temple Swing, Richard H. Ullman, and Frederic A. Morris (rapporteur). We are particularly indebted to Council President Bayless Manning who organized and chaired the discussion group; to Francis M. Bator who patiently and persistently tried to educate us about the issues of Chapter 7; to Dean Donald Stokes of the Woodrow Wilson School of Princeton who organized and chaired a seminar on problems of Congressional organization; to Philip H. Trezise who helpfully reviewed the entire manuscript; and to Stephanie Gould who critiqued every page more carefully and helpfully than we deserved. Richard Huff served ably as research assistant, identifying illustrations, clarifying thoughts, and finding citations. Barbara Phillips in Cambridge and Kathy Tanner in

Washington did their remarkable best to turn squiggles in two hands into prose. The freedom of one of us to devote full time to the book was made possible by grants from the Ford and Rockefeller Foundations; the "May Group" of the John F. Kennedy School of Government at Harvard provided partial support for the other.

Our largest debt by far is to the patience, hospitality, and critical reading of one mother, two wives, and three children who, for twice as many months as we had promised them, saw neither of us except when they saw us both.

G.T.A.
P.L.S.

Remaking Foreign Policy

Chapter 1

The Argument: Organization Matters

IN November 1969 President Nixon reversed a policy that had stood for fifty years. He renounced U.S. use of biological weapons, forswore first use of chemical weapons, and ordered the destruction of existing stockpiles of biological munitions. He also announced his intention to sign and submit to the Senate the Geneva Protocol of 1925, the treaty banning chemical and biological weapons (CBW), which had previously been ratified by more than ninety nations, including the Soviet Union, but not by the United States.

While this decision was difficult and controversial, former aides of President Johnson believe that if the issue had reached Johnson in the last year of his administration he would have decided it just as Nixon did. That judgment is conjectural but plausible, and it raises a question: What brought the issue to one President and not to another?

During the war in Vietnam, the United States had made extensive use of chemicals—tear gas and herbicides. The practice was supported by the Joint Chiefs of Staff (JCS) but was criticized, occasionally in public, by officials of the State Department and the Arms Control and Disarmament Agency (ACDA). Annoyed by the criticism, the chiefs in 1967 asked Secretary of Defense McNamara to seek from the President a formal affirmation of the policy of no restraint on use. The procedures of the Johnson administration, like those of most administrations, brought an issue of this sort to the President only if a Cabinet officer were prepared to urge the President to adopt a particular policy. The JCS request thus confronted Secretary McNamara with three alternatives: endorsing the chiefs' proposal despite probable opposition elsewhere; opposing the proposal and urging the President to overrule the JCS; or finding a way to put the issue off. Engaged in other disputes that seemed to him more pressing, McNamara chose to defer conflict; he forwarded the proposal to the State Department for comment.

McNamara's letter confronted Secretary of State Rusk with the same dilemma. He solved it in a similar manner, forwarding the proposal to his Politico-Military Bureau (PM) for preparation of a State Department position. There was no agreement within PM, and when other State bureaus were consulted the deadlock deepened. In March 1968 President Johnson announced that he would not seek reelection; in the remaining ten months of his term the White House searched for issues whose resolution might contribute to a "peace legacy." Renouncing CBW would have offered precisely such an opportunity, but the dispute remained locked in the State Department. It never came to White House attention.

With the arrival of a new administration in 1969, the Joint Chiefs of Staff again requested the Secretary of Defense to seek presidential affirmation of CBW policy. The new administration had adopted a new procedure for policy review; it produced a different result. According to the new system, disputed or newly proposed policies reached President Nixon after having been subjected to interagency studies, formally requested by so-called national security study memoranda

(NSSMs). Under the new rules, these studies were to present to the President not simply the positions championed by particular Cabinet members, but a full array of options for action together with the arguments for and against each.

The new Secretary of Defense, Melvin Laird, had no firmer substantive view of the chiefs' request than his predecessor had, but he did have a new procedural alternative. He used it: Laird proposed an interagency study looking to presidential decision. The analysis was undertaken, and in the course of the study the possibility of renouncing biological and chemical weapons was raised. The JCS objected to discussion of that possibility, but were overruled on the ground that standing instructions required all alternatives to be presented. The completed study became the basis for discussion in the National Security Council, where the chairman of the JCS asserted that CBW was "vital to the national security." But he was expressing views on many other issues at weekly NSC meetings; it was impossible to project equally intense concern about each. And as it turned out, the JCS did not feel very strongly about biological weapons; they were mainly representing the views of the Army Chemical Corps. After this meeting President Nixon made the decision to reverse previous policy.[1]

Here, then—if the conjecture as to President Johnson's probable response is right—a change in decision process made a decisive difference. A change in the method by which an issue was prepared for decision, and a change in the level of government at which the issue was addressed reversed the outcome. Neither the constellation of forces concerned with the problem nor the politics of the issue had substantially changed between 1967 and 1969. The essential difference was organizational. Yet, organizational changes alone rarely make so decisive a difference. More commonly, organization shapes performance in subtler ways. Consider, for example, the Nixon administration's handling of the oil import issue.

On March 25, 1969, President Nixon commissioned the Cabinet Task Force on Oil Import Control. Labor Secretary George

Shultz was appointed chairman, and members included the secretaries of State, Defense, Commerce, Treasury, and Interior, and the director of the Office of Emergency Preparedness. After a year-long investigation of oil import policy, the task force reported to the President in February 1970 that, despite its national security rationale, "the present import control program is not adequately responsive to present and future security considerations." Stressing the need for increased oil imports to meet U.S. energy needs, the report recommended the gradual abandonment of the quota system of import controls and its replacement by a tariff system designed to discriminate against insecure sources of oil. In reaching its conclusions, the study explicitly considered a number of oil embargo scenarios for the years 1975 and 1980, with varying durations and numbers of participating countries for each. The report asserted that an embargo was unlikely but that the risk "may nevertheless be real enough to warrant expenditures to guard against it." It concluded that if appropriate emergency measures were taken, the United States should be able to cope with embargoes rather comfortably.[2]

Such optimism was understandable in 1969. Oil then glutted world markets, the Organization of Petroleum Exporting Countries (OPEC) had demonstrated little cohesiveness, and the number of significant oil-exporting nations was expected to continue to grow. But the report's optimism was based on faulty projections of future supply and demand. As it later turned out, demand had been seriously underestimated, and U.S. production and the availability of Canadian and Latin American oil all overestimated. The report did, however, recognize the uncertainty of its forecasts and propose that future oil import controls "be the subject of an annual report and adjusted periodically if import volumes or domestic production significantly exceed or fall short of projections and/or if the security of imported supplies either worsens or perceptibly improves."[3]

The report's recommendations triggered strong opposition

from the domestic oil industry, and as a result were shelved. Oil continued to receive intermittent government attention, but the results were inconclusive. The interagency Oil Policy Committee that was established in 1970 under the aegis of the Office of Emergency Preparedness proved wholly ineffective. A small energy office was set up in the Treasury to share responsibility for oil import policy with Interior's Office of Oil and Gas, and finally, in early 1973, the Energy Policy Office was created as part of the White House staff. But none of these entities had much weight; none—not even the White House office—enjoyed presidential support. All viewed the issue through essentially domestic lenses, as a problem of ensuring supplies to match U.S. consumption. The foreign policy aspects of the problem passed largely unnoticed by State, Defense, and the NSC.

Meanwhile, the assumptions on which U.S. policy as well as the Shultz Task Force report had rested were being steadily undermined. U.S. and world demand for oil soared, while U.S. production declined. Canada and Venezuela, the main sources of U.S. oil imports, imposed export restrictions. U.S. oil imports from other sources, especially from the Arab nations, increased rapidly. A series of world oil price hikes demonstrated the possibility of effective cartel action by OPEC. At the same time, participants in Mideast affairs began warning the United States of the tension between U.S. policy toward Israel and the growing U.S. requirements for Arab oil. By 1971 King Faisal of Saudi Arabia was insisting to every high-level visitor that unless American policy became more "even-handed," the "oil weapon" would be used, even against the United States, his primary military supplier and residual security protector. Although expert opinion was divided on the probabilities, it recognized that a new round of hostilities in the Mideast might produce a solid front among the Arab oil exporters, with resulting production cutbacks and dramatic increases in the price of oil. It was clear that the supply of imported oil might be interrupted and that the U.S.

was becoming steadily more vulnerable to such a possibility. The Shultz Task Force report had warned that "total abandonment of all import controls might on present evidence be deemed to threaten security of supply."[4] On April 18, 1973, the fourteen-year-old mandatory oil import control program was abolished. The Arab oil exporters announced their embargo six months later.

The resulting oil shortages; the quadrupling of oil prices; the impact of those price increases in pushing all industrial nations to double-digit inflation in 1973–74; the resulting $70 billion increase in world oil costs; the problems associated with this transfer of wealth and its financing; the inability of Fourth World nations to pay for their oil imports—all this is now history. But during the four crucial years 1969–73, the U.S. government had taken no action to forestall, offset, or diminish those effects. Indeed, between those years U.S. dependence on imported oil had risen from 24 percent to 35 percent of daily consumption, and the proportion of imported oil coming from Arab sources had jumped from one-fifth to one-third.

Could a feasible change in the organizational design of the U.S. government, or in its decision processes, have prevented the embargo and price rise, or made the United States wholly invulnerable to it? Almost certainly not. Yet means might well have been found to blunt the oil weapon. U.S. Mideastern policy might in fact have become more "even-handed," as it did in the aftermath of the embargo. Plans for responding to an embargo could have been developed, and standby authorities might have been proposed, and perhaps enacted. Non-OPEC sources of supply might have been cultivated; fuel stockpiles could have been expanded. There is good reason to believe that appropriate organizational arrangements would have led to the construction of at least one of those defenses. Many organizations—military services are a good example—routinely identify threatening contingencies, and despite their improbability, guard against them. In fact, the U.S. Navy had insured against exactly such a contingency: in 1973 the navy controlled four major oil reserves, with known supplies sufficient to meet navy needs for three hundred years.

Anticipation of unfamiliar contingencies is a hard test. Neither people nor organizations do it consistently well. But what about more familiar contingencies? What did the U.S. government do after the 1973 embargo, when the nature and severity of the problem had been demonstrated?

The Federal Energy Office was established, developed a staff of three thousand, and became in 1974 the Federal Energy Administration (FEA). President Nixon announced "Project Independence," nominally intended to achieve American energy independence by 1980. Little action followed. Secretary of State Henry Kissinger sought to establish an internationally agreed minimum floor price for oil to stimulate expanded domestic and world-wide oil production, but Secretary of the Treasury Simon opposed that initiative; no clear U.S. policy resulted. Eight congressional committees undertook hearings. The Departments of State, Treasury, Commerce, Transportation, Interior, Justice, Defense, and Agriculture (for farmers); the Federal Power Commission; the Interstate Commerce Commission (for truckers); the Civil Aeronautics Board (for airlines); and the Environmental Protection Agency (Alaska pipeline, auto pollution standards), each asserted jurisdiction over pieces of the problem.

The FEA developed the first solid government data on fuel consumption rates, production and processing costs, oil company profits, and petroleum reserves. It quickly became a focus of public concern, and a useful source of information. But the energy problem interacted with U.S. policy toward Israel, Europe, and Japan; it affected the management of the U.S. economy, the relation of the federal government to the states, and the profitability of several huge industries—oil, utilities, and automobiles. A new sub-Cabinet agency was in no position to assess all of those interactions; still less could it impose a national policy that so sharply affected so many interests.

The issue was in the deepest sense political; it involved the distribution of gains and losses—mostly losses. Only a strong President working effectively with the Congress could have won acceptance of a policy adequate in scope, firmness, and equity to the dimensions of the issue. But President Nixon was shadowed and then destroyed by Watergate, and presidential leadership could not quickly be restored by an inexperienced and unelected successor. The power of Congress was dispersed among committees attentive to particular interests—and energy affected many interests. In short, the system defaulted. By mid-1976 U.S. international initiatives had contributed significantly to potentially important agreements to stockpile oil and to share existing supplies in the event of future embargoes. But domestic energy policy remained paralyzed, unable either to enforce serious conservation or to stimulate expansion of domestic supplies. By summer, 1976 the United States was dependent on imports for more than 40 percent of its oil, and the figure was still rising.

It might be argued that government should not be expected to master an issue as complex and difficult as this one—even the second time around. Yet the harder one looks at the future, the clearer it is that a government capable of no better performance is likely to prove inadequate to the challenges— the risks and opportunities—of the next quarter century. The risks, at least, will be substantial, as a final set of facts suggests.

The pressure exerted by the growth of world energy demand on the finite supply of fossil fuels has resulted not only in sharp increases in petroleum prices, but in increasing emphasis on nuclear power to help meet that demand. More than 290 nuclear power plants are now in operation, under construction, or on order outside the United States and the Soviet Union, and the number is expanding steadily. World commercial nuclear power capacity is likely to triple or even quadruple within the next ten to fifteen years.[5] Reactors are or soon will be operating in most of the volatile areas of the globe, including India and Pakistan, Israel and Egypt, South

Africa, Brazil, Korea, and Libya. While expanding reliance on nuclear power is logical in view of the world energy situation, two very troublesome consequences follow: nuclear technology is being widely disseminated, and growing quantities of spent nuclear fuel are being produced.

As former Director of Defense Research and Engineering John S. Foster has noted, "the only difficult part of making a fission bomb of some sort is the preparation of a supply of fissionable material of adequate purity; the design of the bomb itself is relatively easy . . ."[6] As Foster indicates, the limiting factor controlling the spread of nuclear weapons has been the availability of weapons-grade nuclear material. Ordinary nuclear power plants burn a uranium fuel that has been enriched to a concentration of only 3 to 5 percent U-235, far below the 90 percent strength needed for an atomic bomb. But plants that enrich uranium for fuel can also enrich it to weapons-grade quality. The gaseous diffusion technology that until recently was the only practical method for uranium enrichment is enormously expensive and consumes a vast amount of electric power. It is simply not economically feasible to build such a plant without an assured market for the fuel from several dozen reactors. Hence, for the past two decades, virtually all of the non-Communist world's nuclear fuel has come from three diffusion plants built by the U.S. government in the 1940s and 1950s to produce uranium for atomic bombs.

As world demand for enriched uranium soars, however, those plants will soon reach the limits of their capacity. To assure themselves of a continuing source of nuclear fuel, therefore, other countries that have hitherto depended on the United States for enriched uranium are developing alternate sources of supply. As leader of a European consortium, France, for example, is building a gaseous diffusion plant of commercial scale. And new and potentially far less costly enrichment technologies are currently being developed in Britain, West Germany, the Netherlands and South Africa.

The security problems posed by expanding nuclear technology are further complicated by the problem of spent fuel. Until recently, the waste products of nuclear power reactors have mainly posed a disposal problem. With the growing scarcity of uranium, however, the reprocessing of spent nuclear fuel may become economic, especially as a hedge against disruptions in uranium supply. But reprocessing recovers plutonium which, like uranium, can fuel a power reactor, but which—unlike reactor-grade uranium—can also fuel nuclear weapons.

Still more worrisome is the probability that future technology may produce an abundance of both highly enriched uranium and plutonium, each suitable for weapons. If the new high temperature gas-cooled reactor (which uses weapons-grade uranium as fuel) and the fast-breeder reactor (which produces more plutonium than the uranium it consumes) come to be widely used, the plutonium and weapons-grade uranium they will require or produce will be sufficient to fuel thousands of Hiroshima-sized bombs annually.

At present, the main safeguard against such use of uranium and plutonium is the inspection of reactors and reprocessing facilities by the International Atomic Energy Agency and the incorporation of IAEA standards in the Non-Proliferation Treaty (NPT). But the quantities of weapons grade fuels are rising to such levels that the undetected diversion of very small fractions of the reprocessed fuel would suffice for a small number of weapons. Many governments abiding by IAEA standards but having physical access to plutonium will have, at a minimum, a "nuclear weapons mobilization base," the capacity to construct nuclear weapons within a period of months. Others may be tempted to create a standby capability to assemble bombs should the need arise. States that neither possess nor have tested nuclear weapons may in this way be able to assemble them in a matter of days. (According to CIA estimates, Israel assembled ten to twenty such weapons during the 1973 Mideast War.)[7] In a period of international tension the temptation to take this route may be intense. But what appears a prudent precaution to one government may look like a deadly threat to its neighbors.

The prospect of the proliferation of nuclear weapons to small and unstable nations is chilling enough, but there are worse prospects. The widespread availability of fissionable material will make it quite possible for dissident or terrorist groups to acquire bombs—with potentially awesome consequences for international order and American security. Commenting on this situation in January, 1976, David Lilenthal, the first chairman of the U.S. Atomic Energy Commission, expressed the feelings of many who have seen matters become steadily more dangerous. "I'm glad I'm not a young man," he said, "and I'm sorry for my grandchildren."[8]

The U.S. has so far failed to establish policy commensurate to this problem. Our capacity to control the nuclear genie is necessarily limited. We cannot halt the development of nuclear technology abroad. (Indeed, we are obliged by the NPT to assist it.) Nor can we veto the policies of other exporters of this technology. The United States can, however, lead, pressure, and cajole current nuclear powers toward much less risky arrangements, arrangements which would include more stringent international controls of nuclear technology and fuel, internationalization of various phases of the fuel cycle, and tightened safeguards at nuclear power facilities.

Given the extraordinary dispersion of its authority over the various aspects of nuclear policy, it is hardly surprising that the U.S. has proven unable to formulate and implement a farsighted policy. Defense, State, ACDA, the Energy Research and Development Administration, the Interior Department, and the Nuclear Regulatory Commission share responsibility for nuclear energy policy with a dozen Congressional committees and sub-committees, and with substantial private interests. Non-proliferation policy is only one aspect of nuclear policy. It may conflict with economic and environmental objectives, or with the strategic requirements of alliance relations. This

is legitimate and unavoidable. But just as was true in the oil
case, no mechanism exists for integrating the various pieces
of policy to form a coherent whole. Another nuclear genie,
in short, and a wildly dangerous one, may soon escape its
bottle. The U.S. government, with greater capacity to cap
that bottle than any other entity on earth, moves slowly and
erratically, tangled in inter-agency disputes and battles with
private interests.[9]

The CBW case and the oil and nuclear energy situations
suggest several propositions that underlie this book. Let us
state them directly.

The first is simply that *organization matters*. We define
"organization" to include the combined effect of three factors:
(1) the *structure* of government, which is to say the existence
of agencies having particular missions, authorities, and com-
petencies and the nonexistence of others; (2) the *processes*
by which issues are identified and assessed, decisions made
and put into effect; and (3) the *people* whose energy, skills,
and values more nearly than any other factor determine
whether government works. This definition is broader than
that employed in traditional discussions of government organization, but we think it essential. Processes (as we will show)
and people (as everyone knows) have fully as pronounced an
effect on performance as does formal structure. The full effect
of organization on governmental performance can only be
appreciated by examining the interaction of all three.[10] Balanced organizational structures, efficient decision processes,
and competent people appropriately placed do not guarantee
good policy performance. But they greatly improve the odds.

Second, *current organization is clearly inadequate*. Chapters
2 and 3 detail our argument. Very briefly it is that current
organizational arrangements embody three major defects: they
are out of balance; they deploy too little competence in tasks
of special importance; and, above all, they make almost impossible the effective integration of policy.

The imbalances are several. Current arrangements accord
excessive weight to the problems of the late 1940s as against

those of the late 1970s; to institutions focused on domestic as against foreign concerns; to the making of "policy" as against its effective implementation; and to the maintenance of stability as against the anticipation and management of change.

The effects of imbalance are compounded by critical deficiencies in competence. The ability of foreign service and intelligence reporting to assess the probable response of foreign societies to alternative U.S. policies is poor, and poorly used. The generalist agencies in foreign affairs—State Department, the Office of Management and Budget (OMB), and presidential staff—contain too little expertise in military, economic, and technical subjects, and too little capacity to plan or forecast. And despite the recent mushrooming of congressional staffs, the ability of congressional committees to apply genuine expertise in their own service remains weak. Throughout the government, competence in identifying longer-run problems and in foreseeing future effects of U.S. actions is both inadequate and underutilized.

Finally, the means for insuring the integration and coherence of policy are everywhere meager, while pressures toward the disjointed and conflicting treatment of related issues are uniformly powerful. The clamor of varied views is unavoidable: our relations with the external world are now far too diverse and specialized to be managed by any single central agency. Responsibilities are necessarily decentralized, and decentralization inevitably presses toward the disintegration of policy. But the corresponding responsibility of government—there is no task more important—is to ensure that particular interests are accommodated within some coherent conception of the nation's larger needs. That task is now feebly undertaken even in the executive branch, the branch with a chief. Congressional efforts are feebler still, handicapped as they are by the systematic diffusion of legislative power, the recent weakness of congressional leadership, and the fact that the two branches have long been controlled by opposing parties.

Our third proposition is that, as one looks to the future,

*the gap between the capacities of government and the dimen-
sions of the likely problems grows larger.* Viewing the future
with alarm is a common tendency and common failing. But we
think the evidence suggested by the oil and nuclear problems
and presented more fully in Chapter 3 portends real trouble.
We are entering an era in which our foreign relations are likely
to be marked by issues that, like energy, arise from the tightening economic and physical interdependence of nations.
Problems individually complex will be still harder to resolve
because of their interconnection with others. Important issues
will combine foreign and domestic aspects, will occur in great
numbers and affect everyday life, making them intensely political. Moreover, these issues—difficult both intellectually and
politically—will be faced by a government whose authority
is likely to be even more broadly diffused than it is today as
the number of executive agencies concerned with pieces of
the problems continues to grow, and the Congress is drawn
toward deeper involvement by the effect of these issues on
prices, jobs, and the conditions of ordinary life. Finally, the dispersion of authority within the United States will be mirrored
in the external world. Our power relative to other nations—
still very great—is nonetheless diminished; in most respects
it will probably continue to decline. The United States will be
increasingly forced to design policy, and to build domestic
backing for it, while negotiating its terms with an increasingly
pluralistic world. Good instincts, great brilliance, heroic solo
performances may still suffice to manage single issues of great
difficulty, or multiple problems of a straightforward sort. But
the steady pressure of numerous problems marked by high
complexity, great uncertainty, striking importance, and the
pulling and hauling of multiple interests—such pressure will
overwhelm a shaky structure. The best estimate we can make
of the future, and a quite conventional estimate it is, is that
it will be characterized by many issues of exactly this kind.

    The conclusion we derive from these propositions will come
as no surprise: *Changes in the way the U.S. government is*

organized to formulate and conduct foreign policy are impera-
tive. This book develops the case for that conclusion, discusses
the nature and purpose of the changes required, and makes
many specific proposals.

Yet it is essential to recognize that organizational reform
is hard and uncertain work, and to understand why. One reason is that any pattern of organization advantages certain view-
points and disadvantages others. It focuses attention on some
problems and slights others; makes more probable the emergence of some policies rather than others; strengthens certain
officials and weakens others. That, of course, is why organizational reforms are so often proposed and so bitterly resisted:
there is something important at stake.

The tension between conflicting interests in organizational
reform reflects the complexity of organizational objectives.
All important organizational reform must seek to achieve not
one or two aims, but an appropriate balance among a large
number. There will inevitably be tension between parochial
objectives and those of the system as a whole; between those
of short-term advantage and others looking to the longer term;
between consistency and the ability to capitalize on special
circumstances; between prompt action and the capacity to pro-
long the period in which choices are kept open; between the
needs for secrecy and the desirability that policy be widely
understood and broadly supported. Such tensions reflect the
nature of government, not imperfection in policy or policy
making. Organizational design must recognize and balance
them, not try to eliminate them.[11]

To ignore the fact that organizations are multi-purpose entities is to invite trouble. Yet pushing a single objective is a
popular approach to organizational design. In the early 1960s,
for example, many proponents of organizational reform sought
simply to enhance presidential control of foreign policy making.
More recently, reformers have sought to reduce the U.S. propensity to intervene in the affairs of other nations and to

restrain presidential power. Such single-minded approaches
have one powerful attraction: they greatly simplify the task
of organizational design. But recent history suggests their
folly. A pluralistic society committed to a political system of
shared authority in a rapidly evolving world must seek to
balance many objectives.

Striking such a balance is further complicated by the fact
that though pervasive, the effects of organization are subtle,
and easily overlooked. An example makes the point. Imagine
asking a friend who had just dined at a Chinese restaurant
what he had for dinner and why. The answer would almost
certainly be posed in terms of personal preference—for twice-
cooked pork, for example—and it would seem both accurate
and complete. But the overriding fact would have been
missed: namely, that the meal had been eaten at a Chinese
restaurant. The friend may or may not have chosen the restaurant, but once that choice was made, the question of having
hamburger or *coq au vin* simply did not arise. The effects of
organizational arrangements on the menu of alternatives presented to a President—on the definition of a "problem" that
requires action by the U.S. government, on the information
presented about any such problem, and on the execution of
any decision—are equally pervasive, and equally easy to
overlook.

Finally, since reorganization changes the terms and conditions of people's jobs and since those adversely affected resist
such changes, efforts to reform organizations expend influence, generate friction, and arouse opposition, especially
from vested interests, often with few—or quite unintended—
results. The series of attempted changes in the status of the
State Department described in Chapter 6 illustrates empty
reform. The imposition in 1921 by the Congress of government-
wide budgetary responsibility on the President is a clear case
of unintended impact. This reform was intended to hold
expenditures in check. In fact, expenditures were little affected
but relations between the White House and the Cabinet were

transformed: the authority to determine the size and composition of departmental budget requests gave Presidents a measure of control over departmental policies and action that none of their other authorities approached. Similarly, the 1947 advocates of the National Security Council believed it would constrain foot-loose presidential initiative in foreign affairs. The NSC was to be "Forrestal's revenge" on FDR's practices of war management; it would force the President, in formal setting, to confront the counsel of his senior advisers and chief lieutenants. But President Truman demonstrated that even Presidents inexperienced in foreign affairs need not be awed by such an institution; President Kennedy largely ignored it; and President Nixon transformed the NSC into a mechanism for centralized presidential control.

All of these problems—the conflict of interest, the multiplicity of objectives, the obscurity of impacts—discourage productive discussion of organizational reform. Most debate tends to be dominated either by high level abstractions ("coordination," "efficiency," or "centralization," for example) or by very particular policy concerns (for example, cutting the defense budget). As a result, organizational advice tends to be either highly abstract or narrowly value-laden. The question thus arises: can useful and concrete proposals for organizational reform be made independent of the substantive policy objectives of a particular administration?

The answer of this book is a qualified "Yes." For administrations of extreme views—deeply isolationist, say, or imperial—many of our specific proposals would not be acceptable. They are not designed to minimize contact between the United States and the external world, or to facilitate reconstruction of an American imperium. To more probable administrations, however, they should be useful for two reasons. They are based on a quite widely shared sense of the major objectives any centrist U.S. government would wish to pursue—to assist the development of a stable and equitable world order, and to build the capabilities, national and international,

needed to manage the growing physical and economic interdependence of nations. They are drawn from an equally common appreciation, backed by a good deal of evidence, of the
difficulties current organization poses for the accomplishment
of those objectives: over-emphasis on short-run considerations
as opposed to future problems, a tendency to let particular
interests dominate collective ones, and an inability to assess
specific issues in terms of larger and coherent conceptions of
the national interest.

A further question is how specific recommendations can be
made in ignorance of the personal characteristics of key
appointees. Who could confidently assign certain roles to the
Secretary of State and others to the President's assistant for
national security affairs without knowing whether Henry
Kissinger, for example, would be the first and William Rogers
the second, or vice versa? The answer is that we do not assign
to key positions roles that any competent official could fill;
instead we suggest the particular kind of competence needed
in particular positions. But we do not require transcendent
gifts of any official. GI's used to be told that the army had
been designed by geniuses for operation by idiots. The top
of our government now suggests exactly the reverse. Genius
can transcend organizational idiocy, but there is no reason to
add that to its burdens.

In short, we approach the problem of organizational design
with an intent less doctrinaire than those who seek a single
end, and more operational than those guided by the traditional
abstractions. Our approach emerges from an attempt to answer
the basic question: Why organization? Why, if no government existed, should a President or Congress want to establish
structures and processes employing people? The answer is
that organized government performs three principal functions:
it creates capabilities, it vests and weights certain interests and
perspectives, and it helps assure the legitimacy of decisions
taken.

Most obviously, organization *creates capabilities.* Structure and procedures that divide assignments among a collection of individuals, and coordinate their behavior toward some common end make possible the performance of tasks beyond the capability of independent individuals. In the making of foreign policy such tasks are many and hard. Ideally they include: (1) developing a coherent conception of U.S. interests; (2) scanning for problems, collecting information, and identifying issues that may require decision or action; (3) developing alternative courses of action and analyzing their relative benefits and costs; (4) making decisions, without undue delay and at the lowest levels having the requisite perspective and authority; (5) taking action, effectively and efficiently; and (6) assessing the results of action and revising policy accordingly.

Adequate performance of such tasks requires structures (a Nuclear Regulatory Commission, for example), processes (for consultation among the many agencies concerned about nuclear power), and the choice and placement of key people (perhaps an "anti-proliferation czar"). Moreover, the question is not simply whether a capability exists or not, but what level of performance is reached, and at what costs. Poor organization produces lower levels of performance than are needed at higher costs than are required.

Second, organization *vests and weights particular interests and perspectives.* Organizational arrangements—the existence or absence of specific departments or agencies, the distribution of powers among them, procedures for concurrence or consultation, the skill and forcefulness of key officials—determine whether and how effectively particular considerations will be represented in policy making. A central question in organizational design, therefore, is *which* substantive perspectives should be introduced, with *what* weights, in the processes of decision and action. An interest can be vested in a number of ways: most vividly, perhaps, by establishment of a new agency dedicated expressly to that interest. The Arms Control and Disarmament Agency, for example, was created in 1961 for the express purpose of giving institutional voice to the arms control perspective.* Interests can also be vested by establishing units within existing organizations (for example, the Arms Control Directorate in the Office of the Secretary of Defense) or by establishing procedures that require existing agencies to take an underrepresented perspective into account (through an "arms control impact statement," for example). Giving weight to an interest or perspective is a different matter. Weight is power. It may arise from formal authority (to take actions or to make decisions, or to impose limits on the actions or decisions of others); from control of resources (mainly budget and personnel); from special competence at some important task; or from linkages to sources of power outside the government, principally money, votes, and publicity. But weight does not follow automatically from vesting; ACDA illustrates that point too.

Third, *organization legitimates.* It makes decisions broadly acceptable by assuring that those with stakes or relevant competence are heard, and that decisions are taken by duly constituted authorities. Contrast the nation's probable acceptance of a decision to use military force made by the President alone with the likely response to the same decision taken only after the Cabinet, the JCS, and the Congress had all publicly concurred. As in all spheres where reasonable men can disagree about ends, legitimacy depends on adherence to established procedures. Constitutional government consists of processes designed to give competing interests a fair hearing in the making of decisions affecting them. Congressmen represent the interests of particular citizens, districts, or states; the President stands as the sole official elected by all the people; the departments embody specialized knowledge and capacity. Interaction among President, Congress, and the bureaucracy assures the representation of multiple interests, and enhances the likeli-

---

*ACDA can also be regarded as a "divestiture." Thomas Hughes has characterized ACDA, the Agency for International Development, and the U.S. Information Agency as "monuments to the State Department's disinterest in their functions."

hood that even those who sought a different result will accept the decision taken.

This triple conception of the purpose and effect of organization pervades the chapters that follow. For each of the major realms of foreign policy we ask: What *capabilities* must government have? Which *perspectives* should be introduced, with what weight, in the major processes of decision and action? What interests must be represented to *legitimate* decisions?

Chapter 2

The Problems:
Recent Cases

To say that the government of the United States is really improperly organized is a massive understatement.

Donald Rumsfeld (November 1975)

THE American response to the foreign policy challenges of the years just after World War II stands as a triumph of historic proportions. U.S. leadership was decisive in creating the United Nations, the International Monetary Fund (IMF), and the General Agreement on Tariffs and Trade (GATT); in restoring the economy of Europe and the polities of Germany and Japan; in assuring the defense of Europe and East Asia against what seemed an imminent Communist threat; and in encouraging Western colonial powers to free their former colonies. The nation's success in organizing to accomplish its ambitious foreign policy goals was no less impressive. Three main organizational challenges emerged during the post-war years: to integrate diplomatic and military policy making, to improve the reliability of foreign intelligence, and to develop a new command structure for the huge new U.S. defense establishment. The United States met these challenges with organizational inventiveness on a grand scale. The National Security Act of 1947 created the National Security Council, the Central

Intelligence Agency, and a unified Department of Defense. The organizational framework established by the act endures essentially unchanged to this day.

But the foreign policy problems of today are not those of 1947, and recent U.S. experience in meeting them is far from reassuring. The record is not entirely dismal; it has included far-reaching trade agreements like the Kennedy Round; important accords with the Soviet Union—the hot line, the nuclear test ban, agreements on peaceful uses of space and the seabed, and SALT I; international monetary reforms; and the opening to China. Moreover, the failures in U.S. foreign policy cannot be attributed simply to poor organization. They have sprung largely from dubious values, limited comprehension, and weakness of will on the part of presidents, cabinet officers, leaders of Congress, and others. Nonetheless, two propositions seem beyond dispute: U.S. performance in foreign relations has fallen well below the standard the nation requires, and poor organization is an important source of that failure. The first of those propositions is argued by a considerable literature which we do not rehearse here.[1] The second is the subject of this book.

To aid in analyzing the relation of policy failures to organization, we present here brief descriptions of six incidents of recent foreign policy making. The cases do not represent either the full array of issues or the normal level of performance in recent foreign policy making. But they do illustrate shortcomings most observers of American foreign policy making will recognize as characteristic and damaging. They thus can serve as a basis for diagnosis.

"Offsets": The Problem of U.S. Troops in Germany[2]

Throughout the 1960s, a recurring issue in relations between the United States and the Federal Republic of Germany was how many troops the United States would station in Germany, and what share of the foreign exchange costs of those troops Germany would cover, or "offset." The contingent of 200,000 American troops in Germany served many purposes: it stood as an earnest of America's commitment to fight for Europe, deterring Soviet attack or military pressure; it provided the backbone of NATO's capability actually to defend Europe if war should occur; it encouraged the confidence and stability of Germany as a democratic state (and the confidence of Germany's neighbors that German militarism would not be permitted to revive); and it gave the United States influence over developments in Europe and bargaining leverage with all parties involved. But U.S. troops in Germany also cost some $600 million annually in foreign exchange at a time when U.S. balance of payments was a matter of growing concern. Thus, the related questions of troops and offsets became a major issue in the periodic meetings between Presidents and Chancellors throughout the 1960s, most dramatically in 1966.

Viewed whole, the problem was to ameliorate a pressing but secondary economic concern without raising doubts about our commitment to the defense of Europe or jeopardizing political relations with a major ally. The most visible and measurable piece of the problem, however, was the balance of payments, an issue that directly engaged the departments of Defense and Treasury. In particular, it concerned a Secretary of Defense determined to observe White House injunctions to reduce the payments deficit attributable to his department, and a Secretary of the Treasury displaying his department's normal sensitivity to the issue. The combination of those concerns produced a U.S. insistence on maintaining a separate subaccount for military payments and on forcing the Germans to cover deficits in that account through military purchases alone.

There existed a third department with responsibility for broader American foreign policy interests and for the maintenance of coherent policies toward our allies: the Department of State. But throughout the mid-1960s State kept to the sidelines of offset decision making, largely because Secretary Rusk was reluctant to contest the issue with Secretary McNamara, but also because of internal weakness. Though of all U.S. agencies, State had the best means of assessing political and economic developments in Bonn, it failed to exploit them at critical junctures. By late 1965, the Germans regarded their military reequipment program as complete. Moreover, their economy had slowed, producing a budget deficit and a severe political problem for Chancellor Erhard. For the better part of a year, State failed to recognize or report that these circumstances might cause Erhard to slight his offset commitments, and that unrelieved U.S. pressure on the point might precipitate the fall of his government. At the last moment, in the fall of 1966, the severity of Erhard's problem became obvious. White House intervention produced a more accommodating U.S. stance, but by then it was too late; deeply compromised, the Erhard regime collapsed in October, and the United States was implicated in its fall.

In 1969, after the Nixon-Kissinger revisions in the procedures of the National Security Council, a review of the offset issue— a NSSM—was commissioned. On the basis of that study, the President decided that U.S. interests required the maintenance of existing levels of U.S. troops in Europe and that, while German coverage of the foreign exchange costs was desirable, the security the troops provided both the United States and Europe was essential. A National Security Decision Memorandum (NSDM) was then issued, decoupling the specific number of U.S. troops in Europe from the particular level of German offset payments and instructing the U.S. negotiators of the next offset agreement to be more generous about terms. The White House then dropped the matter; little effort was made to monitor the subsequent negotiations. But since the NSDM had not clearly explained the grounds for the decision, the apparent change in policy had little practical impact. U.S. negotiators continued to press the German government as hard as they had done before.

To many Americans, moreover, the maintenance of 300,000 men in Europe (200,000 of them in Germany) a quarter century after the war seemed an expensive anomaly. A number of senators favored unilateral reductions of the American garrison. Rather than addressing these concerns, the administration simply tried to hold the line—quietly. A Senate effort to impose a unilateral cut in American forces was resisted largely by recruiting public figures from previous administrations to carry the burden of argument. But no effort was made to articulate a coherent set of current objectives and to show how existing levels of U.S. forces in Europe served them. The absence of such a showing guaranteed that the issue would remain an irritant in executive-congressional relations and a puzzle to the American public.

The Panama Canal

Under the terms of its 1903 treaty with Panama, the United States controls "as if sovereign" and "in perpetuity" both the Panama Canal and the bordering ten-mile-wide zone of Panamanian territory. "We shall have a treaty," said Secretary of State John Hay, who negotiated it, "vastly advantageous to the United States, and we must confess, not so advantageous to Panama."[3] The generosity of the terms was attributable partly to the fact that they had been negotiated for Panama by a Frenchman with a $40 million personal interest in the matter, and partly to the recency of Panama's independence from Colombia, accomplished with U.S. assistance.

Minor revisions of the treaty in 1939 and 1955 increased Panama's share of the canal's revenue, but the territorial terms remained, smacking of colonialism and producing growing tension. Ill will was exacerbated by the discrepancy between the comfortable living standards of the 40,000 American "Zonians," and the $700 per capita income of the surrounding

Panamanians. Resentment occasionally boiled over into violence, as in the 1964 "flag riots" in which twenty-one Panamanians and three Americans were killed.[4]

The riots and the break in diplomatic relations they precipitated forced Washington to reassess its policy toward Panama.
The military value of the canal had declined ever since World
War II, when the U.S. Navy organized itself around aircraft
carriers too big to transit the canal. Similarly, the economic
importance of the canal, while still substantial, was also
waning. Most modern commercial vessels and virtually all
bulk carriers are too large to use it, and air freight and over-
land transport within the United States compete for much of
the canal's business. The most likely threat to the canal, moreover, is sabotage by Panamanians, a largely indefensible
danger given the canal's length and number of locks. These
considerations led the Johnson administration to begin negotiations with Panama for a new treaty in 1965. But since
Washington was still not ready to consider substantial modifi-
cations, the talks stagnated for eight years.

In 1973 Panama broke the impasse by internationalizing the
issue. Panama's president, General Omar Torrijos—a moderate
with strong nationalist and populist leanings—adroitly invited
the U.N. Security Council to meet in Panama City to discuss
the issue. The discussions produced a resolution for a restora-
tion of Panamanian sovereignty over the Zone. The United
States vetoed the resolution, but prodded by the vote, the
Nixon administration appointed former Ambassador to Saigon
Ellsworth Bunker as a special U.S. negotiator, and early in
1974 Secretary Kissinger signed an "agreement on principles"
with Panama's foreign minister, calling for Panama, in time,
to "assume total responsibility for the operation of the Canal."

Talk of a new treaty aroused vociferous opposition. The
civilians who live in the Zone, together with the U.S. Army,
whose plush Southern Command Headquarters (known as
"Southern Comfort") is sited there, mounted a forceful lobby-
ing campaign. Their opposition was reinforced by a strong

undercurrent of nationalist public opinion. Advocates of a new treaty enjoyed no comparable intensity of support. Accordingly, in 1974, thirty-seven senators (more than the number necessary to block a treaty) co-sponsored a resolution declaring that the United States "should in no way cede, dilute, forfeit, negotiate, or transfer any of [its] sovereign rights . . ."[5] And in June 1975 the House cut off all funds for the U.S. negotiators, an action recast in conference into a "sense of Congress" resolution calling upon the administration to "protect the vital interests of the United States in the Canal Zone."[6]

As of this writing, negotiations are still stalled, Ronald Reagan having made the canal an issue in the Republican primaries. But time is running short, and the pressure in Panama continues to build. Having already elicited the unanimous support of all Latin American nations, Panama has appealed to the "Group of 77" developing countries, whose demands for a "new international economic order" find perfect expression in the unresolved issue of the canal. Moreover, President Torrijos has let it be known that he cannot indefinitely suppress the more radical segments of Panamanian opinion. If violence erupts again, he has warned, "we will have two alternatives, to smash it or to lead it, and I'm not going to smash it."[7]

The "New Economic Policy"[8]

On August 15, 1971, President Nixon announced his "New Economic Policy," a sweeping set of measures designed to strengthen the U.S. economy at home and abroad. That package included a suspension of the convertibility of the dollar into gold, a 10 percent surcharge on all imported goods, and a thinly veiled demand that the United States' major trading partners permit a unilateral devaluation of the dollar against their currencies. The new policy ended the era in international economics that the United States itself had begun at Bretton Woods in 1944.

The Bretton Woods system had established the dollar as the foundation of the international monetary order. The United States had pledged itself to maintain the dollar's value at $35 per ounce of gold, while other countries pegged their currencies to the dollar at fixed exchange rates. The dollar thus became a form of international money, an unofficial legal tender for the world economy, since the strength of the U.S. economy made other countries willing to accumulate dollars and to treat them "as good as gold." Thus, during the first two decades of the Bretton Woods regime, the American balance of payments deficit was not only tolerated but welcomed: it was an important source of the liquidity needed to finance the economic recovery of Europe and Japan. By the late 1960s, however, that recovery was largely complete. Continuing deficits were no longer useful; instead they were producing a massive "overhang" of dollars held abroad. And during the Vietnam years U.S. demand for imports increased, while overvaluation of the dollar made American goods less competitive abroad. The result was a rapidly worsening U.S. trade and payments position, culminating in a massive hemorrhage of capital from the United States in early 1971—the United States' official reserves transactions balance was headed for a record deficit of $30 billion for the year.[9] Something had to be done.

The Nixon administration's response was formulated during the summer of 1971 by a handful of advisers dominated by newly appointed Secretary of the Treasury John Connally. Important but supporting roles were played by the Federal Reserve chairman, Arthur Burns; the chairman of the Council of Economic Advisers, Paul McCracken; and OMB director George Shultz, but no representatives of either the State Department or the NSC participated in the deliberations. Hence the discussion proceeded with little consideration of the broad foreign policy implications of the proposed measures and with no participation by any official responsible for managing their international consequences.

Not that adverse foreign reaction was unanticipated: the international aspects of the New Economic Policy were part of a conscious "get-tough" attitude toward the Europeans, Japanese, and Canadians. But the decision process precluded any serious effort to assess how the NEP would affect other important foreign policy issues: SALT and European fears of a U.S.–Soviet deal at their expense, the China summit and Japan's uneasiness over the sudden American policy reversal, or U.S. relations with the expanded European Economic Community, among others. It also lacked any representative of the view that U.S. actions, whatever they were to be, should not ignore the procedures for international consultation that the United States had itself worked painstakingly to develop since the Second World War.* In the event, the United States consulted with none of its economic partners before announcing its decisions. The sudden display of U.S. economic nationalism shook the confidence of other nations in the international economic order, and set a risky precedent. It reversed the steady movement toward free trade, contributed to a developing world climate of "neomercantilism," and weakened the practices of international economic collaboration, which most observers believe need marked reinforcement to manage the growing economic interdependence of nations.

Nuclear Options[10]

In January 1974 Secretary of Defense James Schlesinger announced a "change in targetting doctrine" that would provide "a wider variety of strategic options for the President in crisis situations."[11] Schlesinger's proposals, stressing the need for a capability to make limited, "selective" nuclear attacks on Soviet targets in situations short of all-out nuclear war, were not new. In 1961 President Kennedy had replaced the "mas-

* Whether and how those perspectives might have made a difference, given the need for some action and the extraordinary influence of Secretary Connally, is discussed in Chapter 7.

sive retaliation" doctrine of the Eisenhower years with a policy of "flexible response"; in 1962 Secretary McNamara had advocated a "no-cities" nuclear strategy in many respects similar to Schlesinger's. In 1970, in his first foreign policy report to the Congress, President Nixon had asked rhetorically, "Should a President, in the event of a nuclear attack, be left with the single option of ordering the massive destruction of enemy civilians in the face of certainty that it would then be followed by a mass slaughter of Americans?"[12] What was new about Schlesinger's proposals, then, was not the doctrine but the prospect of its imminent implementation.

Why was it that in 1974, after thirteen years of pronouncements by Presidents and Secretaries of Defense, U.S. strategic plans still provided for nothing smaller than a massive nuclear attack? Several reasons can be identified. For one, the path from the expression of a presidential or secretarial preference about strategic doctrine to an actual change in the SIOP (single integrated operating plan), the plan for the use of American nuclear weapons, is long and winding. It runs through the Joint Chiefs of Staff, the commander of the Strategic Air Command, and the Joint Strategic Targetting Staff, each of whom have preferences about doctrine and options that differ substantially from those of Presidents and Secretaries of Defense. Another reason is that American nuclear planning was centralized in 1960 under the domination of the Strategic Air Command, an organization dedicated to maintaining an alert capability to destroy an enemy by particular means: nuclear bombs delivered from manned aircraft. The vulnerability of U.S. bombers to Soviet air defenses meant that those defenses had to be destroyed first, largely with Minuteman or Polaris missiles, in order to enable the B-52s to reach their targets. Bombers, therefore, could not be used to carry out a constrained, selective attack. Moreover, military planners are traditionally reluctant to consider limited uses of force. They fear not only that constrained attacks may prove unreliable and insufficient, but that politicians may not recognize their limits. A military commander's worst nightmare has the United States entering a nuclear exchange with the Soviet Union while political constraints forbid operations he believes indispensable to national survival. Finally, Presidents and Secretaries of Defense have involved themselves in the issue of limited attack capability only sporadically. They have made pronouncements about doctrine, but have not joined the extended, continuous, and technically difficult process of implementation. Hence, lower-level officials have been able to discover more difficulties—some quite genuine—than Presidents and Secretaries of Defense have been determined to surmount.

Hard as it is to believe, the problem is not yet solved. At the time of Secretary Schlesinger's dismissal from office, the SIOP still did not incorporate significant limited-attack options. It remains to be seen whether future Secretaries of Defense will be more successful than the last five in providing Presidents with strategic alternatives to all-out nuclear war.

Peruvian Expropriation of the International Petroleum Company[13]

In June 1963 Fernando Belaunde Terry was elected president of Peru. A democratic reformer and a friend of the United States, he seemed exactly the kind of Latin leader for whom the Alliance for Progress had been intended. Yet Belaunde's inauguration was greeted by the United States with a partial embargo on new AID loans to Peru. The measure aimed to induce Belaunde to fulfill his campaign promise to settle a dispute over ownership of substantial oil fields between Peru and the International Petroleum Company (IPC), a subsidiary of the Exxon Corporation and Peru's predominant oil company. No settlement occurred, but the freeze continued until early 1966, when a thaw produced only a trickle of aid before loans were embargoed again, this time in reaction to

Peru's decision to purchase supersonic Mirage jets from France. As a result, in the years 1963–68, Peru received only about one-fourth the American aid per capita received by Colombia and one-tenth that given to Chile, a factor that contributed to the stagnation of the Peruvian economy.

In October 1968 the military deposed Belaunde, bringing to power a military government headed by Army General Juan Velasco Alvarado. The coup put an end to prospects for democratically led development and social reform in Peru. A government friendly to the United States was replaced by a radical, nationalistic regime much less receptive to American policy and even less friendly to American investors. Among its first acts, the new government expropriated certain IPC properties; soon thereafter it took the entire company.

The IPC affair posed a difficul problem for U.S. policy makers. On the one hand, the State Department had little choice but to back the company's claims; in 1962 Congress had enacted the Hickenlooper Amendment, which mandated a complete aid cutoff to any country that nationalized U.S. property without taking "appropriate steps" toward compensation, and Exxon had many friends on Capitol Hill. Not only did State wish to forestall the application of the amendment; American officials feared that if Peru was permitted to threaten expropriation, the climate for investment in all of Latin America might be chilled and the whole Alliance for Progress jeopardized. Yet Belaunde appeared politically incapable of reaching any settlement that IPC could live with. More than once he backed away from nearly concluded agreements.

Still, whatever chances there may have been for a negotiated settlement were clearly diminished by the U.S. government's handling of the problem. The aid freeze began as a temporary and ad hoc measure, but its nature and purpose were not revealed to the Peruvians. No alternatives to the embargo were seriously considered, nor were its probable effects assessed. Washington failed to notice that the same nationalistic pressures impeding Belaunde's settlement with the company operated even more strongly to prevent his submission to U.S. arm twisting. And as the embargo dragged fruitlessly on, the U.S. government avoided reexamining the merits of the issue that had become the focal point of U.S.–Peruvian relations. Such an examination might have made clear that the United States was pursuing two essentially contradictory objectives in Peru, and that it would have to choose between Belaunde and IPC. Instead, the United States continued to seek both objectives. It ended with neither.

Vietnam[14]

The Vietnam War was fought under extraordinarily close political-level observation; indeed, senior military officials constantly complained about the level of detail at which the White House attempted to direct military operations. Yet in many respects, the U.S. conduct of the war lay beyond the reach of civilian policy makers, despite their close attention and their apparent power. That is the least-told story of Vietnam: the story of how the conduct of the war was determined as much by the goals, incentives, and standard operating procedures of the armed services as by the choices of U.S. political leadership.

President Johnson dispatched large numbers of American ground forces to South Vietnam to preserve a non-Communist government in Saigon. Those forces were utilized mainly for large-unit search and destroy missions, conducting essentially a small war of attrition. That strategy flowed logically from long-standing army doctrine, training, and equipment. It was the kind of war the United States was best prepared to fight. But it was by no means the only way the war could have been fought, as a number of former military commanders have pointed out. And it involved great disadvantages. It meant high American casualties, minimum effort to improve and use the South Vietnamese army, limited attention to the political job of winning the support of the civilian population (which would have been much easier under an "enclave" strategy, for example), and significant civilian casualties from misdirected firepower. At no point did high level civilian and military officials "choose" the search and destroy strategy; it simply emerged. As former Ambassador Robert Komer has argued, the U.S. Army simply "did its thing."[15]

Organizational factors also affected the conduct of the air war. In February 1965 President Johnson initiated the campaign of regular air strikes against the North. Because his objectives were as much political as military, Johnson attempted to maintain tight personal control over the bombing campaign, involving himself even in the selection of targets. The Joint Chiefs of Staff steadily recommended expansion of the bombing campaign. Offered no alternative to those recommendations, President Johnson acquiesced in steady expansion of the scope and intensity of the air war. He did so despite the repeatedly expressed judgment of the CIA that the bombing campaign was neither curtailing the supply of North Vietnam's forces in the South nor breaking Hanoi's will to pursue the war. By 1968 all the targets requested by the JCS had been attacked.

The White House never fully understood the extent to which JCS recommendations reflected not only professional military judgment, but also far more parochial factors. The organizational interests of both the air force and the navy in more targets and more sorties, JCS processes that guaranteed unanimous military advice, and rivalry between the air force and the navy over the relative effectiveness of land-based vs. sea-based aircraft—each of these factors influenced the JCS recommendations. (During a period of munition shortages in 1966, one air force officer commented, "Our planes were flying with half loads, but bombs or no bombs, you've got to have more Air Force over the target than Navy.")[16] The President's acceptance of the JCS recommendations reflected not only the necessarily heavy weight of the chiefs in the internal counsels of government during time of war, but also the wider political support in the Congress and in the country for punishing the enemy and expanding any effort once begun to a level at which it succeeded. Yet, the original decision to initiate bombing was made without serious attention to the pressures that action would unleash, or to the way those pressures would constrain later decisions about the war.

American chemical warfare in Vietnam contains the whole story writ small. As McGeorge Bundy has testified:

. . . there is . . . one specific lesson from the past that seems to me worth holding in mind. Both in the case of herbicides and in that of tear gas, the initial authorizations for military use in the early 1960s were narrowly framed, at least as understood by civilians in Washington. The first authorized use of herbicides, as I recall it, was for defoliation along narrow jungle trails. I remember no talk of crop destruction at the beginning. The initial use of tear gas was for situations involving the need to protect civilian lives, in conditions closely analogous to those of a civil riot threat at home, and indeed in his first public statement on this subject, Secretary Rusk made it clear that it was the policy of the Administration to authorize the use of such agents only in such riot control situations. But as time passed, increasingly war-like uses were found for both kinds of agents. . . . Thus under the pressure of availability and battlefield urgency, the initial authorizations from Washington had been steadily widened. This is not a matter of bad faith or deception. Nor is it primarily a failure of command and control, although tighter and more explicit guidelines could have been useful in limiting the use of these agents. What happened here is what tends to happen quite remorselessly in war: unless there are sharp and clear defining lines against the use of a given weapon, it tends to be used.[17]

Lessons of the Cases

These episodes illustrate what a much larger body of evidence demonstrates; that recent U.S. foreign policy making exhibits a number of great and characteristic faults. Though related and partially overlapping, these faults can be categorized under three headings: imbalance, incompetence, and incoherence. Each has organizational roots.

Imbalance. The most obvious and most important imbalance is the pervasive weakness of broader foreign policy considerations when pitted against specific military, economic, or domestic concerns.* Both at departmental levels and in higher policy councils, the probable foreign consequences of our acts and the implications of those consequences for ourselves are regularly slighted. A principal cause is that the institutional guardian of those considerations, the State Department, repeatedly fails to compete effectively with the military services, the Secretary of Defense, the Treasury Department, or even with the lobbyists of private corporations. That is the main reason why U.S. demands for offsets could be pressed with so little regard for their likely effects on a decidedly pro-American leader of a major ally; why U.S. interests in Peru were allowed to become so closely identified with the interests of a particular company; and why the Connally initiatives of August 1971 could be taken with so little deliberation about their effects either on major allies or on practices of international collaboration that the United States had been building for a generation.

A closely related imbalance is the excessive weight accorded narrow military requirements as against broader conceptions of American security.[18] Thus, the United States renounced chemical and biological warfare half a century after most other powers had forsworn it; protected the navy but not the

---

* It has been argued that Vietnam demonstrates just the opposite. Since the Army was initially wary of another land war in Asia, since the costs of the war coupled with commitments to Great Society programs were likely to trigger serious inflation, and since the domestic politics of the war proved disastrous in the end, a case can be made that here foreign policy considerations must have overridden "military," "economic," and "domestic" concerns. In fact, however, by 1965 the JCS (including the Army) strongly advocated U.S. military intervention, the economic costs of the war were unclear, (they were to remain hidden for a remarkably long period), and the initial domestic politics of intervention appeared favorable or at least more attractive than their alternative.

nation against an oil embargo; failed to act concertedly against the dangers posed by the development of a global nuclear power industry; and insists still on retaining a canal of little military use, at great potential political cost. The organizational linkage here is not the whole of the problem, but clearly contributes to it. As we have said, the basic structure of foreign policy decision making is still the framework put in place in 1947. The principal forum for foreign policy decision making remains the National Security Council, a structure that includes the Secretaries of State and Defense as statutory members, and the chairman of the Joint Chiefs of Staff and Director of the CIA as steady participants, but accords no regular place to the Secretaries of Treasury or Agriculture, the managers of national economic policy, or the Budget Director. A forum of so narrow a membership impedes consideration of the manifold implications, foreign and domestic, of major policy issues.

Imbalances in the general perspectives brought to bear on policy making are also apparent. One is a notoriously short time frame. The U.S. government mostly reacts to problems, and often only after they have hit the front pages. The fault is hardly limited to government; for most organizations, as for most individuals, deadlines drive action and the immediate displaces the important. But this persistent failure to give adequate weight to long-run considerations incurs very high costs. Slow-maturing problems like oil and nuclear energy may have become insoluble by the time they make headlines; goals like the construction of new international economic arrangements require steadiness of attention over decades.

Another such defect in perspective is the common concentration on decisions and the neglect of implementation. Formulating goals, making decisions, and announcing them to Congress, the bureaucracy, and the public is a main responsibility of Presidents and Cabinet members. It is also the function over which they have the greatest control. But because policy directives are generally broad and often conflicting, they must be interpreted by middle-level officials. Those officials and their subordinates embody perceptions, objectives, and constraints that differ from those at the political level. And as the nuclear options and Vietnam cases illustrate, those differences can have great effect.[19]

Finally, the structure of the U.S. government weights those with stakes in maintaining current activity much more heavily than those charged with making change. Where the problems to be dealt with are relatively familiar, that imbalance has advantages. But the issues of the cold war are being superceded. If the oil and nuclear energy issues, for example, are typical of the future foreign policy agenda, it cannot be managed by a structure deeply weighted toward the maintenance of things as they have been. At the root of this problem is the "permanent government," a foreign policy and national security establishment of more than 3 million people, virtually none of whom change with administrations. Organized by department and agency, each responsible for a special piece of the problem of "foreign affairs," each taking a deliberately parochial view of the larger problem, this structure deeply affects the situations identified as problems, the information made available about them, the specification of feasible responses, the making of decisions, and the taking of actions. Proponents of change are often tempted to circumvent the permanent government, concentrating on issues that can be managed wholly at the political level. But there are few such issues. The cases—and much history—suggest that unless political appointees are able to anticipate, understand, and effect the processes they are charged with managing, required changes will not take place, and "policy" will prove empty.[20]

Incompetence. Incompetence is not a problem across the board. The agencies engaged in foreign relations contain large numbers of skilled and devoted people. But the capacity for performing certain limited but crucial tasks is clearly inadequate. One such task is the assessment of likely foreign developments. In both the IPC and offset cases, for example, the

United States took actions without understanding their probable effects on foreign governments. In both cases such an understanding could have been obtained, and in both cases it would—or should—have altered U.S. policy choices. A second incompetence is the inability of the organizations intended to play generalist roles in foreign policy formulation to deploy sufficient technical expertise to enable them to probe and question the assertions of more specialized agencies. Part of State's inability to inject broader foreign policy concerns in the August 1971 decisions resulted from its perceived incapacity to deal with the details of the economic and monetary questions involved. Similar deficiencies in the legislative branch hinder effective congressional oversight of executive activities. Particularly on matters of defense policy, Congress has been handicapped by the absence of an independent and expert analytic capability.

A third incompetence afflicts government across the board; it is the absence of a capacity to foresee problems of implementation. By concentrating on the making of "decisions" and neglecting questions of how to get from here to there, Presidents and Secretaries make it inevitable that some decisions will be put into effect only slowly and partially, or in distorted form. Moreover, the orientation toward "deciding" leads to policies preferable in theory only over courses whose actual consequences might well have been preferable. President Johnson's failure to foresee how his Vietnam policies would be affected by the procedures and incentives of the organizations charged with carrying them out makes the point painfully; the inability of four Presidents to achieve nuclear options could prove more painful yet.

Incoherence. In a complex and changing world, where the nation's objectives are many and partially conflicting, neatness, consistency, and the subordination of all actions to some grand and overarching plan cannot be expected. But the ability of separate agencies and particular interests to determine pieces of policy independently, and autonomously to start (or stop) its implementation must be subjected to at least partial control. Special interests and particularistic proposals must be comprehended and confined by a framework of larger national purposes and priorities. Such purposes evolve over time and priorities shift, but at any given moment they must be understood and observed. Over the next decades, many entities, executive and congressional, public and private, will play a part in America's international relations. The largest problem, and the most difficult to solve, will be to impose minimum levels of order, consistency, and coherence on a system in which power is so widely diffused.[21]

Chapter 3

The Future Will Be Harder

> Progress in dealing with our traditional agenda is no longer enough. A new and unprecedented kind of issue has emerged. The problems of energy, resources, environment, population, the uses of space and the seas now rank with questions of military security, ideology, and territorial rivalry which have traditionally made up the diplomatic agenda.
>
> Henry Kissinger (January 1975)

IT is now widely accepted that new and unfamiliar issues have been added to the traditional agenda, and that they present difficult challenges to American foreign policy. Almost equally well recognized are the facts that power among nations is becoming more widely dispersed; that U.S. preponderance is diminished; and that influence outside the United States is not confined to a rival superpower, or to a small group of dominant states, but is substantially if unequally shared among dozens of nations. What has so far attracted much less attention is that these two phenomena—the new agenda and the dispersion of power—are likely to place even greater strain on the most vulnerable aspects of U.S. policy making. They will have powerful implications for the ways the United States must organize to formulate policy and to conduct its foreign relations.

This chapter tries to spell out those implications, relating them to six apparent trends: an emerging global economy; growing physical interdependence; reduced preponderance of American power; multiplication of important actors; diminishing utility of military force; and erosion of the postwar consensus. Slicing complex and connected circumstances into such categories is somewhat arbitrary, but the reality of the main developments described is not in serious dispute. Indeed, our description of these characteristics of the present and near future is quite conventional.[1] Our purpose in this chapter is not to propose an original vision of the near future, but to examine the organizational implications of projections now widely accepted and solidly based.

An Emerging Global Economy

Over the last quarter century, economic interactions between the United States and the rest of the world have become far more direct, numerous, and consequential as a global economy has emerged. The significance of this development for Americans is not that, say, the reflation of the German economy in 1975 was importantly affected by actions of the U.S. government; that would have been even more true in 1950. The significance is that the interactions now run both ways. A German revaluation of the mark, or poor crops in the Soviet Union, or oil price hikes imposed by OPEC now change prices, jobs, and profits in the United States.

Degrees of interdependence vary, and many aspects of our economy are far less vulnerable to external forces than are those of Japan or of Europe. Yet for all its unqualified misuse, the concept of "interdependence" captures a large and still growing truth, underlined for Americans by the oil embargo:

our daily lives can be powerfully affected by economic or political events abroad. Numbers provide the reasons. In 1950* exports of U.S. goods amounted ot 3.5 percent of our GNP; in 1975 they represented 7.0 percent.[2] In 1950 multinational corporations mattered little; in 1975 their business accounted for one-seventh of the world's gross product and production outside of their headquarter nations exceeded the level of world trade.[3] In 1950 the management of national economies could concentrate almost entirely on the control of domestic factors; in 1973–74 half of the double-digit inflation experienced by the United States was caused by foreign-imposed increases in fuel and grain prices, and at least another fourth by the depreciation of the dollar on international money markets and the circumvention of U.S. price controls by American manufacturers through exporting.[4]

The principal significance of those developments can be summarized in a single assertion: During just that period in which the U.S. government, like all other central governments, assumed full responsibility for the nation's economic stability and growth, its power to fulfill that responsibility through autonomous action slipped away.

That fact has at least three implications for government organization. One is simply that the processes by which the American economy is managed must insure that probable developments abroad are identified, assessed, and factored into policy making. That will require good economic and political intelligence, attention to the most dangerous of U.S. vulnerabilities, and strengthening of the international mechanisms for concerting national economic policies—the International Monetary Fund (IMF), the General Agreement on Tariffs and Trade (GATT), the Organization for Economic Cooperation and Development (OECD). Since leaders of foreign govern-

---

* We use 1950 as a base year not because it was economically "normal" but because it well represents the period of the late 1940s and early 1950s in which current organizational arrangements were established.

ments, held accountable by their own citizens for full employment, price stability, and economic growth, depend even more on our economic policies than we do on theirs, U.S. "domestic" economic decisions must be taken with understanding of their likely impact abroad.

More fundamentally, economic interdependence implies that important economic issues simply cannot be classified as "foreign" or "domestic." Energy and the Soviet wheat sales most obviously exemplify the overlap, but other examples abound. The decision of the Johnson administration in 1966 not to seek a tax increase, for instance, was on its face a wholly domestic matter, and was certainly so regarded at the time. But the decision not to absorb excess purchasing power through new taxes made inevitable a rapid U.S. inflation which, in turn, fueled the European inflation of the early 1970s. Few U.S. actions of the 1960s had a greater effect on the international economy. Such a blurring of the traditional distinction between "foreign" and "domestic" issues means that the machinery of government whose membership, competence, and responsibilities are grounded in that distinction—the NSC, the Domestic Council, the foreign relations committees of the Congress, for example—will find themselves increasingly unable to grasp the problems they are charged with managing.

Third, economics is the stuff of politics. Not very many Americans care deeply about U.S. base rights overseas, our treaty relations with Korea, or troops in Germany. Most Americans, however, do care a great deal about the price of bread, the prosperity of the U.S. auto industry, and the rate of U.S. inflation. As a result, foreign policy cannot be nonpolitical. The notion that politics should "stop at the water's edge" has become untenable—or, more precisely, meaningless. "Foreign" policy will increasingly engage domestic interest groups, "domestic" departments of government, domestic politics. The Congress will become ever more fully engaged—and not merely (indeed, not principally) through the committees with international or foreign relations in their titles. The processes by which foreign policy is formulated, and support for it built, will become even more complex than they now are. And since economic interests are, by definition, particular interests, the "economization" of foreign policy will tend to increase pressures toward the fragmented and disjointed treatment of related matters, putting additional stress on the very thin resources of our government now devoted to the integration and coherence of policy.[5]

Physical Interdependence

Americans have historically taken pride in their "splendid isolation" from the rest of the world. Oceans to the east and west, friendly and relatively weak neighbors to the north and south, abundant natural resources gave us genuine insulation. As late as 1950 there was virtually no direct external threat to the physical well-being of American citizens.

The emergence of a sizable Soviet nuclear capability ended that kind of independence for all time. Soviet strategic forces create physical vulnerability in its most acute form; at any moment, a Soviet decision can put tens of millions of Americans to death. The proliferation of nuclear weapons to other states presents risks of only slightly less catastrophic attack, or of radioactive fallout resulting from a nuclear war among third parties. As suggested in Chapter 1, the growing reliance on nuclear reactors for domestic energy raises another specter: every nation with a need for electricity will be able to acquire a standby nuclear weapons capability; weapons-grade fuels together with the now well-understood technology of bomb design and fabrication may become accessible even to splinter groups and terrorists. Given the highly porous nature of U.S. borders—which, on average, some 450 unidentified aircraft cross each day—such developments may create almost unthinkable prospects.

Physical interdependence entails not only the possibility of instant destruction, but also of slow degradation of the conditions of life. Again, borders do not protect. New technologies (aerosol sprays, supersonic aircraft) may degrade the atmosphere; industrial processes can change the earth's climate or pollute the atmosphere and oceans. Discoverers and publicists of such threats frequently exaggerate, and the celebrated claim that we will soon exhaust the earth's nonrenewable resources is certainly overstated; but few informed observers will deny the developing danger.

Finally, the dramatic growth of world population presses on our insularity. It took from the beginning of time until 1930 for the globe's population to reach 2 billion; a third billion was then added in thirty years and a fourth in fifteen. The U.N.'s "medium" forecast for the year 2000 is 6.4 billion people. (Current fertility rates would produce 7.8 billion.) The direct effects of such a population explosion on the physical well-being of Americans defy prediction, but the social and political implications of Americans' awareness that tens—perhaps hundreds—of millions of other human beings are starving will not be negligible. To ignore such misery would badly strain national values, traditions, and moral consciousness. Although modern weapons in the hands of desperate rulers of starving countries would undoubtedly sharpen our sense of responsibility, the essence of the matter is not threat, but national values. The history of moral development evidences a steady expansion of the group for which responsibility is assumed: from the family to the tribe, town, and state, the outer boundaries of responsibility are now marked, for most people, by the nation. And the process is continuing, greatly speeded by the ability of modern communications, especially television, to make vivid and personal the condition of distant peoples. A global consciousness is beginning to emerge.

The implications of these facts for organization are several. Our vulnerability to nuclear terrorists creates new intelligence priorities, both for monitoring and, in the last resort, for action.

The possibilities of climatic change and environmental damage demand that we establish means of anticipating novel dangers and of sensitizing policy makers and the public to their implications. The developing global consciousness suggests that officials and institutions sensitive to the external effects of our policies should play larger roles in the making and execution of policy. Finally, the fact that all physical processes ignore national borders further diminishes the utility of the "foreign" vs. "domestic" distinction on which much government organization is now based; and it underlines the need not only for changes within the U.S. government, but also for new international mechanisms.

Reduced Preponderance of American Power

Economic and physical interdependence create new substantive problems. Other new conditions complicate their resolution. One such condition is the reduced preponderance of American power. National power is an elusive concept, yet most observers of international affairs agree that the ability of the United States to set the rules that guide international relationships and to influence the actions of foreign governments is markedly less today than at the outset of the postwar era, and that the U.S. position in the future will be more like that of 1975 than like that of 1950. In most currencies of power—military, economic, political, and perhaps moral—increases in the standing of other nations have reduced U.S. influence. Outside the Communist world, the United States remains the majority stockholder, but it no longer owns the corporation.

Table 1 documents some of the changes.

Reduced preponderance is not impotence. If our influence is now smaller than Americans familiar with the postwar years recall, it is much greater than those whose perceptions are

TABLE 1*

	1950	1975
Military		
Total expenditures (U.S. % world military):	50	25
Nuclear position	U.S. effective monopoly plus invulnerability	U.S.-Soviet parity plus proliferation
Economic		
U.S. % of world GNP	40	27
U.S. % of world manufactured products	60	30
U.S. % of world monetary reserves	50	7
Political	Reconstructor of Germany and Japan; organizer of the Free World; leading proponent of U.N. and decolonization; model for new governments	Member of multipolar world; the key ally of Japan and Europe; partner in détente

* Data from U.N. *Statistical Yearbooks* for 1951 and 1975, and U.S. *Statistical Abstracts* for same years.

dominated by Vietnam realize. In some regions, the United States may have greater usable influence today than in 1950. And in most arenas, if we cannot impose our own will, we can nonetheless block developments we oppose. Nor is reduced influence a license for withdrawal. Indeed, many analysts, here and abroad, believe that the growing difficulty and number of global issues and the dispersion of the influence of the former great powers enlarge the need for American initiative. But the style of leadership required has changed. Leadership is going to prove a subtler and harder task.

We now must bargain hard to attain our ends, and from a position, in Marina Whitman's phrase, of "leadership without hegemony."[7] To bargain effectively, and to enlist the uncoerced support of large numbers of other nations, the United States will require better capabilities for understanding the forces at work in foreign societies, for assessing the interests and internal politics of other governments, and for identifying the points at which U.S. leverage can be exercised effectively. Reduced preponderance also requires closer coordination of the remaining instruments of U.S. influence. We can no longer rely on the postwar assumption that however maladroitly we managed, our power sufficed for our purposes. As the margin for error has diminished, the need to use our still considerable resources in careful combination has correspondingly enlarged.

The Multiplication of Actors and the Multilateralization of Issues

When the United States negotiated with other states in 1950, it negotiated seriously with few. Outside the United States (and the USSR) power was relatively concentrated. The international monetary system established at Bretton Woods required the concurrence in fact only of Britain, and the establishment of NATO hinged almost entirely on the agreement of France. Serious negotiation was mostly bilateral.

Again, the contrast with today is dramatic. The economic recovery of Western Europe and Japan quickly changed the balance on economic issues. The emergence of the People's Republic of China created a new source of great influence in Asia. The number of nations with nuclear weapons, two in 1950, is now six or more. Membership in the U.N. has risen from 50 to 143, and while many of the new states are small and weak, they command large majorities in forums whose rule is "one nation, one vote." (Indeed, coalitions voting against U.S. positions often command majorities on the basis of "one person, one vote," as well.) A number of the newer nations control important raw materials; other states previously inactive beyond their borders are becoming regional powers, Brazil and Iran, for example.

The number and importance of nongovernmental actors in international affairs has also increased dramatically since 1950, as multinational corporations most vividly illustrate. As noted, the product of multinational enterprises in countries outside their home bases now exceeds the total level of world trade among developed countries.[8] Personal contact among nongovernmental leaders of many nations encourages recognition of common professional and ideological interests. Transnational associations—of bankers, corporate executives, commercial fishermen, and scientists, for example—press national governments to serve the interests of their members. Terrorists and paramilitary groups deploy other forms of influence.

As the number of actors with influence has grown, the forums of negotiation have become multilateral. For the resolution of energy, food, arms trade, or oceans issues, many nations must agree. International organizations therefore become more important—not necessarily as decision-making bodies, but as forums for negotiation, alliance building, consciousness raising. The importance of such organizations is suggested by the fact that, in 1975 official U.S. delegations attended more than 800 international conferences; in 1950 the number was 291.[9]

This multiplication of actors and multilateralization of issues shifts the locus of decision making. When major policy issues affect many countries, the perspectives of officials oriented toward a single nation or toward a small group of them are inevitably partial—often in both senses. Decisions sensitive to all relevant considerations can be taken only where all these considerations are understood—in Washington, if anywhere, and at relatively high levels. This has the effect of further centralizing U.S. decision making, and further eroding the position of ambassadors.

Secondly, because international agreements emerge from bargaining, conflict, and compromise, effective organization

for negotiations with other nations becomes almost as important as organizing to establish initial American positions. The
growing importance and difficulty of international negotiations
enlarges the conflict between the needs of negotiators on the
one hand—especially for secrecy about minimum positions,
and grants of bargaining discretion—and the requirements
for accountability and openness in the development of U.S.
positions on the other.

Finally, multilateral diplomacy requires practices and institutions based on the steady collaboration of many states. Effective U.S. leadership in building such practices and such institutions will require that U.S. policy be developed in a framework
that encourages stability of purpose, long time horizons, and a
willingness to abide by rules not entirely of our own making.[10]

The Changing Role and Diminished
Utility of Military Force

In 1950 the dominant concern of American foreign policy
was to assure the physical security of the nation and its allies
and to contain the pressures of Communist expansion. Those
pressures appeared intense, the product of what seemed a
monolithic commitment to make the world Communist, backed
by the two largest armies in the world. Over the last twenty-
five years, those concerns have faded and altered.

Though the Soviet Union's actual military capability to
harm the United States has increased from near zero to near
infinity, a stable "balance of terror" has evolved. The certainty
that our strategic nuclear forces could destroy the Soviet Union
even after any Soviet attack on the United States has lessened
both the apprehension and the probability of such an event.
The continuing SALT negotiations provide some regulation
of the competition in weapons of ultimate destruction. The
conventional military strength of the United States and its allies

has apparently discouraged direct Soviet military intervention outside Eastern Europe; China, now hostilely independent of Moscow, has thus far shown little interest in military undertakings beyond her own borders.

In 1950, and for many years thereafter, U.S. military force had uses other than deterring the Soviets and Chinese. In Korea, Lebanon, the Dominican Republic, and finally Vietnam, we employed conventional arms to achieve, or attempt to achieve, foreign policy objectives; but now the growing of nationalism in the developing world makes the exercise of U.S. force far more costly, both politically and militarily. These costs have been underscored by the experience of Vietnam and by the deep domestic opposition to a U.S. role as world policeman. And in a world of many nuclear powers, the dangers of escalation are far greater than in 1950. The security of the United States and its allies is still subject to threats, but many are not susceptible to standard military response. For the United States, as for our major allies, the most likely external threats of the next decades concern the denial of important resources (or their supply only at prohibitive prices), or severe environmental change, or attack by terrorists. None are likely to be relieved by conventional military strength.

Thus, a paradox emerges: much of our military strength is essential without being usable. Powerful U.S. forces are indispensable. They underwrite the safety of the United States and its major allies from attack, and they reduce the degree to which international relations generally can be dominated by the weight of arms. But those forces provide little positive influence for achieving objectives of our own.[11]

One implication of these changes is a need to reassess the concept of national security. The National Security Act of 1947 viewed security in narrowly military terms and organized a military response to protect it. Well suited to its time, that perspective is much less useful now. U.S. policy must seek a broader security, attend a wider spectrum of threats, and develop novel means of countering them.

Second, the reduced American interest in the political complexions of foreign regimes, coupled with our diminished capacity to affect developments abroad by military means, suggests that our alliances, foreign bases, troop deployments—and indeed the size of our forces—are all ripe for review by officials holding a broad view of the nation's security needs. Finally, the design of our military forces as well as their deployment and use needs rethinking. As former Secretary of Defense Schlesinger has argued, U.S. strategic forces must be designed with attention not only to their potential use, but also to Soviet leaders' perceptions of our capabilities, especially in crisis contexts. At the same time, a revolution in weapons technologies is occurring, illustrated most vividly by the so-called precision-guided munitions—weapons able from great ranges to detect virtually any target and to hit almost any target they can detect. The new weapons raise serious questions about such military mainstays as aircraft carriers and tanks. But the design of military forces is a notoriously conservative process. It accords little weight to the probable perceptions of potential foes, and permits dogged attachment to weapons and tactics made vulnerable by new technologies. If our forces are to match the subtle and partly subjective purposes for which we need them, and to respond to objective changes in their vulnerabilities, substantial changes in the processes of defense planning and weapons procurement will be necessary.

Erosion of the Cold War Consensus and Loss of Confidence in Government

Except for the McCarthy period in the early 1950s, the officials conducting U.S. foreign policy in the postwar period could count on public and congressional support. The country had great faith in the established institutions that conducted foreign policy. Neither condition now holds. The nature of international politics has become both more complex and apparently

less threatening, a state of affairs nicely symbolized by the fact
that only months after the loss of a war launched largely to
contain China, the U.S. Secretary of Defense could publicly
suggest that we might supply China with weapons. Moreover, in 1950 the issues that dominated the foreign policy
agenda were perceived as threats affecting all Americans
equally. In contrast, issues like food, energy, inflation, and
oceans now divide farmers and consumers, labor and management, East and West Coast fishing industries. They also divide
the Congress, and move it to intervene more directly, if sporadically, in policy formation.

The dissolution of the anti-Communist consensus was docu-
mented by the Chicago Council on Foreign Relations poll of
December 1974, which found that the public put "containing
Communism" ninth in importance in a list of eighteen foreign
policy goals, behind "securing adequate supplies of energy,"
"protecting the jobs of American workers," and "combating
world hunger." Defense treaties continue to commit the United
States to more than forty nations, but Canada was the only
country a majority of Americans favored defending with U.S.
troops if she were attacked.[12]

At the same time, confidence in all national institutions has
declined sharply. For the majority of voting-age Americans
in 1976, the formative historical experience, the experience
that shaped the world in which they became politically conscious and active, was not Munich and the failure of the
West, not the confidence of being morally right in World War
II, not the potency of the American war effort, or the shatter-
ing of hopes by Communist aggression after World War II. It
was Vietnam. That long agony, followed by Watergate and exacerbated by the secretive style of recent foreign policy
decision making, accounts for the finding of a January 1975
survey that 69 percent of the population agreed with the
proposition: "Over the past ten years this country's leaders
have consistently lied to the American people."[13] Changes in
levels of confidence in the people running key U.S. institutions
ran as follows:

TABLE 2*

Key Institutions	Percentage Expressing "Great Deal" of Confidence					
	'66	'72	'73	'74	'75	'76
Military	62	35	40	33	24	23
U.S. Senate	42	21	30	18	13	9
U.S. House	42	21	29	18	13	9
Executive Branch	41	27	19	28	13	11

* U.S., Congress, Senate, Committee on Government Operations, Subcommittee on Intergovernmental Relations, *Confidence and Concern: Citizens View American Government*, 93rd Cong. 1st sess., 3 December 1973, pt. 1: 33; also *Chicago Tribune*, 22 March 1976.

But public confidence in U.S. leadership, and a measure of consensus about the nation's goals, is indispensable to effective foreign policy. Viable international action requires steadiness of purpose and tolerance for the compromises unavoidable in bargaining among nations. To effect such compromises, negotiators need some discretion—discretion based on trust. Rebuilding public confidence in government, and a measure of consensus about the nation's foreign policy are therefore priority tasks. The need for such reconstruction should affect both the substance of foreign policy choice, and the process by which decisions are made.[14]

The Scope of the Challenge

In briefest summary, then, the changing conditions under which foreign policy must be made and executed over the next decades will force the United States to face harder problems in a more difficult environment. The issues themselves will be complex, systemic, numerous, and partly unfamiliar, harder both to understand and to manage than those of the postwar period. They will involve a larger number of players: many nations, regional and special interest organizations, varieties of private interests. Expected to lead the management and resolution of these problems, the United States will lack the broad military, economic, and political authority it possessed in the first decades after World War II. And the internal processes by which we formulate our policies will involve more participants, executive and congressional, public and private. The notion that politics should stop at the water's edge will have disappeared. Interest groups will press the system hard, and that pressure will no longer be confined by a framework of general agreement on U.S. purposes and responsibilities in the world.

These circumstances would be challenge enough for a government well-organized for the making and carrying out of foreign policy. But that is not the U.S. government today. Indeed, the challenges of the near future are likely to demand in greater measure exactly those qualities—alertness, adaptability, high capacity, a regard for the long view, and the ability to draw agreement and action from many participants—that U.S. policy making now most characteristically lacks.

The problem thus posed is formidable. Indeed, it may ultimately prove insoluble within current constitutional boundaries. Perhaps by the 1990s the density, complexity, and importance of international relations, and the difficulty of dealing with them through widely dispersed centers of authority, will force us to consider radical measures—constitutional changes within the United States, grants of what are now national powers and prerogatives to supranational bodies. But that is not likely to occur in the decade next before us. The task of this next period will be to see whether less radical measures can suffice; whether the shared authority of existing constitutional arrangements can be exercised in such a way as to meet the minimum conditions of coherence, decisiveness, and consistency that effective foreign policy requires.

Chapter 4

The President's Tasks

> Energy in the executive is a leading character in the definition of good government. It is essential to the protection of the community against foreign attacks; it is not less essential to the steady administration of the laws, . . . to the security of liberty against the enterprises and assaults of ambition, of faction, and of anarchy.
>
> *The Federalist*, no. 70

THE growing difficulty of effective foreign policy making will bear most heavily upon the President. The issues that come to him for decision will be painfully hard. Problems of the new agenda, like nuclear energy, will jumble domestic causes with foreign effects; political sensitivities with technical complexities; present perceptions with future realities. It is a defining characteristic of "systems" that changes in any portion of them affect other portions; the United States is now part of a global economic, physical, and (consequently) political system of the greatest complexity. So in his role as chief decision maker the President will find that, even more than has been true for his predecessors, the goals he seeks are many and conflicting; the information he must digest is voluminous and incomplete;

the uncertainties he ponders are large and irreducible. The still growing U.S. dependence on foreign oil, the spread of nuclear reactors, the Panama Canal—what to do?

Presidents cannot escape such decisions. As the sign on Harry Truman's desk said, "The Buck Stops Here." And the number of issues that must be brought to the President is growing. With the jurisdictions of executive departments deeply entangled, the questions that can be resolved within departments are only those of lesser importance. Meanwhile, Congress seeks an agenda, a program to support or oppose, and it is in the President's interest to propose one. Events abroad impose their own exigencies. So a stream of choices flows to him, decisions sought by staff or Cabinet officers or congressional leaders, imposed by statutory deadlines (the annual budget, the State of the Union message), or forced by external events.

To the making of these choices, the President brings something unique. He is the single point in the American system of government at which "civil" and "military," "foreign" and "domestic," "legislative" and "executive," "administrative" and "political" merge. He is the sole official elected by the whole nation, the only figure whose authority can effect those mergers. As Richard E. Neustadt has put it,

his mind has become the major source available from which to draw politically legitimated judgments on what, broadly speaking, can be termed the political feasibilities of contemplated action *vis-a-vis* our world antagonists: judgments on where history is tending, what opponents can stand, what friends will take, what officials will enforce, what "men in the street" will tolerate—judgments on the balance of support, opposition, indifference, at home and abroad.[1]

But the President serves not only as the focal point of governmental decision. His larger role is to *lead*. He must assert some control over the demands and deadlines thrust upon him, establish his own priorities, understand which of them he can effect by decisions that will come to him unbidden, and which only his initiatives can advance. He must organize, lead, and manage an administration. He is not merely—indeed not principally—a chief decision maker; he is the chief executive.

This is not to imply that the President embodies the national interest. Organizational reformers have frequently assumed so, but the Constitution is constructed on a quite different principle, and our history confirms its wisdom. Only so broadly based a body as the Congress can legitimately confer legislative authority. Only so insulated a body as the Supreme Court can be trusted to pronounce the meaning of our basic law. But only the President can articulate the nation's purposes, propose policies and actions appropriate to advance those purposes, and induce the machinery of government to formulate and to execute them. A system as diffuse, plural, and complex as ours requires presidential energy to make it work.

The major organizational tasks of the President reflect his unique responsibilities as leader and manager of the executive branch.[2] These are tasks that only he has the perspective and incentive to perform. As regards the *capabilities* of the government, he must guarantee that the structure and processes of all agencies, and the people within them perform to a level of distinction, and economically, the jobs that must be done. In particular, he must seek to ensure that critical new sectors of the front (the risks' inherent in the spread of "peaceful" nuclear technology, for example) are guarded by an appropriate organizational entity. Moreover, he must attend to the organizational implications of insuring that those priorities are advanced special priorities of his administration by processes and people who bring appropriate competence and perspective to the tending of such issues.

With respect to the interests vested and weighted by government, he must look to the *balance* of organizational arrangements and to the *integration* of policy. He must seek to ensure that in the forums of national policy making all relevant perspectives are represented—and represented in some rough relation to their real importance. If, for example, the security of Americans is affected by nuclear devices made from by-products of American uranium supplied to Indian nuclear power reactors, officials appropriately concerned about those security implications need some voice in decision making about such supplies. Moreover, he has a special responsibility for ensuring that these processes effect closure—that the decentralized actions of the many departments and agencies stand in some consistent relation to one another, and cumulatively serve the nation's larger interests.

Finally, the President must guard the *legitimacy* of the governmental process. He must strive to ensure that government merits the trust of the people. Public confidence in the institutions of government is a precious national resource—perhaps the most precious. The sources of that confidence include not only the evident integrity and competence of the President and his chief officials, but a more general assurance that the processes of decision are balanced and fair, and that the priorities and policies of government are truthfully stated. Each of these ingredients has been absent in recent years. Public uncertainty about our purposes in the world has been exaggerated by a decision-making process in which for too many issues only Secretary Kissinger, the President, and a few key assistants have been privy to the "real" definition of the problem or the "true" reasons for our actions. That uncertainty is exacerbated by the disparity between reality and official rhetoric: a lost war merchandized as "peace with honor"; a relaxation of tensions with the Soviet Union treated as an end to hostility; a presidential visit to China staged as "the event of the century"; a fragile international environment declared a "stable structure of peace." In light of the peculiar history of the past decade, the President bears a special burden for ensuring balance, breadth, and openness in the processes of policy making, and candor and directness in communicating to Congress and the public our purposes in foreign policy.

The scale and complexity of these partially overlapping organizational tasks is suggested by a glance at the several concentric circles of the executive branch. The innermost

circle contains the White House itself, the President and his
closest staff. Until Kissinger moved from the National Security
Council to the Department of State, Assistants to the President
for National Security Affairs had for over a decade over-
shadowed the Secretary of State. From two personal assistants
in the time of President Hoover and eleven White House aides
to FDR during World War II, the number of "assistants to the
President" grew to fifty-two in 1972. President Ford achieved
some reduction in those numbers, but pressures for expansion
persist, generated by issues that cut across departmental lines,
Presidential distrust of the departments, and the increasing
political attention focussed on the President personally. As
assistants to the President expand in number, however, they
diminish in individual utility; few will have responsibilities
sufficiently broad or a relationship sufficiently close to the
President to understand the extraordinary range of his concerns.

Just beyond the White House lies the Executive Office
of the President, the "institutional presidency." This circle too
has swelled, from 1,175 persons in the early Eisenhower period
and 1,664 in Kennedy's last year in office, to over 5,000 under
Nixon. The Executive Office is intended to serve only the
President, but its growing size makes it both distant from him
and hard to distinguish from the cabinet departments.

The third circle is the "appointive government." The several
hundred secretaries, under secretaries, assistant secretaries,
and their deputies who comprise the "administration"
expect to direct the departments, linking the President with
the operating levels of government. But the ascendancy of key
White House advisers has reduced many members of the
appointive government (especially in domestic affairs) to
ministerial tasks. Recent Presidents have seen many appointees
rarely or not at all, and then for purposes more ceremonial
than substantive. Presidents know that many members of their
administrations are hostage to special interests, and doubt the
competence of others.

Finally, there is the "permanent government," the more than three million people (some two million of them military) who do not change with Presidents, but carry on the day to day work of all administrations. Organized by department and agency, each with its separate professional career line, these individuals are protected by Civil Service or similar systems and largely "unionized." Contrary to popular impressions, the permanent government has not been steadily expanding. In fact, the executive branch employs fewer civilians today relative to U.S. population than it did in 1947.[3] Moreover, for so large a body, its levels of skill, expertise, and devotion to duty are high. Yet it appears to a new President a behemoth: huge, slow, at least independent, perhaps hostile.

Beyond the executive branch—which for all its unwieldiness, at least is *his* (so he thinks; Congress believes otherwise)—lies Congress, alien territory. Beyond that, the private sector of the economy, another participant in the making and execution of foreign policy; and beyond that, the larger public whose support or acquiescence he must gain and hold.

The President must energize and lead this conglomerate so that its interactions with the external world serve his conception of the nation's broadest interests—checked, corrected, and constrained though this conception must be by Congress and the public. The task is easily stated and difficult in the extreme to perform. As Harry Truman commented in contemplating the prospect of Eisenhower as President, "He'll sit here and he'll say, 'Do this! and Do that!' *Nothing will happen.* Poor Ike—it won't be a bit like the Army."[4]

In considering how organization can assist a President in making things happen, we focus first on the Presidency itself, personal and institutional. Here, the President's goal must be the effectiveness of high policy making: ensuring that issues requiring his attention are identified and that their full dimensions are made evident before decision. To that end we propose making key Cabinet officers the chief substantive counselors to the President; creating a forum for serious substantive discussion among them and the President; and reducing White House staff to staff roles. We then address the departments and major agencies of the executive branch, where the main task is to assure that the day-to-day actions of the departments effectively serve not only their own specific purposes but the broader interests of the nation. The means to that end, we believe, include giving Cabinet officers the authority and support to become in fact the chief line managers of the government, improving relations between the appointive and permanent governments, and strengthening one weak and crucial department, the Department of State. Finally, we turn to executive-congressional relations, where workable levels of trust and comity between the branches must be restored, and the incentives and abilities of the Congress to appreciate the foreign implications of its actions must be strengthened.

The Presidency

Recall the history of U.S. oil policy recounted in Chapter 1. It illustrates how a large and unfamiliar problem is likely to be handled in the absence of strong presidential direction:

1. Warning signs of increasing vulnerability to embargo went unnoticed; no action was taken to defer or to hedge against that contingency.

2. When the embargo and the hike in oil prices occurred, they were met by "Project Independence"—an attractive label for an almost certainly infeasible course of action.

3. Two years passed before the administration was able to sort out its proposals; the bill then submitted to Congress represented a least common denominator proposal that avoided most of the hard issues.

4. A divided executive encouraged divisions within Congress; after hearings by eleven committees and subcommittees,

Congress passed a bill even weaker than the one the administration had proposed.

5. No consistent and supportable view of the issue was presented to the public; popular skepticism of the very reality of an energy crisis was thus left uncountered, and the task of building a consensus for responsible policy was barely attempted.

6. Though important international agreements have been reached, the United States depends more heavily on imported oil today than it did in 1973, the degree of dependence continues to rise, and no U.S. policy now in place or in prospect offers much promise of changing that fact.

The need for presidential decision and coordination is not confined to novel issues. To a White House Task Force on government organization a decade ago Francis Bator provided this account of circumstances far more routine than those of the oil crisis:

Recall that in the autumn of 1964 a new Labor Government took over in London in the midst of a foreign exchange crisis. Mr. Wilson decided against devaluation at that time but it soon became clear that the foreign exchange bind, and more generally too many claims on not enough resources would, in the absence of extraordinary luck, force on the United Kingdom difficult choices involving the British military presence east of Suez, Britain's NATO forces, foreign aid, trade policy, the exchange rate, domestic economic policies, et cetera. Obviously the United States had a great interest in what HMG would decide about all these matters during the course of the next several years. And it is not surprising that different parts of the U.S. Government had different priorities. The Treasury and "the Fed." were primarily concerned to avoid a British devaluation and, by the autumn of 1965 to assure London's support in the SDR negotiations. The Economic Bureau of State and STR were mainly worried that London might impose protectionist restrictions that would endanger the Kennedy round. Commerce, also concerned with a good industrial bargain in the Kennedy round, had its mind on such things as textiles. Agriculture was preoccupied with the Kennedy round and the inequalities of the common agricultural policy. The European Bureau of State, and a part of the Seventh Floor, were primarily concerned with the British role in Western Europe and Germany in NATO, and with United Kingdom policy *vis-a-vis* the Common Market. They were scared to death by any large drawdown of the British Army on the Rhine (especially given the effect on our troop levels, in the light of congressional sentiment). Last, the top of Defense and State were principally concerned about the British role East of Suez and their stance on Vietnam. Similar differences about priorities existed on the British side, among the bureaucracies of the British Government and within the Cabinet. Moreover, all these issues were to come up for the first time, implicitly if not explicitly, during the first visit by the new Chancellor of the Exchequer to the new Secretary of the Treasury during the early summer of 1965. This would be the first face-to-face contact at any level where these issues would begin to impinge on each other. And as a normal matter such a Treasury-to-Treasury visit would be handled as primarily a Treasury matter. . . . [I]t is obvious that in a situation we faced *vis-a-vis* this United Kingdom during the spring of 1965, allowing each department and each bureau and each Cabinet Officer to communicate to his counterpart his own priorities on these matters would have created an unholy mess in British-American and Atlantic politics.[5]

These two examples, together with the cases described in Chapter 2, help define the problem of central coordination. The starting point is now familiar: virtually no issue of importance in foreign relations falls exclusively within the domain of a single department or agency. The wide-ranging objectives of American foreign policy jumble agency jurisdictions, cut across lines of authority, breach the boxes on organization charts. Relations between the United States and Britain in 1965 could not be handled by State alone, or by State, Treasury, and Defense. Still less could the oil issue be managed by those agencies, even together with Interior, Commerce, EPA, and the new Energy Agency specifically assigned the problem. Nor do categories like "security," "general foreign policy," or "foreign economics" describe separable realms. "Security" considerations are normally tangled with "economics"—the level of offset for U.S. troops, the price of oil. And both "security" and "economics" are components of larger foreign policy objectives.

The latter example also illustrates the extent to which the day-to-day business of international relations is carried out by separate departments dealing directly with their counterpart agencies abroad. Those dealings are inevitably influenced by the perspectives and functions of the department conducting them and by the concerns of its clientele. Even where appointive officials seek genuinely to serve the President, they must do the business and defend the interests of their departments. Each knows that his influence and effectiveness are gauged—by his subordinates, his department's constituents, the press, indeed by the President himself—in terms of the skill and force with which he advances the department's efforts or argues the department's brief.

This decentralized management of day-to-day operations is both inescapable and proper. But it produces problems of several kinds. Departments seek to impose their own priorities on U.S. policy generally, as in relations with the United Kingdom. Or the disagreement of departments sharing pieces of a problem produces stalemate, as in the case of chemical and biological weapons in 1967. Or it leads to logrolling, with compromises meeting the minimum needs of all departments but serving the nation poorly, as true of advice from the military services about progress of the war in Vietnam. Or it yields unresolved conflict, inconsistency, and confusion. That is still the situation with respect to oil.

Only the President can circumvent, dampen or resolve such problems. Congress lacks the unity, the State Department lacks the authority. If the policies and actions of the U.S. government are to fit a conscious pattern, the President must impose it. The processes and the staff that assist the President in imposing such a pattern must follow largely from the President's personal preferences. As Secretary Rusk put it, "The real organization of the government at the higher echelons is not what you find in the textbooks or organization charts. It is how confidence flows down from the President."[6] That flow of confidence cannot be mandated. It follows that efforts to legislate structure for Presidential management and decision rarely succeed. Structures, processes, or people that the President does not find useful will simply go unused. But the history of recent Presidents' attempts to coordinate these decentralized operations does suggest a number of general propositions about strengths and weaknesses of alternative structures—propositions a President can ignore only at his peril.

Central Decision and Coordination

Formal and relatively open White House-centered processes operated in the Eisenhower and early Nixon periods; Kennedy and Johnson utilized informal White House-dominated processes, and Johnson also promulgated but never really tried a formal system centered on the State Department; after 1970, the Nixon years were marked by use of a tightly closed White House system. Careful review of those mechanisms and their results suggests a number of conclusions.[7]

The evidence is clearest in demonstrating the kind of authority necessary to make a system of central coordination work. President Johnson's attempt to lodge coordinating authority in the Department of State failed almost completely and almost immediately—for several reasons. First, State simply did not have the staff to effectively argue security issues with Defense or monetary issues with Treasury. That fault can be remedied over time, and it should. (We suggest how in Chapter 6.) More important, the Secretary of State proved reluctant to use what influence he had on issues of first-order importance to other departments, but only secondary to his own. And when State did attempt to exercise leverage, it found itself at a disadvantage: other departments regarded it as representing not the presidential perspective, but a purpose quite its own, the maintenance of good relations with other countries as an end in itself. But most fundamentally, State simply lacked the power to coordinate the actions of major departments, or to resolve differences between them. Coordination, like decision making, is a function of power. In the executive branch only one power—the President's—is superior to that of Cabinet officers. Central coordination and decision is therefore, inescapably, a presidential function. The President—if he is truly determined—can delegate some measure of authority to a forceful and able subordinate, who visibly enjoys his full confidence. That official can be the Secretary of State,* but a Secretary playing this role serves in his capacity as confidant and adviser to the President, not as chief of a department. The distinction is important. As Presidential adviser the Secretary's responsibilities are broader and as Presidential confidant his authority is greater, than that of the department he heads. The Department of State cannot play these roles at the next levels down; except briefly and on quite specific assignments, no bureaucracy can wield the President's authority.

The record of the recent past also suggests the advantages and disadvantages of informal and ad hoc methods of coordination, as opposed to more fixed and regular processes of decision. Francis Bator has characterized the key features of ad hoc White House–centered systems as the timely formation of task forces tailored to the problem at hand and

consisting of a small number of people who are senior enough to marshall the resources of their agency; not so senior as to make it impossible for them to keep up with detail or spend the time

---

* It has been argued, most recently by Milton Eisenhower, that a new official should assume this role. Eisenhower asserts that the burdens of the current system fall far too heavily on the President, and that they can be lightened most effectively by a constitutional amendment creating two Vice-Presidents, one for international affairs, the other for domestic matters. We differ, believing that the costs in time, energy, and political leverage to achieve the amendment would be great, and that the resulting benefits would be minimal. The Vice-President for International Affairs would have little authority that could not be given, *de facto*, to a National Security Adviser or Secretary of State who met the personal requirements for such a role, and had strong presidential backing. The deeper objection is that such a proposal raises to constitutional dimensions the distinction between "foreign" and "domestic" matters at just the moment in history when, for the largest issues, it has lost its meaning. (Milton S. Eisenhower, *The President Is Calling* [New York: Doubleday, 1974], p. 539 f.)

needed for comprehension and sustained exploration of each other's minds; and close enough to their Secretaries and to the President to serve as double-edged negotiators (each operating for his Secretary in the task group bargaining, and in turn representing the group's analysis of the issues and choices to his Secretary).[8]

Such task forces are assigned to draw sharp "maps" of the issues for the President, specifying the choices open and assessing their probable consequences. Once decisions are made the task force may be used to oversee implementation.

A principal advantage of ad hoc processes, especially important in coping with a large and rapidly changing foreign policy agenda, is flexibility. While formal structures do not respond easily to novel problems, the memberships and mandates of ad hoc groups can readily be designed to represent and weight the interests appropriate to virtually any issue. Such groups offer other advantages as well. Responsibility for a specific cluster of issues is clearly assigned to a particular individual, accountable directly to the President. The key people concerned with an issue can be assembled without extraneous bystanders, and can be encouraged (since the group is presidential) to relax departmental parochialism in their deliberations. Such steady and informal interaction among the officials actually charged with managing problems, and among them only, tends to produce a collegial conception of larger and long-term objectives, and to facilitate implementation by their departments. And dissolution of the group at the close of the task forecloses waste motion.

But such groups also show significant drawbacks. Given the press of other business and the very limited number of White House staffers who can anticipate and represent presidential preferences, important issues may be missed or noticed too late. The procedure produces resentment elsewhere in the government since, from the vantage point of most officials, issues may simply disappear into the hands of unannounced groups of unknown composition and schedule. Departments having legitimate interests may inadvertently go unrepresented, with incomplete information, mistaken decisions, or reluctant implementation the result. And this system tends to operate on the basis of the prevailing understanding of an issue among senior officials; it typically fails to encourage the development of new information or fresh analyses.

Formal White House–centered systems have different virtues, different defects. As exemplified by the Nixon-Kissinger NSC procedures outlined in the CBW story, formal systems provide a visible process for raising issues for interagency examination and White House review, and assure all legitimate parties an opportunity to be heard. When coupled with a study process like that inaugurated by national security study memoranda (NSSMs), they provide the President a broad range of options and arguments, and tend both to dampen interagency differences and to prevent premature acceptance of logrolled solutions. Lower levels of the bureaucracy are drawn into an analytic process likely to broaden their view of the problem, while upper levels are educated in the relevant facts. And such formal systems encourage the explicit communication of decisions taken and of their rationale. Their disadvantages, however, are also real—chief among them the syndrome of all formal committees: membership expands (because additional parties want to participate and can readily claim legitimate interests); agendas become more general and abstract (because participants in the expanded group are not equally competent or interested in more specific issues); the level of representation declines (because secretaries and assistant secretaries are unwilling to discuss abstractions with extraneous parties of lower rank). As a result, serious debate and negotiation often moves to other settings. Moreover, the requirements for extensive documentation and large meetings consume great time and energy, and may prove unsustainable. (In fact the Nixon-Kissinger system functioned as designed for less than a year.) Finally, formal systems do not easily accommodate crises or fast-moving situations. And they do not facilitate secrecy; in spreading information widely, they

raise the risk of leaks to the press and end-runs to Congress or to special interest groups.

These observations lead us to conclude that the instinct of new administrations to choose a *single* new system—more formal or more fixed, regular or ad hoc—is mistaken. Instead, the problem is how to use several systems selectively and in parallel in ways that exploit the advantages of each. Formal procedures are likely to prove particularly useful in the early months of an administration, or thereafter for the limited number of issues which may be ripe for comprehensive reexamination. In 1977 such topics might include the nature of U.S. relations with the Soviet Union, the character of the U.S. response to the Fourth World, and U.S. policy toward southern Africa. Ad hoc groupings are more appropriate for crisis decision making, for managing lesser issues, and for exploring emerging problems not yet ripe for resolution. But convenors of ad hoc groups should take pains to ensure that the groups contain all necessary participants, and that the decisions taken and the bases for them are communicated clearly to all interested parties—cautions especially important in a period when issues routinely cut across many departments, and when rebuilding clear conceptions of U.S. purposes and interests ranks as a high priority.

More critical than their degree of formality is the breadth of participation in systems of central decision and coordination. At one extreme lies the "two-man band" of the latter Nixon years, where the President and his National Security Adviser held to themselves the decisive considerations affecting most of the first order issues of policy. Such closed systems have undeniable advantages. They provide maximum presidential flexibility, permit *faits accomplis* that foreclose potential opposition, allow novel high-policy conceptions to emerge uncompromised by interagency wrangling, and afford drama that can be turned to domestic political advantage. Nixon's China departure well exemplifies all these characteristics. While most Presidents find it necessary to hold one or two major issues to a narrow circle of trusted advisers, extensive reliance on a closed system imposes high costs. One is limited span of control; a very small group can manage only a small number of issues. Another is limited understanding. No small group, however brilliant, can fully comprehend many of the multitudinous issues that affect our foreign relations. It will favor the issues it does understand, ignoring or mishandling others. Reciprocally, the permanent government, while poor at grand conceptions and reluctant to innovate, is an unmatched reservoir of knowledge. When kept ignorant of the issues being considered, its knowledge cannot be tapped. Worse, ignorance and irrelevance destroy morale. Leaks and foot dragging result; implementation goes poorly. More subtly, closed systems engender a peculiar policy bias—toward relations with autocrats. Secret processes work best in dealing with those foreign leaders who can limit the involvement of their own bureaucracies and publics. They work less well in relations with open and democratic states, relations that tend to require actions by hundreds of informed individuals on both sides.[9] Finally, closed systems consume rather than build trust. They impede the building of consensus and support.

How inclusive, then, should systems of central coordination and decision be? In terms of the breadth of major perspectives represented, they should be more inclusive, we believe, than any system recently utilized. Each of the procedures of the past quarter century have been variations on a single theme of the National Security Council. The council's function, defined in 1947, was "to advise the President with respect to the integration of domestic, foreign, and military policies relating to the national security so as to enable the military services and the other departments and agencies of the Government to cooperate more effectively in matters involving the national security."[10] Membership was limited to the President and Vice-President, the Secretaries of State and Defense, and the director of the Office of Emergency Planning (subsequently dropped).

When political-military concerns dominated U.S. foreign policy, that membership matched the problems. But for foreign policy making, the central difference between the world of 1947 and that of today—as so often noted in these pages, and elsewhere—is that our relations with the external world are now systematic, intense, routine, and widely diffused. They impinge on all major interests in our society; they involve virtually all major departments and agencies; they are no longer dominated by military considerations. Under these circumstances, reliance on a body as narrow as the NSC for the coordination and decision of central issues of our international relations is an anachronism.* The intertwining of foreign and domestic issues and the politicization of foreign policy—discussed at length in earlier chapters—necessitates a broadening of the base upon which policy rests. The close ties of department heads to interest groups, Congress and to their own bureaucracies can help bring that about, and at the same time help insure that the full implications of proposed decisions stand out and that the shape and intensity of probable opposition is foreshadowed before decisions are taken. Greater involvement of the departments in the making of foreign policy would also improve the prospects for faithful policy implementation.

Wide-spread recognition of these points accounts for the legislation recently passed by the Congress (but vetoed by President Ford) to make the Secretary of the Treasury a statutory member of the NSC. Given the high economic content of "foreign" policy, that addition represents a step in the right direction. But is it an adequate adjustment to our changed situation? We think not. We propose instead that a considerably more comprehensive body be utilized, a body based on that perennial loser, the Cabinet.

* The narrowness of NSC membership is dramatically evident from the makeup of its eight committees. The same State, Defense, and military officials appear repeatedly. Treasury appears only on one panel; the Council of Economic Advisers on one other, which has long since ceased functioning. Agriculture, Commerce, Labor, and Justice appear nowhere.

Presidents have frequently taken office promising to use the Cabinet fully; they have uniformly behaved otherwise.

With regard to the Cabinet as an institution, as differentiated from the individuals who compose it, as I have seen it operate under three Presidents, it is a joke. As a collegium, it doesn't exist. Its members, serving as a Cabinet, neither advise the President nor engage in any meaningful consideration of serious problems or issues.[11]

This was the comment of Abe Fortas, and it is not a minority view. The persistent failure of the Cabinet as a collegial body reflects two inherent handicaps. Many issues involve only a small number of Cabinet departments. Secretaries of other departments thus become extraneous, and extraneous participants inhibit serious discussion. Moreover, many Cabinet members are rapidly socialized to departmental roles, becoming spokesmen for the interest groups and congressional committees to which their departments are tied. They appear to a President, therefore, not as counsellors but as special pleaders. "The members of the Cabinet are a President's natural enemies," in the famous words of Charles Dawes.[12]

The first of these handicaps is serious: the full Cabinet is simply too large. But the second, we believe, can readily be turned to advantage; it can ensure that the full range of interests affected by decisions are weighed before policy is made. And broader use of Cabinet members would confer other benefits as well. Presidents need stronger and more responsive performance from key Cabinet departments. Strength and responsiveness are not easy to combine. But making key Cabinet officers the primary substantive counsellors to the President, and insuring steady face-to-face relations between them and the President, will tend to induce both. The recognized participation of Secretaries in Presidential decision making would also sensitize them to Presidential perspectives and to interests other than those of their own departments.

Finally, increased involvement of key Cabinet members in foreign policy making offers a less obvious, but perhaps equally important benefit. Councils and Cabinets are not only forums; they are also opportunities for creating of staffs. Indeed, no consequence of the NSC has proven more important than the development of its staff. The use of a Cabinet-like body as a forum for decision would facilitate creation of a single integrated Cabinet staff. Combining the three principal White House staffs that are now autonomous—those of the NSC, the Domestic Council, and the Economic Policy Board—would create a more efficient mechanism for Presidential staffwork. Some specialization within a broader and integrated staff would obviously be necessary, but a single staff preparing issues for a central forum of broad jurisdiction could address the interacting issues of the future far more effectively than the three specialized staffs do now.

We therefore propose that the National Security Council be abolished and that an executive committee of the Cabinet become the chief forum for high-level review and decision of all major policy issues that combine substantial "foreign," "domestic," and "economic" concerns.[13] Most major decisions about the U.S. economy would fall in this category; so would virtually all key national security issues. Such a committee— it might be called "ExCab"—should surely contain the Secretaries of State, Defense, and Treasury. As the Cabinet officer best situated to represent the concerns of domestic social policy, the Secretary of HEW should also be a member. ExCab should probably include an additional representative of U.S. economic interests—ideally, the secretary of a new department created by a merger of Commerce and Labor, although interest-group and congressional opposition have long prohibited such a merger. Barring that possibility, the President might appoint whichever head of either department possessed the larger perspective and greater competence. John Dunlop, George Shultz, and Elliott Richardson are recent reminders that the two secretarial offices have been occupied by men capable of representing larger economic perspectives than those of either department.

These officials might form ExCab's permanent membership, but other Cabinet officers and agency heads could be asked to join the discussion of issues that concerned them. (Congressional leaders might also occasionally be invited to ExCab meetings, though on a wholly informal basis.) Depending on the issues being discussed, several additional officials might attend: the President's chief substantive staff members and congressional liaison officers; his science adviser, chief intelligence officer, and the director of OMB. At least in the early months of an administration, and at subsequent times of major uncertainty when broad changes in policy are contemplated, issues should be prepared for ExCab deliberation through formal and intensive interagency studies, like those of the NSSM process.

A body like ExCab would yield most of the advantages of the collegial participation of major department heads while avoiding the unwieldiness of the full Cabinet. It would also establish an implicit hierarchy of Cabinet and "super-Cabinet" positions, a means of improving the integration of policy which has attracted many Presidents but proven impossible to achieve through formal reorganization in the face of Congressional opposition. ExCab would possess no formal authority of its own, but might still prove a powerful innovation. It would widen the circle of advisers the President normally consulted before taking major decisions, thus improving the odds that major decisions would be taken with an eye to both their domestic and foreign effects. It would put those advisers directly in touch not only with the President but with each other, helping to generate a collegial comprehension of the varied dimensions of the issues confronting the President. And it would reinforce the standing of Cabinet officers as the primary substantive counsellors to the President. The size, formality, and title of the forum used to accomplish these purposes are quite secondary. What is essential is that some such forum regularly bring together for substantive discussion and decision the senior line officials of the government, the officers who together can best assess the full implications of major issues and who individually and jointly must understand, support, and manage the processes by which decision becomes action.*

ExCab would clearly have to be supplemented by various Cabinet sub-committees, and by ad hoc task forces. As discussed above, such task forces would utilize small numbers of sub-Cabinet officials, together with White House staff members, in addressing particular issues—in some instances providing staff work for presidential decision, in others managing continuing processes of implementation, review, and redecision. Presidential assistants might appropriately chair groups engaged in the first process; departmental officers, selected for personal competence as well as departmental position, would normally be designated "czars" for issues of enduring concern —nuclear proliferation, for example.

Presidential Staff

What the President cannot rely on the machinery of coordination to produce is what he needs most from his staff: help in assuring that issues requiring his attention are identified; that decision makers are faced with adequate maps of such issues; that decisions made are faithfully implemented; and that the President's own judgments at all stages benefit from advice sensitive to his personal and political concerns.

Before issues are brought to a forum such as ExCab, the President's staff must see to it that studies have tested the purported facts, highlighted uncertainties, explored feasible

---

* Since the effectiveness of senior officials is strongly affected by the ease of their access to the President, ExCab members should probably maintain small offices in the White House, and normally spend a portion of each day there. (Indeed, if the rebuilding of downtown Washington were in prospect, one author would be inclined to propose a single circular structure in which the President, his staff, and Cabinet and sub-Cabinet officers occupied concentric rings, and whose design invited informal contact among them all.)

alternatives, and identified linkages to other issues. When issues are handled by more informal groups, staff must assure their timely formation and the balance of their memberships, and should communicate presidential perspectives where these are needed but the President himself need not be directly involved. At all levels, staff must see that all affected parties are clearly apprised of decisions taken, that their responsibilities resulting from those decisions are specified, and that their subsequent actions meet the intent of policy. Staff, in short, must assist the President in ensuring the balance, depth, and integrity of the processes of decision; it must not seek to dominate those processes.

That is a hard role, requiring self-restraint in a place—the White House—where that quality is hardest to maintain. And it has not often been well performed in recent years. Instead, staff members have frequently become the President's chief substantive advisers and assumed major operating responsibilities—for continuing negotiations, for the authoritative statement of policy, and for relations with press, Congress, and foreign leaders. The result has been a confusion of staff and line functions, and poor performance of both.

The arguments against such mixing of roles are compelling (and common); it is therefore important to recognize the powerful forces producing such distortions. To any President, his staff—in contrast to departmental bureaucrats—appears aware of his needs, conscious of his perspectives, and inclined to get on with the job rather than to fuss with difficulties. For staff members, the shift from advising the President to directing his subordinates promises to substitute the satisfactions of visible authority for the frustrations of anonymous service. In varying degrees, all Assistants to the President for National Security have moved from staff toward line functions; the phenomenon was not limited to Henry Kissinger.[14]

But the tendency is dangerous. Almost without exception, Presidents grow insensitive, over time, to the views of their Cabinet officers, the perspectives of the Congress, the moods of the electorate. The absorption by staff of line responsibility speeds that process. It undercuts the Secretaries and their departments. It frustrates the Congress, which finds itself unable to question the sources of real influence or to discover the causes of presidential decision. It increases the risk of decision making without competence, since many decisions reveal their complexities, especially to generalists, only after they have been made and presidential staff is by definition generalist. But the most important reason for trying to maintain the porous distinction between staff and line is that presidential staff suffers from exactly the defects of its virtues. It is too responsive; it has no purpose but to serve its single superior. Staff brings to that service no counterpressure from statutory responsibilities, or from bureaucratic loyalties, or congressional supervision. Staffers lacking strong professional identification or other internal controls therefore tend to become courtiers. This is true everywhere, but nowhere more so than in the White House. The consequence is deepening presidential isolation and unrealism as the White House becomes, in Senator Mathias's words, a presidential "house of mirrors in which all views and ideas tend to reflect and reinforce his own."[15] The mirror effect has been most evident in the Johnson and Nixon Presidencies, but it is not a new or passing phenomenon; the pressures and powers of the modern White House tend to disorient all Presidents.*

One reliable antidote to the mirror effect is steady contact

---

* A story of Dean Acheson's notes similar tendencies in FDR's Presidency, and identifies a powerful remedy:

During the Second World War a weekly news magazine published a pocket edition which the War Department distributed to the troops. One issue contained an article open to criticism as a grossly unfair attack on the President. An intimate of his and a member of the White House staff called on General Marshall reporting the President's wish that this issue be withheld from circulation to the Army. The General replied, "Certainly. The President is the Commander in Chief. Kindly ask him to send his order to me in writing. It will be obeyed at once; and he will receive simultaneously my resignation as Chief of Staff of the Army." The matter was never mentioned again by anyone. (Dean Acheson, *Fragments of My Fleece* [New York: W. W. Norton & Co., 1971], pp. 96–97.)

between the President and his chief line subordinates, the major Cabinet Secretaries. Cabinet members face both ways, combining presidential loyalties and departmental responsibilities; they cannot merely echo a President. But care in the selection of staff is also essential. Intellect, energy, and loyalty will remain the chief characteristics a President must seek in the assistants closest to him, but he would do well to season his staff with persons of skeptical temperament, strong professional loyalty, independence of mind, or concern for procedure—for the balance and openness of the process of decision rather than the triumph of a particular cause.

In addition, many White House staffers should be drawn on a rotating basis from the agencies. This practice would provide a leavening of specialized competence and experience; it would educate to the perspectives of the Presidency a small number of able officials who will later return to their departments; and it would introduce into the White House persons whose time horizons and career expectations extend beyond the President's immediate wishes. It also would help establish rotation as a normal practice. Routine replacement—after perhaps two years—may be the most effective single hedge against a staff's acquisition of excessive power. We suggest below that Cabinet and sub-Cabinet officials, presiding over complex and specialized institutions, need time to master their subjects and their bureaucracies; and in consequence they should normally be kept in position longer than in current practice. But staff should be moved more frequently. Rotation provides a crude but effective purgative.

---

* Recent Presidents' relationships with their Vice Presidents provide a clue about the ways in which Presidents come to relate to both staff and Cabinet officers. Because the Vice President is his colleague in campaigning and presumptive heir, it might be expected that the Vice President would be a major agent of the President. In such a role, however, the Vice President would be an agent exercising Presidential authority whom the President could not fire. This is at least part of the explanation of the consistent experience of all post-war Vice Presidents: beginning with high expectations based on Presidential promises of a major role rapidly followed by deep disappointment about being kept in the closet.

The organization of White House staff must still depend largely on the President's own preferences and disposition. The roles sketched above for line and staff officers suggest, however, that if the President wishes to place a close substantive adviser in the White House, he should allow that person no role in managing the flow of advice from other sources. They suggest also that the total number of White House staff be substantially reduced, though the number accorded direct access to the President might be slightly enlarged. If a forum like ExCab were established, the President's substantive staff* might consist of four principal Assistants to the President, one standing astride the flow of predominantly "foreign policy" issues, one for "domestic" affairs, and one for "economic" issues. (The director of the Office of Management and Budget might be regarded as an equivalent, fourth principal assistant.) The first three of these would each require two or three deputies, the Assistant for "Foreign Affairs," for example, having a deputy for "foreign economics" and another for "defense." The three presidential Assistants and their deputies would be backed by an ExCab staff of several dozen members responsible to them jointly—a single, unified staff replacing the currently autonomous staffs of the NSC, the Domestic Council, and the Economic Policy Board.

In such a system, the sensitive task of assigning particular issues to one or more of the principal assistants, of ensuring that they worked effectively together, and of controlling jurisdictional disputes generated by the necessarily ambiguous boundaries between them, should be assumed not by a chief of staff but by the President himself. Presidents of particularly reclusive temperaments might find that responsibility unwelcome. But most modern Presidents would have performed it willingly enough in view of the probable benefits. For the first time, the President would possess a substantive staff oriented toward a central task previously performed only in his own

* We ignore here other assistants the President will obviously need: press and appointments secretaries, a chief speech writer, and the like.

mind or not at all: the analysis of trade-offs among "domestic," "foreign," "economic" (and "political") considerations, and the integration of policy across those boundaries.

The President and the Departments

However organized, neither mechanisms of central coordination nor presidential staffs conduct foreign policy. The day-to-day business of foreign affairs is carried on by the Cabinet departments, and as the cases recounted above suggest, the departments have often performed poorly. Their failures, in our view, arise principally from mismatches between Cabinet appointees and their jobs; from presidential reluctance to give Cabinet officials the mandates and support necessary to their management function; and from the inability of the appointive government to work effectively with the permanent substructure on which it is placed.

The choice of Cabinet officials provides a President-elect with his single greatest opportunity to address these problems and to establish the character and competence of his administration. Yet those choices are generally made when the President-elect is least likely to make them well—at the close of a long and exhausting campaign. The debts and loyalties of the past year are uppermost in his mind. Constituencies must be reassured through appointments, and debts paid. The importance of such reassurance and the identity of those debts are far clearer to the President-elect than is the design of his new administration. He may be determined that his appointees be people of high quality, and such a determination helps. But it is not enough. The persons chosen must also fit the intended organizational design, just as building materials must bear the stresses of a particular architecture. Unless the main lines of that design have been thought through, the President will have in hand no clear standards against which prospective

officials can be measured. And unless a wide recruiting net is
cast, even clearly defined standards will not be met. The first
injunctions a President-elect should observe, therefore, are
hard but important: before making major appointments he
must decide how he wants the upper levels of his administration to function, and recruit accordingly.

Whatever the specifics of organizational design, Cabinet
officials capable of playing the extraordinarily difficult combination of roles we have suggested above must be individuals
of great competence and breadth. Simply to meet the demands
of Presidential counselling, departmental management, and
representation of Presidential perspectives on the Hill, to private interest groups and to foreign officials—all within the
confines of an eighty hour week—is a feat. As argued above,
performance of each of these responsibilities can make easier
the performance of others. But given the weight of these
responsibilities, we believe it imperative that the President-
elect permit his Cabinet officials to select a team of their own
subordinates. If they are to manage their departments effectively, they will need strong and compatible deputies, undersecretaries, and assistant secretaries. Just as presidential
performance would be facilitated by broader and more collegial consultation with key Cabinet members, so strong departmental performance would be facilitated by the collegial use
of sub-Cabinet officials by Secretaries. But such practices succeed only if sub-Cabinet officials understand that they work
for their Secretaries—understandings a President can enforce
or undermine. Insofar as he can, therefore, the President should
resist selecting sub-Cabinet officials. Where campaign debts
or prior loyalties make such self-restraint impossible, the
appointed officials should know that though they may owe
their jobs to the White House, they owe their loyalties to
their Secretary.* Fortunately, a President who chooses Cabinet

---

* The refusal of Secretaries-designate to accept deputies or assistants
imposed by the White House may be a good test of their own qualifica-
tions for office. One close observer of the preinaugural days of the

officers of strength and scope, and deals with them directly, will find it easier to abstain from making sub-Cabinet appointments. Having good two-way communications with his Cabinet officers, he will feel less need than previous Presidents to protect himself with special agents and personal loyalists at lower levels of the departments.

Presidents whose Cabinet officers meet those standards should also be inclined to keep them in office longer, a most desirable change in itself. Understanding the work of a major department, identifying its points of leverage, learning to deal with the political constraints within which it works, establishing effective relations with its permanent officials—these are large tasks. Typically, a year has passed before senior officials understand both what they are up to and what they are up against. Their second years are often their first productive ones—yet the average tenure of Cabinet officials since Truman's Presidency has been under two years. Such rapid turnover imposes high costs in uncertainty of policy, ragged implementation, and disincentives to long-range thinking, costs underappreciated in recent years.

Having chosen competent Secretaries for his ExCab departments, and encouraged them to create departmental teams of strong subordinates, the President must make clear his major objectives for their departments and must, through his staff, periodically assess progress toward those objectives. The costs of failure to do so are vivid in the nuclear options story, where the stated desires of four Presidents, unsupported by continuing pressure and monitoring, yielded no significant results.

A President will have particular priorities for specific departments (our proposals about priorities for the departments of State, Defense, and Treasury are outlined in subsequent chap-

---

Kennedy administration has commented that Robert McNamara's rejection of Franklin Delano Roosevelt, Jr., as Secretary of the Navy was a good sign of his own qualification to be Secretary of Defense, while Dean Rusk's willingness to accept G. Mennen Williams as Assistant Secretary of State for African Affairs forecast his future passivity as Secretary of State.

ters); but several more general objectives seem valid across the government. For one, the appointive officials of all ExCab departments should assist the White House in building congressional and private support for administration policy. Collegial processes of presidential decision making can educate a large number of participants in the bases of presidential policy. When—as is true today—influence important to the government is widely dispersed among executive and congressional bodies, in state and local government, and in the private sector, that understanding is a significant asset; it should be used.

A second priority results from the fact that time horizons at the top of all departments are now too short. The President should encourage organizational changes that help counteract the pressures on high officials to focus only on Tuesday's congressional testimony or next month's budget submission. Several proposals we discuss below may be helpful: multi-year authorizations and appropriations; Biennial Statements and white papers that set current policy in a longer-run framework. Longer tenure for appointed officials should also help ease the problem. But other devices will also be needed. The President should require that proposals made to ExCab be presented with attention to their possible consequences five and ten years forward. Requests for major capital expenditures in defense and foreign aid should be justified in terms of the probable environments during the years when the products those expenditures produce (Trident submarines, steel plants, dams) will be operating—two or even three decades later. To retain their own sensitivity to the longer-run problems and purposes of their departments, Secretaries may find it useful to establish small groups of knowledgeable private citizens whose judgments they value, and to meet with them informally for wide-ranging discussions several times each year.

To meet the demand for longer-run thinking which such devices should stimulate, Secretaries may wish to establish small staffs with special responsibilities for future projections. Their purpose would not be to monopolize such projections but to stimulate and improve their development throughout the departments. Experience shows that if capable, such staffs are drawn into short-run business; if not, they lack influence. Coping with this dilemma requires that the director of such a staff seek a personal working relationship with his principal, that he find ways of linking longer-run analysis to current deadlines, and that the principal hold his staff to these purposes.

Another general priority for Cabinet officers should be that they come rapidly to understand the processes they are charged with managing. Secretaries, like Presidents, find it natural to focus on decision making. But decisions become action only through the work of subordinates, mostly members of career services. The values and incentives of those services—as the nuclear options and Vietnam cases so clearly demonstrate—are typically different from the values and incentives of political appointees. Appointive officials cannot manage their departments without far deeper understanding of the motivations of their bureaucracies than has been common. In very large and complex agencies, particularly in the Department of Defense, this requirement, as Chapter 7 discusses, might well be pressed to the point of establishing staffs specifically dedicated to what has been called "implementation analysis": predicting the bureaucratic response to policy proposals, and designing whatever changes may be necessary in the form of those proposals, or in the implementing organizations, to ensure that the policies chosen are feasible, and that they are then made to work.

In broader terms, this is the large and underattended problem of the relationship between the appointive and the permanent governments—a relation marked by mutual suspicion and hostility. Since career officials frequently resist the initiatives of political appointees in a new administration, senior political officials often try to work solely through small groups of trusted assistants; they circumvent or distract the bureaucracy and largely ignore the wide range of problems especially those of implementation—on which such practices provide little leverage. Treated in this way, members of the permanent government do their business around and beneath appointed officials, pushing favorite projects when they can be given labels attractive to the present "boss," working through congressional or private allies, or delaying action they oppose until a Secretary or an assistant secretary moves on. (In the last two decades, assistant secretaries have averaged roughly eighteen months in office.) No post-war President has been willing to invest the time, effort and political capital that substantial improvement will require. Viewed from the perspective of individual Presidents, that reluctance is understandable. But its cumulative effects are appalling.

Addressing this problem will require many specific steps, some of which will vary by department. But the measures worth considering in each are similar. They include creating some form of the long-proposed "federal executive service";[16] giving agency heads more flexibility in administering supergrade executives; broadening the perspective of career officers through rotation among related agencies; upgrading management capabilities in labor/management relations within the career services; abolishing the "merit system" embodied in the current civil service; and assuring the career services genuine participation in departmental decision making. The underlying objective of all such reforms is the same. It is to establish conditions in which the skill, knowledge, and energy of the permanent government can be deployed on the issues of greatest importance to the administration, and thereby to create a relationship between permanent and appointive governments of greater respect, trust, and productivity.

The President and Congress

Presidents are inclined to view the Congress as a barrier, an obstacle to efficient administration and rational policy, by which they mean their own. So it is, and so it was intended.

As Justice Brandeis noted, the Constitution divided authority between the branches "not to promote efficiency but to preclude the exercise of arbitrary power."[17] Nothing about recent history suggests that concern to have been excessive. Presidents are also apt to see Congress as particularly unfit for deep involvement in foreign policy making—a more nearly arguable case, as the next chapter suggests. But Congress is now deeply engaged in foreign policy making, partly as a result of the perceived failures of presidential policy, especially in Vietnam, but more durably because of the merger of "foreign" and "domestic" issues, and the impact of "foreign" issues on domestic politics. Future Presidents will have to accept that congressional involvement, and they will find it complicated by the fact that the Congress now feels ill-used by the Presidency—manipulated, deceived, and treated with indifference or contempt. Indeed, the recent insistence of Congress on quite particular changes in policy, some of them dubious—a high and explicit quota for Jewish emigration from the Soviet Union, a cutoff of arms to Turkey—appears motivated almost as much by congressional pique at the administration as by the influence of Greek and Jewish constituencies. As Congressman Donald Fraser observed of the situation in 1975, "The distrust of the executive branch runs so deep in this chamber that members are afraid that any discretion, any grant of authority to the executive branch will open the door to allow the executive branch to again try to make one more effort to do what ten years failed to do."[18]

As a result, the next President will face a great challenge, and a great opportunity: to reconstruct effective working relations with Congress. Here is another "leadership without hegemony" problem, a matter not of imposing presidential plans, or of merchandising them, but of encouraging and accepting genuine interaction between the branches. More particularly, we believe, the President should set two major objectives in congressional relations. First and most important is the reconstruction of comity and trust between the branches. The President has at least as much to gain from such a development as does the Congress, since it is only on the basis of such trust that Congress is likely to allow the executive that discretionary authority and freedom to maneuver which international bargaining requires. The second objective is to strengthen, insofar as a President can, the ability of Congress to assist the integration and coherence of policy, or at minimum to offset the Congressional forces of fractional and special concern. Most helpful to these ends would be the control of the Presidency and the Congress by the same political party—the situation in only eleven of the last twenty-five years. But whether that occurs or not, the President, in our view, should take a number of steps.

Toward the reconstruction of comity, the underlying attitudes of the President will be most important. But changed practices can help. Steady and genuine informal coordination between the White House and the limited number of congressional leaders who for any particular issue strongly influence congressional action is the first requirement. The President, his assistants for congressional liaison, and his Cabinet and sub-Cabinet officials must all make such consultation prime business. It must come ungrudgingly and early, not after press reports of administration action inconsistent with prior assurances to Congress. And the staffs of those officials should develop working relationships with the relevant congressional staffers. For numerous foreign policy issues, especially those that do not arouse strong emotions in particular districts or states, the votes of many members of Congress are not politically constrained. On such issues, unless they happen to be personally expert in the matter, Congressmen tend to follow the lead of colleagues whose values and knowledge they trust. Engaging a sizeable fraction of that informal leadership group in executive decision making would produce benefits far greater than its likely cost in time or compromise. Such consultation should extend both to the development of policy and to the creation of institutions capable of carrying it out. A good model was provided by the Asian Development

Bank, where after several years of stalemate, the Treasury solicited and received genuine and substantive Congressional participation, which produced not only initial appropriations but a proprietary and protective attitude in the Congress toward a valuable international institution.

Executive willingness to share credit with the Congress will also be required. A President should not only involve Congressmen but be seen to involve them in the formulation of policy. Truman's dealing with congressional leadership provides a model both of manner and of result. Even as an apparent lame duck and with Congress controlled by the opposite party, he succeeded (with the assistance of a number of Cabinet and sub-Cabinet officials) in enlisting active congressional support for so sharp a departure in foreign policy as the Marshall Plan. The recipe included steady consultation, informal and formal; willingness to forego partisan advantage; and a determination to share credit as widely as necessary.[19]

A second purpose of the President should be to reinforce Congressional incentives and abilities to view major foreign policy issues more comprehensively, thus at least partially offsetting the powerful pressures in Congress to deal with issues by carving them up to fit committee jurisdiction. This is no easy task, but some feasible reforms would begin movement in the right direction. Probably most important would be presidential assistance in strengthening Congressional leadership through political support and practices of consultation. Here, the President who takes office in 1977 may have a unique opportunity. For the first time in this century, both houses will simultaneously acquire new leadership—leaders certain to be more forceful and energetic than their predecessors. Such leaders could use the party caucuses and their own powers to impose a greater measure of policy consistency among committees. In addition, the President should publicly make the case for hard foreign policy decisions, especially where they impose significant domestic costs. A President visibly and deeply committed to a major policy on grounds that it well serves the general interests of the nation provides an indispensable rallying point for congressional support where the policy is politically difficult.

One formal mechanism also seems to us worth considering. It is that the President submit to Congress every second year a comprehensive statement of U.S. purposes and commitments in the world, a document that would articulate basic foreign policy goals and specify their relation to proposed and continuing policy.* This Biennial Statement might be amplified by occasional "white papers," dealing with specific issues in more detail. For such formal statements of policy, there are, we recognize, a number of unpromising precedents: the Basic National Security Policy documents of the Eisenhower administration, the National Policy Papers of the Kennedy years, and Nixon's "State of the World" messages. Their preparation absorbed great effort in the departments and in the White House; they tended to resolve disagreements by resort to assertions so general as to be meaningless; and they provided little usable guidance for decision makers faced with particular choices. Nonetheless, we believe that if linked to action-forcing processes, especially in the Congress, biennial statements can serve several purposes now especially important. They can encourage rethinking in the executive of the adequacy of current policies and of their relations to one another; they can express a more long-range view of U.S. foreign policy goals; they can articulate policy in a form that invites discussion and enlarges public understanding; and they can provide a framework for coherent congressional debate and action. The Statements might be tied to processes of decision and action in several ways. Relevant portions of the Statements could provide the policy basis for the Defense Posture Statements, the principal justifications of each year's proposed

---

* For a proposal that Congress require of the President a far more comprehensive set of annual reports, see Joseph A. Califano, *A Presidential Nation*, (New York: W. W. Norton & Co., 1975) pp. 284–291.

defense budget; white papers on foreign policy and force posture, presented and defended jointly by the Secretaries of State and Defense could serve the same function in alternate years. Other portions of the Biennial Statement could preface Presidential requests for authorizations and appropriations for foreign aid, military sales, military assistance, contributions to international financial institutions, and the like. White papers—some perhaps specifically requested by Congress—could provide the framework for congressional hearings and debate on issues of particular concern, such as U.S. policy toward South Africa, American interests in Southeast Asia, and programs affecting the spread of nuclear reactors and related technology.

Most importantly, such statements might provide a basis for more coherent congressional debate and action. How that might be done we discuss in the larger context of the role of Congress in "foreign" policy making.

Chapter 5

The Role
of Congress

> To what expedient, then, shall we finally resort,
> for maintaining in practice the necessary parti-
> tion of power among the several departments, as
> laid down in the Constitution? . . . By so con-
> structing the interior structure of the govern-
> ment as that its several constituent parts may
> by their mutual relations, be the means of keep-
> ing each other in the proper places. . . . The
> great security against a gradual concentration
> of the several powers in the same department,
> consists in giving to those who administer each
> department the constitutional means and per-
> sonal motives to resist encroachment of the
> others. . . . Ambition must be made to counter-
> act ambition.
>
> *The Federalist*, no. 51

CURRENT discussions of the relative virtues of Congress
and the executive in the conduct of foreign policy bring to
mind the story about the judge in a singing competition who
awarded the prize to the second of two contestants after
having heard only the first. After Vietnam, many commentators seemed inclined to follow the judge's example and give
the prize to Congress. Students of Congress, however, will

anticipate the end of the story: the judge was made to listen to the second contestant, whereupon he retracted his judgment and cut the trophy in half.

The Founding Fathers would have understood that judgment; the Constitution they constructed declines to choose between the executive and the Congress. In foreign as in domestic affairs, it creates a government of "separated institutions sharing power."[1] In view of the common belief that foreign policy is constitutionally an executive prerogative, it may be useful to recall the relevant provisions. The Constitution designates the President commander-in-chief of the armed forces, specifies that he shall receive ambassadors, and empowers him, with the advice and consent of the Senate, to make treaties and appoint ambassadors. It assigns the President no other powers specific to foreign relations. The Congress is empowered to provide for the common defense, to raise and support armies, to provide and maintain a navy, to declare war, to define and punish piracies and felonies committed on the high seas and offenses against the laws of nations, to lay duties and imposts and to regulate commerce with foreign nations. The constitutional design, in short, assigns ultimate power over foreign commerce, war and military preparedness to the Congress, permits one-third plus one member of the Senate to prevent treaties from taking effect, and requires even the President's appointment of ambassadors to gain senatorial approval. It is hardly a junior role.

Yet the popular perception reflects historical fact: the President has played the dominant role in directing our foreign relations. Why? The causes are several and they appeared early in our history. The necessities of management in the first decades of national independence moved Jeffersonians and Hamiltonians alike to accept more executive leadership in foreign affairs than the Constitution envisaged. Congress was numerous, divided, and ordinarily not in session. It could not stay abreast of the details of foreign relations, could not conduct negotiations nor keep a secret. By 1790 Secretary of

State Jefferson had concluded that "the transaction of business with foreign nations is Executive altogether."[2]

When the business involved crises, the advantages of the executive become all the more important. They had been laid out clearly in *The Federalist:* unity, constancy, expertise, decision, secrecy, and dispatch.[3] From the beginning Presidents did act on their own authority, often with minimal congressional consultation. Thus, though executive authority over foreign affairs ebbed and flowed, the inherent advantages of the executive branch, dramatized by recurring crises, led to widespread acceptance of what Arthur Schlesinger has called the "executive perspective," the view that in foreign affairs, "the executive branch, with superior information and direct responsibility was the source of judgments to which Congress should customarily defer."[4]

War was the ultimate instance, and the Second World War placed in the President's hand virtually unlimited powers in foreign affairs. After a decade of congressional attempts to enforce neutrality and to limit preparedness (the House had come within a single vote of repealing the draft just five months before Pearl Harbor), the war seemed clear evidence that Congress as a body could not be trusted to play a major role in foreign policy. After the war President Truman and Senator Vandenberg established what Vandenberg called "nonpartisanship" in foreign affairs, a principle that gave the President wide latitude in return for early and informal consultation with key congressional leaders. The degree of congressional deference to presidential judgment is reflected in two statements made by Senator Richard Russell, chairman of the Senate Armed Services Committee from 1955 to 1968. In 1954 he counseled President Eisenhower that sending military help to Vietnam would be a "terrible mistake," but assured the President that "I will never raise my voice against it." In August 1965 he told a CBS interviewer: "I guess I must be an isolationist. I don't think you ought to pick up 100,000 or 200,000 or 500,000 American boys and ship them off somewhere to fight and get killed in a war as remotely connected with our interest as this one is." But then he added he would "support the flag."[5]

The dominance of the Presidency in this period derived not only from the authority of the Commander in Chief in times of conflict and recollections of congressional irresponsibility, but from novel factors as well. The emergence of a huge federal bureaucracy had put at the President's service hundreds of thousands of eyes, ears, and hands, enlarging the executive's knowledge, expertise, and capacity for action. A classification system kept from Congress (and the public) enormous stores of information on which wise decision making might depend. The growing involvement of the federal government in the domestic economy greatly increased the President's bargaining power vis-a-vis Congress. The growth of the mass media—especially television—gave him ready access to every voter, largely on his own terms. Finally, diminishing voter identification with political parties made the President the central focus of political emotion.

The protracted failure of presidential war in Vietnam eroded the presumption that in foreign affairs the President knew best; the revelations of Watergate nearly washed it away. Congress is now deeply immersed in foreign policy making, and in our judgment it will remain so. Indeed, we believe this congressional involvement will mark the largest single difference between American foreign policy making in the last quarter of this century and that of the preceding decades. The balance of power between the branches will depend on many factors: whether the same party controls both branches; the degree to which dominant issues are controversial; patterns of presidential and congressional behavior expected by press and public; the strength of congressional leadership; and the unity of the political parties. But whatever the particulars, congressmen, the odd uncles in the family business, will no longer be silent partners.

Our confidence in this prediction arises not from a belief that suspicion of presidential military adventures will remain high. It may or it may not. Memories recede fast, especially memories of distant failure. The emergence of any severe threat to important U.S. interests will realign the electorate where such threats always align it—behind the Commander in Chief. Congress will continue to show strong interest in the resource questions of national security—defense budgets, base locations, weapons systems—but current high sensitivities to deployments and use of U.S. forces may well diminish.*

Instead, the relation of Congress to the executive in foreign policy will be changed by the shifting *content* of that policy. As noted frequently in these pages (and elsewhere), our relations with other countries are no longer dominated by issues like the terms of alliances, the duration of base rights, or the breadth of security guarantees; they are shaped also by issues arising from the tightening economic and physical interdependence among nations. That interdependence is incomplete and asymmetrical, and it may not continue to grow at rates of the last decade. But for the foreseeable future we and the nations most important to us will be part of a single system of trade, resource access, monetary arrangements, and population movement. Our foreign relations increasingly involve efforts to regulate or adjust that system. These efforts affect prices, jobs and the conditions of everyday life; they are the stuff of domestic politics. It is that circumstance which makes congressional activism inevitable.

That activism will be reinforced by a number of other devel-

---

* Indeed, on close examination the supposed congressional revival in national security issues is ambiguous even now. Its most celebrated monument, the War Powers Resolution, was passed eight years after Americanization of the war in Vietnam, and more than two years after the President's only constitutional authority for continuing the war was the claim of inherent power to protect American troops being withdrawn. And the resolution requires only that the President inform Congress within forty-eight hours of the introduction of American forces into combat; that he gain congressional sanctions of his action within sixty days; and that if Congress refuses that sanction, he disengage within another thirty days. Contrast the Constitution's unambiguous requirement of affirmative action by the Congress to involve the country in war, leaving the President only the powers to be inferred from dire necessity in case of sudden attack.

opments, perhaps the most powerful of which is the explosive growth of congressional staff. Since 1954 Congress has more than tripled its personal and committee staffs, which now exceed 17,000 persons, outnumbering the entire Department of State. When the Congressional service agencies are included—General Accounting Office, Congressional Research Service, Office of Technology Assessment, Congressional Budget Office—the number exceeds 23,000.[6] Though perhaps half the personal staffs attend primarily to constituent services, dramatic increases in the numbers of professional staffers give Congressmen the ability to dig more deeply into a wider range of issues and generate staff pressure for more action. The changing composition of Congress itself will also encourage activism: the number of younger senators and representatives with broad experience, advanced education, and considerable understanding of the world outside the United States has increased sharply, and seems likely to continue to grow. This changing in composition has altered the balance of influence within Congress—most markedly in the Senate. No longer, in matters of foreign relations, do junior senators defer readily to seniors, and seniors to the White House. A majority of committee chairmen are now inclined toward activism, and even the newest of senators may appropriate an issue and challenge executive proposals without incurring the opprobrium of his colleagues. Absent direct threats to U.S. security, moreover, Congress will continue to give voice to the special claims of particular ethnic and national as well as economic interests. The dissolution of public consensus on the role of the United States in world affairs will be reflected in Congressional disagreement about whether the United States should meet Soviet initiatives in Africa, for example, or give up the Panama Canal. Finally, the "lesson of Vietnam and Watergate" has deeply affected the public conception of proper Congressional behavior. A senator can no longer explain to himself or his constituents that he simply defers to superior executive judgment in foreign affairs.

Increased involvement of Congress in foreign policy making therefore seems certain. But involvement can be deep without being either effective or responsible. The authors of *The Federalist*, though determined that in foreign as in domestic affairs the Congress should provide the ultimate check and balance to executive power, were skeptical about the capacity of so large and diverse a body to play a leading role in foreign policy making.

The fluctuating and . . . multitudinous composition of that body forbids us to expect in it those qualities which are essential to the proper execution of such a trust. Accurate and comprehensive knowledge of foreign politics; a steady and systematic adherence to the same views; a nice and uniform sensibility to national character; decision, *secrecy*, and dispatch, are incompatible with the genius of a body so variable and so numerous.[7]

Time has confirmed their skepticism.

A larger congressional role in foreign policy making may still fail of its constitutional purpose—to check and balance executive power—and it may deepen distortions in executive policy making, further fragmenting the treatment of related issues and strengthening special interests. Changes in the processes of interaction between the branches, and in congressional organization itself can diminish those probabilities, but only if the changes are grounded in a realistic appreciation of the differing natures of Congress and the executive. The two branches are not simply competing centers of power; they are institutions of fundamentally different kinds. Their functions and responsibilities overlap, but their comparative advantages and disabilities are distinct. Since our recommendations build on judgments about those advantages and disabilities, we outline those judgments and the basis for them.

Characteristics of the Congress

Organizational reformers typically accord high value to rationality, order, and efficiency. Thus, when they turn to the Congress, their proposals often seem aimed at turning Congress, in Congressman Les Aspin's phrase, "into a kind of Brookings Institution or Systems Analysis office."[8] That aim is neither feasible nor desirable, as it ignores the following fundamental characteristics of the legislative branch.

A Headless Body. Each of the 535 members of Congress is elected in his own right, an independent representative of a district or state. None owes his election to another. Though power is certainly not equally distributed among the members of the Senate or House, still less is it concentrated in a single head. At their own discretion, many cooks can add to the broth, turn up the heat, or turn it off. As Senator Mondale has observed, "Congress cannot carry out the laws nor provide symbolic leadership, for the simple reason that a nation with a collective leadership of 535 could not function."[9]

Dominated by Committees. "Congress is a collection of committees that come together in a Chamber periodically to approve one another's actions."[10] Congressman Clem Miller's observation echoes the conclusions of most observers since Woodrow Wilson. Committees guard their jurisdictions, and divide issues among themselves by fixed rules. Everyone knows that a committee's jurisdiction may correspond only to a piece of a major problem; but in practice what everyone knows is frequently ignored. The Foreign Relations and Armed Services committees, for example, still split "diplomacy" and "defense" almost 30 years after the need to view them in combination produced, in the executive branch, the National Security Council. Although issues of great public concern can serve to unite the legislature in some actions (e.g., the 1975 cutoff of funds for Vietnam), and although caucuses and party leadership can

impose some discipline, Congress does not generally accept
responsibility for the integration or coherence of policy. Committees deal separately with related issues and defer reciprocally to each other's actions. The same principles operate
through a lower tier of subcommittees, compounding the dis-
junctions in policy making. And the number of committees
and subcommittees steadily grows.

Serving Particular Interests. To the question "What is the
spirit that has in general characterized the proceedings of
Congress?" Madison responded, in *The Federalist*, no. 56:

> A perusal of their journals, as well as the candid acknowledgments
> of such as have had a seat in that assembly, will inform us that the
> members have but too frequently displayed the character rather of
> partisans of their respective States than of impartial guardians of a
> common interest; that where on one occasion improper sacrifices
> have been made of local considerations to the aggrandizement of
> the federal government, the great interests of the nation have suf-
> fered on a hundred from an undue attention to the local prejudices,
> interests, and views of the particular States.

The source of that spirit is clear. Constituents and supporters
want their own interests advanced—or, at minimum, protected—and the two-year congressional election cycle keeps
those interests evident. On issues about which particular elec-
torates do not care deeply, a Congressman's sense of the
national interest may safely prevail. But a district dependent
on textile production or the manufacture of shoes, for example,
will not long tolerate a representative unduly devoted to the
broader virtues of free trade.

The power of particular interests in the Congress is reinforced by committee assignments. Congressmen seek assignment to the committees that make decisions about policies
most important to their own districts. As a result, flows of benefits are dispensed largely by agents of the beneficiaries. Congressman Robert Leggett of the House Armed Services Committee has described the situation with great candor:

The forty guys on the committee should come from all walks of life. But they don't. Practically all of them have conflicts of interest. Not that any member is getting a piece of the cash or owns stock in a company that will benefit. Such as myself. We have the Mare Island Navy Shipyard in my district and the only nuclear naval shipyard. I like to build lots of those nuclear subs. I've done some personal emissary work to get some of the contracts. In my district is the Travis Air Force Base, the Beale AFB, the Mather AFB, the McClelland AFB, the Sacramento Army Depot and Aerojet General Corp. When it comes to the defense budget, my thinking is jaded. The basic problem with the committee is that it is made up of people who are postured that way because of commitments within their district and region.[11]

Resolving Issues Through Bargaining. Where power is broadly shared among representatives of competing interests, bargaining is the mechanism of decision. The force of proposals frequently derives more from their political weight than from abstract judgments about merits. The fact is neither reprehensible nor avoidable. Congress legitimates policy by obtaining the concurrences of a majority of quite diverse interests, and the concurrence of equals is gained through the broad distribution of benefits.

Muffling Positions. As Aspin has pointed out, "Congressmen feel themselves at the mercy of events—something might happen that proves them wrong. An adage often quoted among Congressmen says, 'No one ever got defeated for something he didn't say.' . . . Making decisions on the basis of rational arguments requires confronting the issues directly, and Congressmen, who are pressured from all sides, who are continually short of time, and who suffer from lack of expertise, are not likely to do that. They will prefer to deal with issues indirectly and procedurally."[12] The end-the-war vote in the House in 1972, for example, was actually a vote on a motion to table a motion to instruct conferees to insist on the House version of the defense authorization bill in the light of the Legislative Reorganization Act of 1970. At least with respect to the House, it is true, as Aspin concludes, that "Besides being used by Congressmen to mask the real effect of their votes and being used to achieve objectives without direct confrontation with the executive, procedure is used by Congressmen to avoid direct responsibility and to protect themselves politically."[13]

Distracted Members. Congressmen must continuously run for office, respond to constituents' requests, vote on bills brought to the floor (more than six hundred in 1975), and participate in committee deliberations. They have more than a fulltime job. Durability and hard work may make them highly knowledgeable across a narrow range of issues, but they cannot be expert, or even well informed, about most issues on which they vote. Especially in foreign affairs, where distance and secrecy limit regular access to some information, Congressmen look to peers they regard as informed and like-minded, or support colleagues who will return the favor on other issues, or support the interest group whose feelings seem most intense or whose spokesmen first win their commitment. They seize issues only sporadically, when their personal or political interest is strongly aroused.

Implications for Organization

What do these characteristics of the Congress imply for organization? The main guidelines seem to us to be these.

The old adage that "the President proposes, the Congress disposes" makes sense. Congress is the check on executive power. It provides the forum for subjecting executive initiatives to second and third judgments, for testing their political acceptability, for conferring (or withholding) legitimacy. It is therefore appropriate that Congress normally look to the President for a legislative program, and in fact the President's program does normally establish the congressional agenda in foreign as in domestic affairs.

But Presidents do not merely propose; they also act, and a huge and pervasive executive bureaucracy acts in their name, or fails to. To check and balance the full measure of executive power, then, Congress must review departmental programs and investigate executive actions. These activities complement the orientation of congressmen toward constituent service, mediating between general programs and the specific needs of citizens, and holding executive action accountable. But the ability of Congress to review does not confer a capacity to manage. The leverage of Congress lies mainly not in requiring, but in revealing and preventing. The principal power of Congress is the power to say no.

Though the line between them is fuzzy, congressional attention should center on ends, not on means. Senator Fulbright distinguished between two kinds of power involved in shaping foreign policy: one pertaining to its direction, purpose, and philosophy; the other to day-to-day conduct of relations. He argued that the former belongs particularly to Congress and the latter to the executive, but that Congress had often reversed them:

We have tended to snoop and pry in matters of detail, interfering in the handling of specific problems in specific places which we happen to chance upon. . . . At the same time we have resigned from our responsibility in the shaping of policy and the defining of its purposes, submitting too easily to the pressure of crisis, giving away things that are not ours to give: the war power of the Congress, the treaty power of the Senate and the broader advice and consent power.[14]

Those who would establish ends must influence means; the power to intervene in particulars gives their larger judgments force. But detailed control should be exercised by the Congress only exceptionally. The broad distribution of power and responsibility in the Congress, its slowness to decision, and its practices of resolving differences through bargaining are traits appropriate to the legitimation of policy but inimical to the management of detail. Lord Bryce's aphorisms on the point retain their timeliness:

> In a democracy the People are entitled to determine the Ends or general aims of foreign policy.
>
> History shows that they do this at least as wisely as monarchs or oligarchies, or the small groups to whom, in democratic countries, the conduct of foreign relations has been left, and that they have evinced more respect for moral principles.
>
> The Means to be used for attaining the Ends sought cannot be adequately determined by legislatures so long as international relations continue to be what they have heretofore been, because secrecy is sometimes, and expert knowledge is always required.[15]

Finally, Congress has no more significant power than its ability to investigate, to publicize, and hence to educate. As Woodrow Wilson argued ninety years ago, ". . . even more important than legislation is the instruction and guidance in political affairs which people might receive from a body which kept all national concerns suffused in a broad daylight of discussion. The informing function of Congress should be preferred, even to its legislative function."[16] The function well suits both the characteristics of the Congress and the needs of foreign policy making. Hearings can make news without requiring that positions be taken. They presuppose little agreement, no joint action. And they can raise new issues (ozone, oceans) to public consciousness; probe executive abuses (Watergate, intelligence), challenge outdated policy (China). In so doing, they offset the principal dangers and weaknesses of executive leadership—abuse of authority, ignorance of novel threats or opportunities, inattention to the longer run.*

---

* The strength of Congress as an educator is its vulnerability as guardian of secret information. Congressmen generate support through public action; this requires disclosure. Even when a jury of twelve would conclude that the national interest lies in discretion, a political body of 535 would be unlikely to concur unanimously. Deeper congressional involvement in foreign policy making will thus probably both force a reduction in the amount of information now unnecessarily classified, and necessitate tighter limitations on disclosure of information with genuinely harmful potential. We discuss below how this might be accomplished.

What Is to Be Done?

Those principles suggest a number of desirable changes within the Congress, and in relations between Congress and the executive. Some would be quite substantial, and equally difficult to achieve. These might include abolishing seniority, putting committee assignments on a random and rotating basis, lengthening representatives' terms to four years running concurrently with presidential terms, reducing the numbers of existing subcommittees and adopting a "sunset" rule limiting the life of new ones, and broadening the jurisdictions and reducing the number of standing committees. But such changes would not only be difficult to accomplish; their implications reach far beyond the realm of foreign relations. This discussion focuses, therefore, on more feasible reforms particularly important for foreign relations that still might have quite important effects. The changes we propose have three purposes: to equip the Congress to more effectively review and check executive action in foreign relations; to offset, at least in part, the tendencies toward fragmented and parochial treatment of issues; and to heighten awareness of the longer-run consequences of government's actions and failures to act.

Reviewing and Checking Executive Authority. Several feasible reforms would strengthen the ability of Congress to serve this purpose. The first builds on the proposal, advanced in the previous chapter, for presidential submission to the Congress of a formal comprehensive Biennial Statement of U.S. purposes and policies abroad. Even without organizational change, such a statement would offer a framework for periodic congressional debate on major U.S. policy objectives, and on the utility of particular programs (U.S. sales of weapons abroad, for example), or particular actions (declaration of a two hundred-mile economic zone in the ocean) in the light of such objectives. But the Biennial Statement could also be used to stimulate more thoughtful and better coordinated congressional response to foreign policy issues. The method might, for example, be modeled after the Joint Economic Committee. The JEC, established by the Employment Act of 1946, receives the President's annual Economic Report, studies means of coordinating programs to further the policy of the act, and as a guide to the several committees of the Congress dealing with economic legislation, reports its findings and recommendations to both Houses. Although the committee has no legislative jurisdiction, it has focused congressional response to presidential economic proposals, has kept disparate committees of the Congress aware of the potential macroeconomic effects of the issues before them, and has speeded the education of the Congress and of the country in the complexities of national economic policy.

In theory, the Budget Committee of each house might provide a more forceful model. Those are the committees through which Congress now limits appropriations and spending to conform to its prior decisions about the total budget and its allocation to major program areas: health, agriculture, defense, and the like. While not yet in full effect, the budget process has passed its early tests. If it operates as designed, it will represent effective coordination of the most sensitive and difficult kind, and itself encourage a more coherent treatment of national priorities affected by spending. But two circumstances make the budget process unique. Its quantitative nature makes the setting of an overall policy relatively simple; ceilings can be expressed in numbers. And the current political climate gives strong support to a reform designed to limit federal expenditure. Foreign policy objectives cannot be precisely stated, and more important, there is no comparable pressure for their consistency and integration.

We propose, therefore, that a new Committee on Interdependence be established in each house to receive and debate the Biennial Statement and the various white papers, and to prepare a comprehensive congressional response. The Interdependence committees would review the issues raised by those documents that transcended the jurisdictional boundaries of existing committees, and would propose means of coordinating congressional action.* Without encroaching deeply on the jurisdiction of any present committee, these new committees would make possible comprehensive and sustained Congressional review of U.S. foreign policy objectives, and of the consistency of those objectives with particular programs and actions. Membership would be drawn from the leadership of each house plus the Appropriations, Armed Services, Foreign Relations, and Economic committees (Ways and Means, Finance, Banking and Currency, and Commerce) and the Atomic Energy Committee. To extend the benefits of membership as far as possible, and to avoid hardening of the committees' perspectives, membership should rotate, with appointments being limited to four or six years, and should include a number of junior members of each house.

The impact of these Interdependence committees would obviously depend on the skill, energy, and seriousness of their chairmen and members, and on the capacity of their staffs, but even under modest assumptions their impact could be considerable. Their hearings and reports would dramatize the growing interactions among societies (Europe's concern about New York City's solvency, the impact abroad of U.S. inflation); and the committees' staffs could serve as brokers among other congressional staffs, encouraging the consistent treatment of related issues. Foreigners might be asked to testify directly (as in Secretary Coleman's hearings on the Concorde) to dramatize the breadth of the population affected by actions

---

* Given these objectives, a Joint Committee on Interdependence might be preferable. But a joint committee would also have several disadvantages. The Senate has a constitutional responsibility for consultation in foreign affairs which the House only partially shares. Separate committees could better relate their deliberations to the principal concerns and working schedules of their own Houses. And joint committees are exceptional instruments. They should be used sparingly, and as we argue in Chapter 9, effective congressional oversight of intelligence more clearly requires a new joint committee.

of the U.S. government. Over time, the committees might become a natural focal point for executive-congressional coordination; they might even evolve toward the budget model, acquiring some measure of coordinating authority.

Related proposals have been made before. The Joint Committee on National Security long advocated by Senator Humphrey and Representative Zablocki is similar in purpose and design. The difference—and it seems to us important—is that the Humphrey-Zablocki bill proposes, in effect, a congressional counterpart to the National Security Council—a committee that would draw its membership solely from the Armed Services, Foreign Relations, Atomic Energy, and Appropriations committees. It is thus designed to meet the coordination problem of the past—that of integrating military and diplomatic considerations—but not the broader difficulty of coordinating military, economic, political and technological policies.

The impact of the interdependence committees should be augmented by a longer foreign affairs authorization cycle. Until the last decade, appropriations—the approval of particular budgets—were voted annually by the Congress, but authorizations, the entitlements of departments and their major programs to continued existence, were renewed only at longer intervals. Partly as a result of the deepening conflict between Congress and the executive and partly because the legislative committees controlling authorizations have sought to regain power that had shifted toward appropriations committees, more and more authorizations are now required annually. State, the oldest Cabinet department, now depends on annual authorization, as do foreign aid, atomic energy, and major defense programs.

The result has been largely pernicious. Fundamental rethinking is simply not possible on an annual basis, and the costs of trying it include protracted and unnecessary executive testimony, and annual delay and uncertainty in the departments. A biennial authorization cycle would link congressional debate of the Biennial Statement to decisions about authorizations, and would also help reestablish the distinct purposes of authorization and appropriation. Such a cycle would have in the Statement a comprehensive and coherent basis for reviewing the agencies and programs being authorized, and it would schedule authorization decisions neither so infrequently as to dilute congressional influence, nor so frequently as to limit serious debate in Congress or make executive programming impossible. Indeed, if serious efforts at "zero-base" budgeting are to be made, a biennial authorization cycle will probably prove essential.

Congressional ability to review and check executive action would also be improved by the attendance of congressional leaders—at presidential invitation—at ExCab deliberations. Occasional and informal congressional participation in such meetings need not bring into question the necessary separation of powers, and its advantage to the Congress could be as substantial as those to the President. It would provide early warning of presidential intentions as well as an opportunity to bring congressional views directly to bear on executive decision making.

An interesting reciprocal of the notion that members of Congress should attend ExCab meetings is Senator Mondale's recent proposal that Cabinet officers routinely appear before the full Senate to expound the bases for current and proposed executive action and to respond to questions.[17] The feasibility of that proposal appears limited by the difficulty of pursuing any issue in depth in a body of one hundred members, a problem which could be circumvented if Cabinet officers appeared before the proposed Interdependence committees. This practice would give Congress an instrument for reviewing executive intentions as well as actions, and at the same time would help offset congressional parochialism and the dominance of particular interests represented in current committees.

Finally, improved congressional review of executive action in foreign affairs will require better access to information now closely held in the executive. While Congress has many sources of information on domestic programs, it must rely on the executive for most of its facts about U.S. actions and commitments abroad, facts partially shrouded in secrecy.

Improving the factual basis for congressional action should begin by widening the access of Congress to information and analyses from the intelligence community. As outlined in Chapter 9, we believe that a new Joint Committee on Intelligence should routinely receive all National Intelligence Estimates, together with all other estimates, analyses, or information (not including the terms of policy advice to the President) that it may request. But while such a practice would greatly assist the proposed oversight function of that committee, it would not answer the need of other congressional committees for access to intelligence about their own substantive responsibilities. That problem, we believe, must be resolved through statutory reform of the entire classification system.

Such a reform is long overdue. The executive orders governing the system have been modified in recent years to reduce overclassification and to permit greater public access. But the basic defects of the system remain. It classifies too much for too long, and protects genuine secrets too little. It involves no systematic procedures for routinely making information available to the Congress. Most remarkably, it rests on no statutory basis at all. With the exception of some kinds of information covered under the Atomic Energy Acts, and material to which, under limited circumstances, the Espionage Acts may apply, the whole mechanism that withholds from public and congressional view virtually all important government documents relating to U.S. foreign and security policy is constructed simply of a series of executive orders.

The Congress should adopt legislation establishing a comprehensive classification system. The details will require careful working out, but the broad outlines, we think, are clear.[18] The statute should require classification of specified categories of information with respect to which the need for confidentiality is overriding—military capabilities, and the sources and methods of intelligence, for example. It should exempt from classification other specified types of information—potential violations of U.S. law such as the unauthorized use of U.S. resources or personnel abroad, for example. And the law should then lodge in appropriate officials the discretion to classify or to maintain unclassified all other information on the basis of a principle that the current system ignores, namely, that in the exercise of that discretion the needs for secrecy be balanced against the values of disclosure. Current procedures require secrecy if any potential harm may result from disclosure, without weighing disclosure's possible benefits. Until that guideline is replaced, prudent men will continue to over-classify. The law should also specify sanctions for violators of the system—criminal in the case of unauthorized release of properly classified information; administrative and civil in the case of improper classification.

As part of the statutory system, or through the adoption of related congressional rules, the Congress must also deal with its own conflicting needs: that the committees of either House whose work might be assisted by classified information are able to identify and receive it, and that at the same time the confidentiality of properly classified material is assured. Recent congressional experience with secret material is not encouraging, but neither is it conclusive. The Joint Atomic Energy Committee has handled highly sensitive information for thirty years without any leakage. A classification system based on statute, adopted by the Congress itself, and containing sanctions against its abuse should be quite capable of producing congressional attitudes toward secrets that are no more casual than those of political-level officials of the executive branch.

Offsetting Congressional Parochialism. A second major purpose of our recommendations is to counterweight the influence current organizational arrangements lend to particular as opposed to general interests, and to partial as opposed to comprehensive assessment of major issues in the Congress. The nature of Congress places sharp limits on the feasibility of reforms with this intention. But framing sensible national policy for the complex and crosscutting issues of the future, made difficult by the centrifugal tendencies in the executive, is made still harder by congressional fractionalism. Recall, for example, that twenty-eight different committees and subcommittees have jurisdiction over parts of the energy problem. Whatever can be done to slow the centrifuge is worth trying.

Several of the measures already discussed would tend to have that effect. The Interdependence committees, for example, while providing Congress with a forum in which to assess executive proposals in terms of their broadest implications, would also make possible the review of proposed congressional action in the same perspective. Similarly, the proposed Biennial Statements and white papers should provide a framework into which various elements of presidential policy are supposed to fit, thus facilitating the intellectual task of relating portions of policy to larger objectives. The proposed question period for Cabinet members should also tend to offset parochialism, sensitizing Cabinet members to congressional perspectives outside the committees to which their departments normally respond, and giving members of Congress some basis for making independent judgments about proposals emanating from those committees.

A further step can somewhat limit another form of parochialism. Issues having both foreign and domestic consequences are generally considered by the Congress principally in terms of their domestic implications. The oil case, the Panama Canal situation and the International Petroleum Company (IPC) affair all illustrate the point. The tendency is powerful and understandable; foreigners do not vote. Organizational changes cannot alter that basic fact, but they can somewhat offset it. The hearings and reports of the Interdependence committees would have that effect. So would expansion of the jurisdiction of the International and Foreign Relations committees. Those committees might usefully be assigned responsibility to review and comment on budget proposals having foreign implications, and be given concurrent oversight (together with Ways and

Means and Banking and Currency) over both foreign trade and international financial agencies.

But the most powerful method of limiting the tendencies toward fragmentation in the Congress is to strengthen party leadership. As noted earlier, the election of leaders more forceful than their predecessors now appears likely in both houses. Energetic leaders, operating with the support of party caucuses, could force many of the changes in structure and process that we propose. Quite apart from their possible support for such reforms, however, forceful leaders could impose a common discipline on committee chairmen, and sharply limit the ability of small groups of congressmen to take important actions inconsistent with the will of Congress as a body.

Finally, we offer three proposals designed to enlarge the capability of the Congress, and of the government generally, to assess current action or inaction in terms of its long-run effects.

The "Critical List." The first is a procedure suggested by Joseph Nye and Robert Keohane to capitalize on the effectiveness of Congress as an investigating and educating body.[19] It involves commissioning an independent, nongovernment body of scientists such as the National Academy of Sciences to develop annually a "critical list" of major problems or opportunities arising from the uses of the globe's physical resources and environment or from new developments in science and technology. Had such a procedure been in effect in the 1960s, ozone degradation, ice-cap melting, nuclear waste disposal, for example, might have appeared as threats, and sea-floor mining techniques might have appeared as opportunities. By itself, such a list would confer small benefit; but if congressional hearings regularly followed its publication and focused public attention on threats regarded by the scientific community as most dangerous, the government's tendency to defer decisions—even about matters that become vastly more difficult to manage over time (oil, population, nuclear proliferation)—would meet a substantial counterpressure. Nye and

Keohane have suggested further that following such hearings, the President, through his science adviser, should report on the administration's estimate of the seriousness of the threats, and spell out the steps he proposes to take in response to them. In this way a new competence, external to government, would be brought to bear on the early identification of novel issues—a task government performs poorly—and congressional hearings would serve to amplify signals that might not otherwise be heard.

Second Decade Projections. The second and third proposals, both suggested by the Committee for Economic Development's report, "Congressional Decision-Making for National Security,"[20] are addressed principally to the defense budget, but could have important effects in other realms as well. It is characteristic of major modern weapons, as of other major capital investments, that they enter service a decade after first being authorized and reach the midpoint of their working lives a full human generation after being designed. The B-52 bomber, whose basic characteristics were fixed in the early 1950s, will remain the principal U.S. strategic aircraft in the early 1980s. Trident submarines now in construction will form the backbone of undersea strategic forces into the twenty-first century. The huge costs of such programs—the latest nuclear aircraft carrier will cost $5 billion—are worth expending where the systems they buy provide necessary capabilities over such long lifetimes. Typically, however, the systems are procured without close attention to the strategic, technical, or political environment in which their future operations will occur. While those environments obviously cannot be predicted with certainty, the size and importance of the investments, coupled with the pace of technological change, makes it essential to attempt such predictions, however uncertain they may be. The army is now seeking to spend several billion dollars on new tanks, for example. But the rapid development of cheap, accurate, and lethal antitank weapons is well advanced, as the 1973 Mideast War demonstrated. Congress should therefore require that requests for funding of long-lived systems be accompanied by the best estimates the Department of Defense can present as to probable environment of the second and third decades in which those systems are expected to operate. And the Congress should review those assessments with care. Similar procedures should govern authorization of other major capital expenditures.

Five-year Authorizations for Defense, Foreign Aid, and Contributions to International Lending Institutions. The defects of single-year authorizations discussed above are particularly severe in budgets containing costly and slow-maturing capital items. The defense budget is the extreme case, though not the only one. There, single-year authorizations make tempting the appropriation of the relatively small sums necessary in each of the initial years of a weapon's development. In form, the vastly larger costs of production are not committed. In fact, however, after several successive years of development, a weapons system takes on a life of its own, acquiring supporters and sometimes even production facilities, thus making its cancellation extremely difficult. Whether or not the two-year authorization cycle we propose is adopted generally, the Congress should shift to a four- or five-year rolling authorization cycle for major weapons systems. Each year's authorization process could add a new fifth year to the sequence, and amend, as necessary, the earlier authorization for the four years ahead. For quite different reasons, similar practices would be appropriate for the authorization of foreign aid, and for contributions to the World Bank and other international lending institutions. There, the necessity of international institutions and of foreign governments to plan programs of many years' duration, and to count on the funding for them, argues strongly that U.S. commitments, once made, should not be subject to annual or biennial cancellation. Just as most federal grant programs to states and localities operate on three- to five-year authorizations, so should U.S. commitments abroad.

Chapter 6

A Function
for State

PRESIDENT KENNEDY: "What's wrong with
that goddamned department of yours, Chip?"
AMBASSADOR BOHLEN: "You are, Mr. President."[1]

NO Cabinet department is as much criticized as the Department of State, and none is more resentful of the limitations
placed upon it. Both attitudes are captured in the celebrated
exchange between President Kennedy and Ambassador Bohlen
above. Some criticisms of the department reflect attitudes toward the Secretary; State has been regarded as "elitist" under
Acheson, indecisive during the Rusk years, "domineering" and
"secretive" under Kissinger. But for at least two decades, criticism of the department as a bureaucracy has been quite
consistent. It has been repeatedly asserted that State was
bloated in size, incapable of management, incompetent at staff
work, and more pointedly, that it represented the interests of
foreign nations rather than those of the United States. The
cures proposed have centered correspondingly on cutbacks in
personnel, "managerial" training, appointment of more non-
career officers, exhortations to dynamism, and forced tours for

foreign service officers in domestic political settings. In varying measure, all have been tried. None have markedly diminished dissatisfaction with the department.[2]

The department's own principal complaint has been that extraneous actors were crowding the foreign policy stage. If they could not be removed, State at least wanted the lead role among them. "Subject only to the higher power of the President, [the Secretary of State] should have authority to direct not only the activities of the Department of State, but all activities conducted by other departments of the government, including economic, social, military, informational, intelligence-gathering, etc., which have a significant impact on the nation's external relations."[3] That view, expressed by George Kennan in 1974, reflects clearly the deep sentiments of the department, and it has commanded general support among students of foreign policy organization.[4]

In theory if not in fact, that injunction too has been observed. President Kennedy formally proclaimed the primacy of the department in Washington and of the ambassador in the field, naming the Secretary the "agent of coordination in all our major policies toward other nations"; President Johnson established a formal system of State-chaired interagency committees to reinforce that authority; President Nixon reaffirmed the "position of the Secretary of State as his principal foreign policy adviser." More tellingly, two Secretaries during this period—Dulles and Kissinger—were forceful men, sensitive to the play of domestic politics and strongly backed by their Presidents. Yet neither delegations of formal authority nor powerful Secretaries have enabled the department to direct or coordinate important activities of other departments.

 This history strongly suggests that the performance expected of State has been inherently impossible. We believe that, for at least the past decade, this has been exactly the case, and that it will be even more clearly so in the decades ahead. We therefore believe that State should no longer be asked to play the role it has most cherished, been repeatedly assigned, and regularly failed to perform. Rather, a serious effort must be made to define a principal role for the department that is both useful and feasible. For that purpose, some understanding of State's recent inadequacies is essential.

The Withering Away of State?

Recall the German offsets episode, a representative problem of the 1960s. How to cover the foreign exchange costs of U.S. troops in Germany was a question central to the business of both Treasury and Defense, and both were under direct presidential pressure in the matter. State could not "direct" or "coordinate" the policies of those two great departments on matters clearly bearing on their own main responsibilities. State might well have played a stronger hand than it did; and had it done so, the outcome almost certainly would have been improved. But its "coordination" or "direction" of national policy was simply not possible. As we have argued above, coordination and direction across departmental lines require that the interests of some departments be sacrificed to those of others. When those interests are important, departments do not accept such sacrifice without appeal. Decisions of such issues, therefore, are accepted only when taken by the highest political authority. State does not have such authority; only the President does. Indeed, rather than attempting to direct other departments, State has more frequently sought what I. M. Destler has called "tacit non-aggression pacts" with them, hoping in that way to retain control over "diplomacy."[5]

The issues likely to be typical of the next decade reinforce the point. In the offset case State had to contend only with Treasury and Defense, next to itself the departments most nearly presidential in viewpoint and least pressed by special interest groups. Contrast this with the oil problem, which involves six times as many executive agencies, three times as many congressional committees, and far more powerful private interests. In a period in which much of "foreign" and "domestic" policy will be indistinguishable, when issues having impact abroad will engage multiple agencies, numerous interest groups, many congressional committees, the role State found unmanageable in the 1960s will prove wholly impossible.

If the department cannot "direct" in Washington, still less can it do so abroad. The speed and economy of modern communications make possible the concentration of decision making in Washington; the importance of the issues, and the numerous parties to them, make it necessary. Increasingly, the major issues negotiated between the United States and other nations are not bilateral in nature. They are not questions, say, of U.S. base rights in Japan or of the terms on which products unique to Brazil will enter U.S. markets. Instead, they concern the shape of an international monetary agreement, or the positions the two nations will take in an international conference on the law of the sea, or the terms of a commodity agreement involving a dozen producing nations and twice that number of consumers. On issues of this kind, U.S. positions are not simply a function of relations with one particular country or another. They derive from far broader and interconnected considerations that our ambassadors in Tokyo or Brasilia can only partially assess. They can be seen whole—if anywhere—only in Washington.

To an increasing degree, therefore, major issues of policy must be managed in Washington, and no matter how clear their foreign implications, they cannot be controlled by the Department of State. That situation is not new; it has been unfolding since before World War II. Nor is it unique to the United States; the autonomy and influence of all foreign offices are shrinking and ambassadors of many nations lament their reduction to reporting and housekeeping roles. If it was ever true that foreign affairs was a technical specialty, best managed by experts, it is true no longer.

Then what is the function of State? Shall it resign itself to supplementing the foreign reporting of the CIA and *The New York Times,* and to providing guide and hotel services for visiting dignitaries? Or should it be abolished? The experience of business organizations, it is worth noting, suggests that State might in fact wither away. Students of business have identified a recurring pattern in the development of international corporations. First the business sets up an international division to handle the unfamiliar problems of doing business abroad. Ten or fifteen years later, if the corporation has succeeded abroad, all its major functions—finance, product development, manufacture, marketing—have become internationalized. All its specialized operating arms have developed their own international contacts and familiarities. At this point the separate international division is extraneous, and it is generally disbanded.[6]

But government-to-government dealings are political as well as economic, and in all states political authority is centralized. Governments must therefore maintain some capability for dealing directly with the chief political officers of other nations, and for keeping track of the full range of their interactions with other societies. So a State Department, unlike an "international division," retains a function: it is at least a useful source of information and staff support to the President. But is that all? We think not, at least for the next several decades. Though ill-suited to dominance in foreign policy making, State displays many characteristics well-suited for a different role, hardly less important, and so far poorly played.

Advocacy, the Major Role for State

Consider the main characteristics of the State Department. By tradition, its chief is the senior Cabinet officer and chief foreign policy adviser to the President. It is the principal repository of knowledge about foreign societies, our institutional memory in foreign affairs; and a main source, through political and economic reporting, of new information about events abroad. It commands the main political channels of contact with foreign governments, and is organized internally along country and regional lines. Its most desired assignments are located abroad; an ambassadorship remains its professionals' highest aspiration. Functional competence in military, economic, scientific matters is thin. The culture of the department is cautious and placid (the principal duties for younger officers abroad are observation and reporting, for which alert passivity is an appropriate style, and foreign service officers are typically assigned little authority until well into middle age). Yet the Foreign Service attracts officers as capable as any in government.

What are the major tasks that, with feasible reforms, such a department might undertake, and that need performing? Recall the poorly met needs of U.S. foreign policy making: first, the need for integration, for the assurance that the decentralized actions of many agencies bear some consistent and intended relation to each other. Achieving integration, we have argued, requires presidential power. But the White House needs help, and help of a kind that State can provide. Second, policy making must be accepted as legitimate; it must be understood and supported by the Congress and the public. There is work for State here. And finally, with sharpest relevance for the department, policy making must be balanced; sufficient weight must be given to collective interests as against particular ones, to longer run versus immediate goals, to the enhancement of security through means other than traditional military capability or autonomous national strength.

Together these policy-making needs suggest a role that is appropriate for State, that with feasible reforms State could perform well, and that—if performed well—would sharply improve the making of U.S. foreign policy. The role is *advocacy:* the forceful argument, at every stage of the policy process, that the interests of the United States are most reliably advanced by policies and actions that meet the legitimate requirements of all nations. Such advocacy looks to longer-run American interests rather than to immediate foreign concerns, it focuses on decision making in Washington rather than on representation abroad, and it requires full engagement in the bureaucratic and political warfare from which policy emerges. State has frequently performed exactly this function, but only as one function among many, and rarely to the level its importance demands. What we think essential is that the department accept such advocacy as its central role and main responsibility, and that its structure, processes and staffing be adapted accordingly.

Well played, such a role cannot be popular. It will frequently require opposition to proposals that serve powerful domestic interests, and whose costs to the United States may appear only after some remote and contingent foreign reaction. (Remember the August 1971 and IPC and Panama Canal cases, as well as the offset and oil issues.) But its performance is essential. Some agency—and State is far the best candidate—must keep steadily before the makers of policy the fact that America's security depends on a fragile network of international relations, and that actions serving short-run U.S. interests, or venting nationalistic emotions, can damage that network or provoke costly foreign reactions. Fortunately, State will not stand alone. The domestic interests directly affected by foreign reactions are becoming more conscious of their own stakes in responsible American policy—the support of free trade by U.S. farmers and consequently by the Department of Agriculture is an example. Moreover, most agencies of the government, like the divisions of international businesses, are now engaged in foreign relations of their own, especially with their counterpart agencies abroad. And all have substantial international staffs attuned to the interests of other societies and aware of the ways foreign actions can affect U.S. interests. An important element in State's role as advocate, therefore, is to mobilize support from such staffs, and from the private interests they serve.

Making State an effective advocate for this perspective will require greater clarity about the primacy of the role and greater capacity to perform a number of tasks. What are the tasks?

Rethinking U.S. Purposes. U.S. foreign policy making in the next decade will be greatly complicated by the dissipation of the broad popular agreement underlying the nation's foreign policy after World War II. The need for some agreement on national objectives will become increasingly evident as domestic political considerations intrude more deeply into foreign policy making. For many of the issues of the future, moreover —like access to ocean resources, the terms of international trade, the control of nuclear fuels—satisfactory solutions can be achieved only through the development of international mechanisms for mediating disputes and enforcing agreements. These mechanisms will probably develop as the European Common Market evolved—slowly, painfully, step by step. Such development can be sustained only by uncommon vision, persistence, and clarity of purpose—characteristics that, in the foreign policy of a democracy, require broad agreement on the nation's interests and responsibilities.

The necessary consensus cannot be obtained by executive fiat; But neither can the executive abdicate the role of leadership in seeking consensus. The White House is the one point in the government where trade-offs between domestic and foreign concerns, between long and short term purposes, between economic and political goals can authoritatively be made. But of all departments in the executive branch, State is best suited to assist the White House in formulating coherent conceptions of U.S. responsibilities in the world, and articulating those responsibilities to Congress and the public. State is not so sensitive to particular economic concerns as Treasury or Labor or Agriculture, not so exclusively concerned with military strength as Defense. Its purposes are relatively broad; its time horizon relatively long; and what it lacks in sensitivity to domestic politics it makes up in awareness of the international ramifications of U.S. decision making. It should bring those perspectives forcefully to bear on all formulations of U.S. purpose (such as the Biennial Statements proposed in Chapter 4) and it should actively promote those perspectives outside the executive branch.

Balancing Decision Making. A coherent and responsible conception of purposes serves as a vow: it establishes expectations but guarantees nothing. The framework of U.S. objectives must be defended, advanced, revised, and acted upon in the making of specific decisions. As those decisions are hammered out in the executive branch and in the Congress, the particular interests most affected will be well represented. In the IPC case business interests and the Commerce Department pressed the domestic arguments, with powerful broad congressional backing. The Defense Department, "Zonians," veterans, and patriotic groups lobby against changed status for the Panama Canal, and have even stronger congressional support. Banking, business, and labor interests, especially those in industries hit hard by competition from imports, urged the August 1971 actions on tariffs and exchange rates.

Who will assert the contrary interests: the weakness of IPC's claims, the global vulnerabilities of extractive industries controlled by foreigners and their declining importance to the United States; the legitimacy of Panamanian expectations and the risks to both the canal itself and the larger pattern of hemisphere relations if they are grossly ignored; the consequences of failure to consult with our trading partners before withdrawing from a world monetary arrangement we established and maintained? U.S. groups adversely affected will speak up—as did U.S. importers in the August 1971 case, for example—if they are aware of the issue early enough. But such groups are often diffuse, and they are rarely able to predict with authority the probable foreign response. More important, they are not well situated to propose alternative formulations of U.S. policy that could accommodate domestic needs at lowest cost to legitimate foreign concerns, and at

lowest risk of foreign retaliation. Those tasks must be undertaken within the U.S. government; there the Department of
State has a clear comparative advantage. While not now
ideally equipped to perform these tasks, State is better suited
than any other department. And feasible changes—addressed
below—can improve its abilities.

Executing and Monitoring. Policy takes its direction from
high-level decision making, but its content from actions at
lower levels. At those levels, State has two main functions. As
the only department aware of the full range of U.S. interactions
with the other nations, and having routine access to their
central officials, State should generally lead the nation's international negotiations, a traditional function that (in the main)
has been well performed. Secondly, State is well situated to
monitor the activities of those agencies that now do business
directly and routinely with their foreign counterparts. Such
direct dealings are necessitated by the technical, detailed and
continuous character of many international issues, but they
are also risky. Most U.S. agencies involved in international
matters have a limited knowledge of the foreign governments
with which they deal, only a partial view of U.S. purposes
abroad, and generally no view at all of the interplay between
their business and the business of the rest of the government.
Those limitations make imperative the active presence of an
agency whose strengths can offset them. Below the level of
the White House, only the State Department has the capacity
to monitor the actions of other agencies to ensure that they
accord with larger policy objectives, and to intervene if signs
of breakdown or error appear.

The Skybolt affair of 1962 provides a dated but clear example of the importance of the monitoring function.[7] The
United States had tentatively decided to cancel development
of the Skybolt system, an airborne nuclear missile designed
to allow aircraft to launch their weapons at great distance
from their targets. Britain had been relying on Skybolt to
extend the useful life of its vulnerable bomber force. Secretary

McNamara took responsibility for informing the United Kingdom of the likely U.S. move and telephoned British Minister of Defense Thorneycroft. The U.S. government then waited for the United Kingdom to propose a substitute arrangement. For various reasons neither Prime Minister Macmillan nor Thorneycroft were willing to broach the problem of an alternative weapon simply on the basis of a warning from McNamara; they assumed the U.S. would take the lead in offering a substitute. The problem might have been resolved had McNamara made an originally scheduled trip to London, but for unrelated reasons that trip was repeatedly postponed. When McNamara finally arrived in London without a substitute offer, the British erupted. The issue then had to be addressed on an improvised basis at the Kennedy-Macmillan summit meeting at Nassau, and the deal hastily contrived there—the U.S. supply of Polaris missiles to be committed by the British to NATO—provided at least the excuse and perhaps the incitement for de Gaulle's veto of British entry into the Common Market.

The problem had developed entirely outside the purview of the U.S. ambassador in London, David Bruce. Respected and competent, Bruce had easy access to Whitehall, and his cables were "must" reading in the White House. Had he been instructed to monitor the Defense Department's handling of the issue, Bruce could readily have spotted the differences between London's assumptions and Washington's. But Bruce not only lacked such instructions, he received no information whatever from his department on the state of play. Indeed, he knew of the warning to Thorneycroft only through military channels, and therefore believed that he had no mandate for involvement.

Early Warning and the Management of Assigned Secondary Issues. Issues should be resolved at the lowest levels having the requisite authority and competence. The question arises, how best to manage interagency relations at these levels. The selection of issues for interagency resolution, the choice of particular participants in the process, and the initiative for making the process work could be left to the White House, but at the risk of further centralizing responsibility in the White House staff or of having important issues noticed only belatedly, or both. Alternatively, a formal system could be established around standing committees, presumably chaired by State. Like all standing committees, however, this alternative risks time-wasting, deadlock, or disuse. Thus it seems preferable to us that State be assigned lead responsibility for the early warning function, where necessary bringing issues to White House attention. The White House can then establish an appropriate ad hoc group, provide its mandate, and designate its chairman. Ordinarily, the chair should be occupied by State for reasons we have stressed so repeatedly: more than any other department State, if suitably charged and led, is likely to counter the overweighting of particular rather than general interests and shorter- rather than longer-run perspectives.

Foreign Assessment. As we have noted, State will frequently need to oppose policies with attractive domestic and political implications, and to do so in arenas containing few allies and many opponents. That role is hopeless unless played with some resource other advocates do not possess. That resource can only be the ability to assert with authority the probable foreign responses to such policies, and the resulting consequences to the United States. The early warning, negotiation, and monitoring functions all need to be backed by the same authority. But State's current political reporting does not provide such authority.[8] State will need to improve its reporting and assessment of possible developments abroad until they reach high orders of insight into the dynamics of foreign politics and of the economic, military, and social forces underlying those dynamics; and until the Department is able cogently to relate that insight to the design of American policy.

What Will It Take?

These, we believe, should be the main tasks of the Department of State in the next decades. They are assignments that only the department is well positioned to accomplish, and that badly need doing. But even partisans of the department would concede that State is not now performing them well. Their more effective performance, and State's consequent success at its central role of advocacy should therefore form the principal goals of reorganization in the department. It is in relation to these tasks that State's key officials should be chosen, its relations with other departments redefined, and its internal organization revised.

Reasonable Expectations. The prerequisite for effective performance by any agency is that it be assigned important functions within its capacity, and not others. Another round of assignments of "lead responsibility" or "overall coordination" to a department that cannot perform them would only precipitate another cycle of failure, confusion, loss of morale, and resignations among the abler younger officers. State should be prized and used for what it is: a potentially effective advocate for a particular perspective of increasing importance that has typically been undervalued in American decision processes.

An Appropriate Secretary. At every stage of the policy process—in the articulation of national purposes, in the formulation of specific decisions, in the resolution of lower level differences, in leading or monitoring implementation—the quality State needs most is aggressiveness backed by relevant competence. Those requirements have implications everywhere in the department, but nowhere so clearly as at the top. If the department is to play its principal role of advocate, and if it is to develop the capabilities necessary to support that role, then the Secretary of State must possess not only intellectual breadth, relevant experience, and political sense, but initiative and energy. Lacking these characteristics, the Secretary

will not long remain the President's chief foreign policy adviser. Nor will his department intervene in policy debates over
issues more central to other agencies than to itself (e.g., Defense with Panama, Energy with oil, Treasury with offsets),
especially if those agencies are technically more competent
and politically more powerful. Secretary Kissinger's aggres-
sive performance, together with recollections of Dulles and
Acheson may encourage the impression that Secretaries of State
normally meet those requirements, but the record in fact is
quite mixed. Of the four Presidents since Hoover who first
came to the White House through their own election, three—
Roosevelt, Kennedy and Nixon—selected a more passive man
to lead the department. Each wished to be "his own Secretary
of State." But future Presidents will find that the interpenetra-
tion of domestic and international issues will give them an
ample dose of foreign relations however forceful the Secretary
of State. Simply being President will give them the dominant
hand in the nation's foreign affairs. They will need a strong
Secretary to help them play that hand.

The Secretary's Team. A strong Secretary does not guarantee
a forceful or effective department. Both Dulles and Kissinger
essentially ignored the department, drawing staff support
from a small group of trusted associates and leaving the rest
of the department to routine and demoralization. Other Secretaries, more concerned for the department as an institution,
have found themselves only nominally in command of it,
faced with undersecretaries, assistant secretaries, and ambassadors who had been appointed separately by the President,
and who operated as independent entrepreneurs. Neither
situation is satisfactory. An effective Secretary requires allegiance and support from his subordinates; an effective department requires guidance, specific assignments and delegated
authority from its Secretary. Both requirements argue that all
principal officers of the department should be appointed and
employed as part of a single team.

First, then, the President should allow the Secretary to

make—or at least to veto—all high-level appointments, and to control firings as well. The Secretary should provide himself with one Deputy Secretary capable of functioning as an alter ego across virtually the whole spectrum of his own responsibilities. A true alter ego relationship is hard to establish, but its ability to broaden the neck of the bottle may be crucial. The responsibilities of the Undersecretaries for Political and for Economic Affairs should be clarified and their staffs upgraded as discussed below. If the undersecretaries are to represent, as they should, the main functional concerns of the department—defense and foreign economics—then the traditional practice of treating them as free-floating staff officers must be forsworn. For special negotiating or troubleshooting tasks, ambassadors-at-large should be substituted. The management of the department, moreover, will have to be conceived as a purposive endeavor; the deputy undersecretary charged with such management will need both guidance and support from the Secretary.

Finally, the Secretary's team should include key ambassadors. Major posts should be assigned to individuals in whom the Secretary personally (and, if possible, the President) has confidence, and they should be encouraged to return frequently to Washington. Travel between Washington and the field, traditionally constricted by congressional limits on travel allowances, can improve foreign assessment, since it sensitizes officers based abroad to the information Washington needs while enlarging Washington's sense of what the embassies might provide. But more importantly, such travel enhances the department's performance as advocate: the envoy fresh from the scene bears an authority and an intensity of concern that home-based officials can rarely duplicate. The point was well demonstrated in 1973 by Patrick Moynihan, then U.S. Ambassador to India. The United States had amassed an account of some $3 billion in rupees from years of concessionary grain sales to India, a massive debt that clouded all U.S.–India relations. State had long sought its settlement at a substantial discount, but the administration was divided and the Congress was opposed. In a series of trips to Washington, Moynihan personally argued the case with Secretaries Schultz and Butz, some forty congressmen and senators, and the President. The result, by a narrow margin, was a settlement of the debt at a two-thirds discount. Of course, Moynihan's political credentials were superior to those of most ambassadors, but his political clout appears to have been less critical than his aggressive view of the nature of his job.[9]

Functional Competence. Effective advocacy will require higher levels of functional competence than State now commands. State cannot and need not supplant Treasury in monetary expertise, or Defense in military judgment, or the Energy Administration in estimating national fuel requirements. But it must become a respected participant in discussions of those subjects. It must be able to hold its own in interagency argument, developing its own proposals and analyzing those of others on the basis of solid technical skills. Those skills are most conspicuously lacking in the department's military and economic areas.

Curiously, there is no high level focal point within the department for "politico-military" affairs. A small politico-military staff (PM) is now headed by a director nominally equivalent to an assistant secretary, but not confirmed by the Senate. The department's third-ranking official, the Undersecretary for Political Affairs, has sometimes assumed responsibility for State's high-level involvement in national security issues, but not at other times. The matter has depended entirely on his own interests; his job is not so defined. Nor is anyone else's. Meanwhile, Congress in 1971 established the post of Undersecretary for Security Assistance, a lofty position with a very narrow slice of the politico-military responsibility. It became clear thirty years ago that the military security of the United States and of our allies was this country's first foreign policy objective, and that attaining it would require the closest integration of diplomatic and military skills. But no senior official of the State Department is yet charged with the routine management of high-level issues concerning both State and Defense.* Nor are the other officials in the department well served by staff competence on defense-related issues. PM has undergone some recent strengthening, but it is still far from adequate to the task. As one recent PM director has remarked, "There are not a half-dozen people in the building who have any understanding of the strategic consequences of the SALT agreements."

Several reforms are required. Responsibility within State for defense-related issues should be clearly designated as the main business of a single undersecretary, probably the Undersecretary for Political Affairs. That official should be made expressly responsible for State's efforts to review and reformulate national security policy (including security assistance) and to monitor its execution. His position might be retitled accordingly. The Bureau of Politico-Military Affairs should be placed under his direction, and its staff renovated—principally by recruiting from outside the department, not by employing additional foreign service officers—until it possesses a solid competence in strategic doctrine, military planning, logistics, and costing. The position of Undersecretary for Security Assistance would then become superfluous and should be abolished.

Unlike military responsibility, responsibility for economic affairs is already well focused in the department. That responsibility is not, however, backed by the requisite capability. The Undersecretary for Economic Affairs has little direct authority over what should be his principal staff—the department's semiautonomous Bureau of Economic and Business Affairs—and this bureau is grossly undersupplied with trained economists (3 Ph.D.s in economics out of a professional staff of 126). The department's tactic of filling economic slots with foreign service officers having some interest or brief, intensive

---

* The Defense Department is not correspondingly disadvantaged. Its Office of International Security Affairs, established in the 1950s and well staffed during most of its history, has normally been headed by a senior and capable assistant secretary. The position has recently been upgraded to that of deputy secretary.

training in the subject serves passably abroad and in the geographic bureaus of the department in Washington, where the issues addressed are likely to be less technical or less critical and where the problems of recruiting and retaining professional economists may be insuperable. But the absence of full professional competence in the staff intended to support the department's intervention in economic issues of high policy is a mistake.

Improving State's performance in defense and economic matters is thus partly a matter of clear assignments of responsibility and appropriate lines of authority—neither now present, but both relatively easy to establish. The harder problem will be to acquire and retain high competence at the staff level. The problem is not one of numbers: if the functional staffs need expansion, it is by tens, not by hundreds. The difficulty will be creating a working environment in which specialized, Washington-based, functional talents are respected and rewarded in a department dominated by a generalist tradition, an overseas orientation, and a regional pattern of organization.

More Authoritative Foreign Assessment. Improving State's capacity for foreign assessment will require—most basically— explicit recognition of the priority of this task. Assessment must be clearly acknowledged as the central skill and great comparative advantage of the missions abroad and of State's country and regional desks in Washington. Once the Secretary has established this point, responsibility for forcing improvement, and for managing the many institutional changes required, should be clearly lodged in a single senior official—the Deputy Secretary or Deputy Undersecretary for Management. That official should be primarily concerned with improving the ability of the missions to anticipate the kinds of information and analysis most important to policy debate in Washington. The real burden here, however, is on the department to ask pointed questions and insist on useable answers—a burden assumed belatedly or not at all in the Offset, IPC, and August 1971 cases. Mutual sensitivity would probably be enhanced by more use of informal methods of exchanging information—more use of the telephone, for example, and more routine visits of desk officers to the field and of senior mission officers to Washington.

Equipping the missions to provide penetrating answers, once pointed questions are asked, will require innovations of several kinds. Entry into the department for persons with analytic training, experience and demonstrated capacity should be made easier and more attractive. Special training of Foreign Service officers at the Foreign Service Institute and at universities should be expanded. Assignment patterns should be revised to permit more extended experience with particular nations and regions. Perhaps most important, the performance of Foreign Service officers should be evaluated for the relevance of their reporting contributions to policy making, and promotion decisions should weigh those evaluations heavily. Finally, the department must find ways, formally or otherwise, to tap the insights of Americans outside the government (businessmen and scholars especially) into foreign societies. That is a long agenda, and it will take many years to work through. But much might be done in a shorter period, with potentially useful results both in selectively improved assessments, and in developing models of change that the whole department might later be led to emulate.*

* Specifically, an experimental effort along these lines might be tried. For each of several foreign countries, three or four panels would be established. One would be composed of eight or ten interested Foreign Service officers; the second of professionals from other agencies interested in the same countries. A third panel would be composed of experts drawn primarily from the universities and think tanks. Finally, private individuals with reputations as "wise men" about developments in each country might be identified and induced to participate.

Then, for each country ten or twenty major issues of concern to the United States would be identified. Each panel would be asked to formulate explicit predictions about those issues, and to make plain the basis for those predictions. The resulting estimates would then be compared with each other, and with emerging events. The better estimates would be noted, and the more effective methods for making assessments and predictions identified. After wide review of the results, the process would be repeated, by the same panels or others. In this way the current —largely impressionistic—means of making foreign assessments would be employed in a more pointed, focused, and competitive way, and at the same time the effort to improve those methods would have begun.

Taking the Initiative with Congress. Finally, we propose some reform in the handling of State's relations with Congress. Diplomats are accredited not to governments generally, but to heads of state. Many of them are accustomed to regarding diplomacy, moreover, as a business "executive altogether," in Jefferson's words. Mixing in the domestic politics of foreign nations, as those politics are played out in legislatures, is regarded as faintly reprehensible. The Department of State displays a residue of that attitude toward the politics of its own country. Its relations with the Congress are largely formalistic, belated, concentrated at the top, and for those reasons inadequate.

As we have argued at length above, Congress is likely to remain deeply involved in American foreign policy. If State hopes to provide a focal point for the formulation and conduct of that policy, it must change its relations with the Congress. The present status of the Panama issue provides an excellent example of the costs of current practice. A resolution calling for "the retention of undiluted U.S. sovereignty over the Canal Zone," which sharply constrained the ability of the Department of State to negotiate a new treaty, was introduced into the Senate by Senator Thurmond, with thirty-seven co-sponsors, in early March 1975. The co-sponsors had been enlisted during the preceding three weeks—a period during which State made no substantial effort to head off the resolution. Ambassador Bunker has explained that State traditionally does not go to Capitol Hill unless it has a treaty in hand; otherwise it "stirs up debate" and may narrow its options.[10] That tradition has been reinforced by the current Secretary's determination to hold his principal subordinates on very short leashes, especially in their dealings with the Congress. Consequently, while Secretary Kissinger has spent a great deal of time in congressional appearances and in less formal briefings and discussions with members of Congress, these efforts have typically been made late in the processes of decision, after trouble has already emerged, and they have been necessarily limited by the other demands on his own time.

Several reformers have proposed that State's congressional links would be improved by enlarging the staff or responsibilities of the department's Congressional Relations Office. That course seems to us wrong, reflective of a notion that relations with Congress, like diplomacy itself, are best left to specialists. On the contrary, if State seeks congressional trust and support, it must build them in the same way other departments do: by cultivating continuous informal interaction at Cabinet, sub-Cabinet, and assistant secretarial levels, and through staffs as well. No single conduit can manage all the traffic that should be moving back and forth between the department and the Congress.

With these proposals for assigning State a role more modest than it has sought but far greater than it has played, and for enlarging the department's capacity to perform it, we conclude the discussion of the three institutions central to the making of foreign policy: the Presidency, the Congress, and the State Department. But at least three major organizational questions remain. How should foreign economic and defense policy—the two main strands in our foreign relations—be formulated? And what can be done to insure more useful products and more defensible behavior from our large and expensive intelligence community? These questions are addressed in the remaining chapters.

Chapter 7

"Foreign" Economics

> Economic policies today are strategic decisions, and economic decisions today have almost the same political impact on the history of the world as formerly decisions on SALT or NATO had.
>
> Helmut Schmidt, Chancellor of the Federal Republic of Germany (1976)
>
> "[Expletive deleted] the lira."
>
> Richard Nixon (1972)

WAR and the prevention of war aside, foreign economics is what most international relations are about. Foreign economic policy encompasses the most substantial, sustained, and difficult relations most nations have with each other. As we saw in Chapter 3, moreover, the growing internationalization of the economies of advanced industrial nations makes international economic issues crucial not only to relations among such states, but also to the achievement of basic economic objectives within them. The subsidized U.S. sale of wheat to the Soviet Union in 1972 raised the price of American bread in 1973. OPEC manipulation of oil prices in 1973 accounted for almost half of the increase to double-digit inflation in 1974.

The U.S. devaluation of the dollar in 1973 accounted for another one-fourth of the increase in our rate of inflation. For the foreseeable future, and for better or for worse, the United States is joined to a world economy of production, trade, and money. That linkage contributes to a more stable international political order and a higher standard of living than would otherwise be possible. But it also makes U.S. prices, profits, wages, and jobs sensitive to events abroad. Other nations are still more dependent on what happens in the United States; the United States comprises by far the largest national component of the world economy. The impact of American economic policy on employment and price levels abroad puts issues of economic policy near the top of the agenda of every head of state who comes to Washington. For some people in developing countries, foreign economic policies of the United States and other advanced industrial powers can literally mean the difference between life and death. Many observers of international politics therefore predict with former Undersecretary of State U. Alexis Johnson that "economic considerations will dominate foreign policy over the next two decades, as security concerns dominated the last two."[1] Whether dominant or not, economic issues will clearly provide much of the substance of America's international relations in the decades ahead. *

As is becoming increasingly apparent, however, American

---

* Historically, the major concerns of U.S. foreign economic policy makers have been:
  1. Trade: What kinds and levels of tariffs and nontariff barriers, subsidies and rules will govern imports and exports of raw materials, manufactured products, and services?
  2. International money: What monies and payment arrangements will finance international trade and capital flows, and govern foreign exchange markets?
  3. Private investment: What rules will regulate U.S. private investment abroad and foreign investment in the United States?
  4. Aid: What kinds and levels of direct grants and loans will be made to which developing countries and with what restrictions?
  5. East-West trade: What policies and procedures will control U.S. sale and purchase of goods and technology to and from Communist countries?

While these issues remain central, more specific problems of energy, oceans, and the coordination of the domestic macroeconomic policies of national governments have recently become more prominent.[2]

foreign policy machinery has not adapted well to the shifting
currents of international economics. The international economic regime created at U.S. initiative during the 1940s and
embodied in the Bretton Woods Agreement and the General
Agreement on Tariffs and Trade (GATT), stood for more
than two decades as one of the proudest achievements of
American policy. In the last decade, that regime came under
strain. The sources of pressure were many: changes in basic
economic conditions, recalcitrance of other nations, conflict
among U.S. objectives, and misunderstanding and mismanagement by the United States. In the end, these forces brought
the key features of the Bretton Woods system to an end, and
endangered the GATT. No similarly comprehensive framework
has been constructed in its place. Instead, the United States
has hesitated for the last several years, making occasional fits
and starts, but mostly confused and immobilized. The United
States now possesses neither a coherent approach to international economics, nor effective machinery to formulate,
adopt, and implement a policy that can be sustained at home
and negotiated abroad. Yet without effective American leadership, no new international economic regime will emerge. We
remain the world's largest and most important economic entity;
that position entails the obligation of leadership.

The August 1971 decisions sketched in Chapter 2 provide
so clear an illustration both of recent mismanagement of our
foreign economic relations, and of its organizational connection, that the story is worth examining more closely. President
Nixon's sudden announcement of his "New Economic Policy"
in August 1971, which dispatched the Bretton Woods system,
showed no understanding of the dual purposes—economic
and political—of the former arrangements. The experience
of the 1930s had taught the architects of the postwar international economic system that the institutions, procedures, and
habits that govern behavior in international economics have
crucial political consequences; if those arrangements are vulnerable to crises, or fail to meet the minimum requirements
of important participants, international political stability can-

not long be maintained. International economic practices of the 1930s had exacerbated national recessions by encouraging nations to compete in the export of unemployment. Economic collapse had led to political breakdown, to the emergence of radical politics in Italy and Germany, and ultimately to military tragedy. The designers of the postwar system therefore aimed to create a web of rules and practices that would restrain nations from causing serious economic injury to others. Their goal was not only economic prosperity, but a basis for sound political relations.

The Bretton Woods–GATT regime proved more successful and more enduring than its architects had hoped. But by the mid-1960s the world economy had evolved so far from that of the late 1940s that basic changes in the regime were clearly required. Serious negotiations were begun with some success: the "Kennedy Round" of tariff reductions was concluded; special drawing rights (SDRs), a form of "paper gold" that provided international liquidity, were created. Other important changes were in train. But in 1971 a feeling of crisis seized Washington: the U.S. was headed for a substantial trade deficit, while the related loss of confidence in the dollar was causing a massive outflow of short-term capital from the United States, all on top of stagflation and the need to stimulate the U.S. economy at home. Something had to be done, and correcting the overvaluation of the dollar relative to other currencies—a chronic problem since the mid-1960s—clearly had to be part of it. Yet the action taken—President Nixon's abrupt and unilateral suspension of the dollar's convertibility into gold and imposition of a 10 percent surcharge on all imports—rocked the international economic system. It violated the principles of cooperative action and of free trade, two pillars of the West's unprecedented postwar prosperity. Even more than the substance of the decisions, U.S. shock tactics in taking them raised questions about the U.S. commitment to orderly international processes and unnecessarily threatened cooperative practices in which the United States had a very large stake.

The short-sighted character of that decision clearly reflected the unbalanced process that produced it. The group President Nixon relied upon to make the decision was dominated by a newly appointed Secretary of the Treasury, John Connally. It included the Chairmen of the Federal Reserve and of the Council of Economic Advisers, together with the director of the OMB. Domestic perspectives were therefore weighted heavily. But the group contained neither the Secretary of State nor the Assistant for National Security Affairs, nor any senior subordinate of either. Thus, no one was engaged whose job required him to think hard about the consequences of the decisions for larger foreign policy objectives. Yet the purpose of those decisions was exactly to affect the relation of our economy to those of our closest allies and trading partners.

The flavor of the discussion at Camp David from which the decision emerged is captured in notes published by William Safire:

McCracken (to Connally): You want to close the window and let the dollar float in addition to a border tax?

Connally: It's more understandable to the American people to put on a border tax. I know it's inconsistent; you are right. But the tax may make a change in the exchange rate possible.

The President: Arthur, your view, as I understand it, why is it not possible to do all the things that get at the heart of the problem and then to close the gold window if needed? The Treasury objection to this is that reserve assets will be depleted quickly.

Burns: I think they are wrong. If they are right, you can close it a week later . . .

The President: The argument on the other side is that domestic opinion would not give it a chance . . .

Connally: What's our immediate problem? We are meeting here because we are in trouble overseas. The British came in today to ask us to cover $3 billion, all their dollar reserves. Anybody can topple us—anytime they want—we have left ourselves completely exposed. There is no political risk—Reuss wants you to do it. (He showed us a batch of clippings about Democratic Congressman Henry Reuss's support of the idea.)

Burns: Yes, this is widely expected. But all the other countries know we have never acted against them. The good will—

CONNALLY: We'll go broke getting their good will.

VOLCKER: I hate to do this, to close the window. All my life I have defended exchange rates, but I think it is needed . . . But don't let's close the window and sit—let's get other governments to negotiate new rates.

CONNALLY: Why do we have to be "reasonable"? Canada wasn't.

BURNS: They can retaliate.

CONNALLY: Let 'em. What can they do?[3]

Why Is Foreign Economic Policy So Hard?

As the circumstances of August 1971 make clear, issues of foreign economic policy are hard. The reasons why emerge more clearly from the more commonplace problem of U.S. soybean exports.[4] In 1973 the Cost of Living Council, an agency whose responsibilities and perspectives ended abruptly at the water's edge, reacted to a rapid increase in soybean prices by advocating an embargo on U.S. soybean exports. The embargo was then initiated by President Nixon after only perfunctory consultation with the departments of Agriculture and State. The result was both an economic and diplomatic fiasco. Speculative prices for soybeans declined, but without measurable impact on consumer price levels. The apparent shortage of soybeans on which the embargo and the licensing arrangements that followed were premised turned out to be unreal, and they were rescinded within three months. But the Japanese, who depended on the United States for 90 percent of this staple of their diet, had been shocked almost beyond belief; both the President and the American ambassador had assured the Japanese government that no such action would be taken. The embargo not only damaged U.S. relations with a close ally, but caused a large loss of subsequent soybean exports. The Japanese moved quickly to develop alternative sources of soybean supply; by 1976, 40 percent of their imports came from Brazil.

The first difficulty of foreign economic policy making, illustrated alike by the August 1971 and the soybean cases, is that it cannot be approached either as principally a problem of foreign relations, or as primarily a matter of domestic economic policy, or as essentially a monetary or trade or agricultural issue. It is all of these, and all at the same time. The United States had undeniable interests in stable domestic food prices, in inhibitions to trade restrictions, in good relations and a growing market in Japan, and in the prosperity of American agriculture.

Second, because issues of foreign economics do have so many dimensions, they necessarily engage many government agencies together with associated interest groups and congressional committees. To the Cost of Living Council, rising soybean prices were a threat to American price stability. An embargo could blunt that threat; any other effects would be secondary. From the perspective of the State Department, soybeans represented a challenge to our commitments to the rules of trade, and to maintenance of good relations with Japan; compared to these, a small increase in U.S. prices was trivial. For the Department of Agriculture, the overriding issue was that farmers had been urged to grow soybeans in expectation of worldwide demand and thus deserved their full reward. If the information and perspectives of each of those departments were partial, they were nonetheless each partially right. Agriculture's data on soybean supplies showed that a shortage was unlikely. The Cost of Living Council was correct in seeing the inflationary impact of sharply rising soybean futures on politically sensitive U.S. food prices. State understood how powerfully the blow would strike Japan. In each case, expertise ran in specialties.

In this situation (archetypal in foreign economy policy decision making) no single department could—given the limits of its responsibilities—appreciate the full ramifications of the problem. And no individual—given the extraordinary complexity of the problem—would be likely alone to fully comprehend it. In such situations, the organizational challenge is to devise processes of decision that explore those ramifications and illuminate those complexities through the expertise and perspectives of everyone concerned.

Since objectives are multiple and partially competing, foreign economic policy often requires hard trade-offs among them, sacrifices of some objectives to others. Processes of central coordination and decision must guarantee that no such sacrifice is made without weighing its costs; they may sometimes reveal that no substantial sacrifice is in fact required. Soybeans was such a case, and in spite of Secretary Connally's eagerness to force a trade-off between U.S. interests and those of its closest allies in August 1971, a more subtle U.S. strategy could have avoided most of the costs of that episode as well.

Characteristics of Recent Performance

The history of U.S. foreign economic policy making is not one of predominant failure. The United States has moved the international monetary system toward more flexible exchange rates; the United States and other industrial nations did avoid beggar-thy-neighbor responses to the oil price increases and the 1973–75 recession; domestic pressures for protectionist policies to limit competition with declining U.S. industries has largely been resisted; international trade continues to expand at an impressive rate. Nor in view of the inherent difficulty of issues involving so many conflicting objectives, should one expect any nation, even the United States, to have a high batting average. Nonetheless, there is widespread agreement that recent performance falls well below attainable standards, and below the nation's needs. The basis for that judgment is suggested by several vignettes:

1. In 1966 the United States helped win acceptance of special drawing rights (SDRs), a form of "paper gold" managed by the major trading nations to meet the liquidity requirements of the world trading system. But more recently Treasury officials acquiesced in French demands that central banks be permitted to buy gold being auctioned by the IMF. This practice will increase the likelihood that gold held by central banks will be revalued to current market prices, thereby dramatically increasing world liquidity, threatening higher rates of world-wide inflation, and undercutting SDRs. While U.S. acceptance of this practice has been opposed by Congressman Reuss and others, including a private group headed by former Secretary of the Treasury Fowler, Treasury has stood pat, and neither State nor the White House has forcefully asserted the case for reconsideration.

2. Secretary of State Kissinger's address to the Seventh Special Session of the U.N. in 1975 presented more than forty proposals addressed specifically to demands of the developing nations for a new international economic order. But the newspaper stories reporting his speech also quoted high-level officials in Treasury, Agriculture, and State as well who opposed many of these proposals and suggested they would not be implemented; subsequent U.S. behavior supports their view. Kissinger's Nairobi address in May 1976 seems destined to a similar future. While the United States has not quite closed eyes to the deepening problems of the Fourth World, the Treasury in particular has proved unwilling to face them, opposing more liberal concessionary loans at the World Bank, for example. Agriculture has successfully resisted creation of international grain reserves. Despite the Kissinger proposals, the U.S. government continues to defer the issue which many observers believe will dominate the last decades of this century and the century to come: international income distribution.

3. Decisions about the management of the domestic U.S.

economy—especially its rate of expansion or contraction—
have greater impact on the economies of foreign governments than any of the traditional instruments of "foreign"
economic policy. European leaders have consequently
called repeatedly for consultation on macroeconomic (fiscal
and monetary) issues and some coordination of national
policies to counteract cyclical swings in aggregate demand.
So far, the United States has resisted those calls, agreeing
only to largely ceremonial meetings of heads of state at
Rambouillet in 1975 and in Puerto Rico during the electoral
season. Differences within the U.S. government block
agreement on any process for more regular and meaningful
consultation.

4. No aspect of recent performance highlights the need for
effective central coordination and control more vividly than
the sustained bureaucratic warfare that has frustrated U.S.
efforts to address newer issues of foreign economics: food,
energy, commodities, and oceans. Public fighting among
Cabinet officers—Kissinger vs. Butz on food, Kissinger vs.
Simon vs. many others on energy—is merely the tip of the
iceberg. Beneath the surface, the struggle has been more
intense and the effects more costly. Accepted practice permits many departmental officials to grab and run with any
issue (or piece of an issue) they can. The unresolved battle
between Kissinger and Simon and half a dozen other
Cabinet and agency heads over energy policy generally
delayed submission of an energy bill to Congress for more
than a year. Though Kissinger has repeatedly asserted U.S.
willingness to negotiate commodity agreements with producing nations, Simon's commitment to free markets for all
commodities has blocked U.S. action. And after several
years of controversy Kissinger and Butz remain at logger-
heads about the need for international grain reserves; an
oft-promised U.S. proposal is still "forthcoming."

5. The twists and turns of U.S. oceans policy almost caricature the now familiar pattern. Faced with the prospect of

an area of ocean as large as the earth's total land mass being annexed by coastal nations, President Nixon enunciated a policy that called instead for preserving oceans as international commons and exploiting ocean resources through an international authority for the benefit of all. The policy was quickly abandoned under pressure from Interior, East Coast fishermen, and multinational companies interested in profiting directly from the oil, fish, and mineral resources of the sea—with a strong assist from developing countries. Shortly thereafter, the assistant secretary at State responsible for oceans policy resigned to protest the fact that the Secretary of State exhibited no interest whatever in the issue. Frustrated by the absence of administration policy and by uncertainty about the timing and terms of an international agreement, Congress unilaterally expanded U.S. jurisdiction over adjacent ocean resources by means of a two hundred-mile exclusive economic zone, meeting the most pointed domestic demands.

These examples, together with the oil, August 1971, and soybean cases display three characteristic and familiar failings of policy making. The first is *inadequate competence*. In the soybean case, for example, though Agriculture's estimates of supply and demand were better than those actually used, they were inferior to estimates in private hands. U.S. macroeconomic policy makers have insufficiently understood the interactions between the U.S. and the international economies; except for the brief Shultz interlude, both the White House and State have lacked professional economic competence at high levels.*

The second fault is *imbalance*. The August 1971 decisions as well as the soybeans and oceans cases display systematic biases in favor of immediate domestic concerns over broader foreign policy objectives; short-run benefits as against more

* Excluding, of course, the members of the Council of Economic Advisers.

enduring advantages, and particular as against collective interests.

The third inadequacy is *drift and incoherence*—evident everywhere. Recent U.S. foreign economic policy making resembles a free-for-all. Within issues and among them, U.S. policy has zigged and zagged: Presidents stating policies that departmental actions contradict, one Cabinet officer taking a position immediately repudiated by another; actions in one area undermining policy elsewhere. This pattern is the inescapable consequence of a policy-making process largely decentralized to the departments, but without the requisite capacity at the center for identifying and analyzing issues that require central management, representing fully the concerns of all departments and interests, presenting issues to the President for timely choice, and insisting on faithful implementation of policy once made.

What Is to Be Done?

Four main tasks, we believe, must be undertaken. The first is principally intellectual: it is to develop a conceptual framework for economic policy making that integrates foreign and domestic objectives. The second is more directly organizational: to design and adopt effective processes for central coordination and decision. The third is to better coordinate governmental policy and private economic decision making. The last involves international organization: it is to foster agreements, authorities, and practices among nations better able to manage the conditions of economic interdependence.

Building a New Policy Framework. The first task is to rethink our basic interests in a novel international environment, and to embody the conclusions in guidelines for future policy. Many issues must be faced:

1. Are the premises underlying three decades of movement toward freer international trade—a politically neutral specialization according to comparative advantage, a more efficient division of labor, and thus a larger international pie —still appropriate?
2. In what sectors and to what extent should the United States set limits to interdependence of its economy with those of others?
3. What role should exchange rates play in adjustment and what rules should regulate governmental intervention, if any, in exchange markets?
4. How should security, economic, and political objectives be balanced in setting the conditions of East-West trade?
5. How important are the Third and Fourth Worlds to us, and does there exist some combination of capital transfers, trade concessions, food assistance, population control, and internal income redistribution that might generate sufficient progress in the developing countries to make an intensive effort worthwhile?
6. What role should the United States play in the evolution of a new international economic system? Having lost predominance, should we adopt a waiting stance as in recent practice or take a more active part?

Though the task is in the first instance intellectual, it has important implications for the selection of key officials, for the mandates assigned them, and for the inclusiveness of the processes by which major decisions are taken. To endure, major revisions of policy must emerge, and be seen by the departments and the informed public to emerge, from a rounded consideration of all relevant concerns, foreign and domestic. Moreover, the new framework must be articulated and defended by key players in many departments and on many fronts, especially in relations with Congress. Competence and interest in international economic issues should therefore characterize both the Secretary and Undersecretary for Economic Affairs in the Department of State; the Assistant to the President for Foreign Economic Affairs (a deputy to the President's Assistant for Foreign Affairs, as proposed in Chapter 4); the Secretaries or undersecretaries of Treasury, Commerce, and Agriculture; the directors of the Energy Administration and OMB, and at least one member of the Council of Economic Advisers. Those officials should be charged by the President with responsibility for jointly reconstructing U.S. foreign economic policy, and for consulting key members of Congress in the process.

Ensuring Central Coordination and Decision. Embodying the new conceptual framework for foreign economic policy in action will require substantial organizational changes. Chapters 4, 5, and 6 spell out most of them. Some seek to build stronger economic competence in State; others, to sensitize the Congress to the international effects of "domestic" economic decisions; but the central reforms look to more reliable processes of central coordination and decision.

Many issues that cross agency lines do not need to engage the President personally, since they can be effectively resolved and managed at lower levels. To deal with the most important of such issues we recommend the establishment of ad hoc working groups. Use of such groups requires initiative and judgment in the White House, and willingness among sub-Cabinet officials to alert the White House to problems justifying such attention. The system is not foolproof, but particularly for foreign economic issues it seems to us more promising than formal interagency committees, like the Council on International Economic Policy (CIEP), which tend to generate routine agendas, to lose the participation of senior officials, and to sink from the mainstream of major economic decision making.

Foreign economic issues necessitating presidential decision would be debated in ExCab by all the relevant Cabinet officers, supported by the staff work of their own departments and of the ExCab staff. More than any other single change, the serious use of such a forum would promote recognition of the characteristic linkages between foreign economic issues and general foreign policy objectives on the one hand, and domestic concerns on the other.

Essential to the effectiveness of both ad hoc task forces and ExCab is an active President.* Indeed, without active presidential attention, none of the main requirements of foreign economic policy making can be met. No new policy framework will be devised, and the central coordination of decisions will break down. Only the President has the perspective to make the hard trade-offs between foreign and domestic, regional and national, "economic" and "political" considerations, and only he can impose such decisions on his subordinates and lead their justification to Congress and the public. In the absence of presidential interest, the organizational changes needed to insure competence and balance in the analysis of foreign economic issues will not be undertaken.

The President cannot perform these tasks alone. He needs a substantively competent White House assistant to identify issues requiring presidential attention, to oversee and participate in their analysis, to shepherd their movement toward decision, to see to it that affected parties are informed of decisions taken, and to monitor implementation. Such tasks cannot be performed as a sideline by a single presidential Assistant for National Security Affairs. Nor can they be delegated to a single-purpose presidential appointee such as the Special Trade Representative or to executive director of a committee such as CIEP, who would lack the necessary breadth of involvement in foreign and domestic decision making. Instead, an assistant to the President for foreign economics seems to us clearly preferable. Technically competent and able to translate technical debate into usable advice, this assistant would link the "foreign"

---

* Creation of the CIEP in 1971 represented a partial attempt to substitute a formal interagency body for the absence of strong interest or competence in both President Nixon and Henry Kissinger. But in the absence of presidential concern, the council could not resolve the difficult and politically charged choices that are the main business of foreign economics.

and "economic" elements of the Cabinet staff, perhaps serving as a common deputy to the Assistants for Foreign and for Economic Affairs.*

To supplement these changes in central institutions, a number of more specific reforms are required—in Treasury, in the "domestic" departments, and at the lower levels of the government. As the department most responsible for international money and contributions to international lending institutions, Treasury must be regularly involved in most decision making about foreign affairs. Within the Department, organizational reform should be principally concerned to broaden the orientation of the individuals who work there. At the highest levels, this is essentially an issue of appointments: the background, competence, and concern of the people chosen by the President. While the Secretary of the Treasury and his key associates must have links to the community of banking and finance, they should also have the stature and insight of a Dillon or Shultz, rather than of a Connally or Simon. Parochialism of the permanent staff at Treasury should be addressed by more extensive exchange of middle-level personnel with both "foreign" and "domestic" departments, and by creation of an Executive Career Service for supergrades (as discussed above).

Secondly, the role of the Deputy Secretary of the Treasury should be revised. Traditionally, he has served as the department's chief lobbyist on the Hill, contributing to the frequently noted fact that Treasury has more clout with Congress than any other department. But this practice leaves the Secretary

---

* To assure coordination of foreign and domestic components of foreign economic policy, both this deputy and the President's Assistant for Economic Affairs should attend meetings of the two groups charged with management of macroeconomic policy. The "troika" (the group that traditionally manages fiscal policy, now comprised of the Secretary of the Treasury, the director of the Office of Management and Budget, and the chairman of the Council of Economic Advisers), and the "quadriad," the four-member group charged with formulating monetary policy, now composed of "troika" members plus the chairman of governors for the Federal Reserve System.

without a real deputy. To preserve the Deputy as an effective alter ego for the Secretary, responsibility for relations with Congress should be more broadly diffused among the senior members of the Secretary's team.

Third, a number of changes should be made in the management of international economic issues within the department. Traditionally, the Undersecretary for Monetary Affairs has had primary responsibility both for U.S. debt management and for the U.S. policy on international money. The growing demands of both jobs (the current Undersecretary for Monetary Affairs spends almost every weekend engaged in discussions of the international monetary system with foreign counterparts) combined with the difficulty of finding individuals competent to deal on both fronts makes a plausible case for splitting these two functions among two undersecretaries. On balance, however, we reject this alternative because it would further deepen the division in the department between foreign and domestic responsibilities. The Undersecretary for Monetary Affairs should retain both functions, but—in contrast to the current situation—he should be chosen with primary regard for his ability to deal with international monetary affairs, and he should be made the operational superior of the bureaus whose work falls in his domain, particularly the Office of the Assistant Secretary for International Affairs (for reasons analogous to those advanced in Chapter 5 for the comparable recommendation concerning the Undersecretary of State for Economic Affairs). Finally, more responsibility and power should be concentrated in the Assistant Secretary for International Affairs, by making the current offices of National Security and Foreign Assistance Contributions report to him and giving him a larger role in trade policy (and thus more leverage vis-à-vis the Assistant Secretary for Trade, Energy, and Financial Resources).

Since the "domestic" departments—Agriculture, Labor, Commerce, Transportation—will now frequently be engaged in the debate and management of foreign economic issues, their international perspectives should be expanded and specific competences within them upgraded. In part, this process is occurring naturally. Over the last three decades all major agencies have established international divisions to manage the overseas dimensions of their work, and the growth of these divisions has been dramatic.* Each major department thus possesses some exposure to foreign perspectives and some concern for foreign interests. Those concerns can be given powerful expression when they accord with the basic interests of the department. In the soybean case, for example, free trade had no more persuasive advocate than the Secretary of Agriculture. International perspectives within departments should be further encouraged by more frequent interchange of middle-level personnel among the various agencies having important foreign economic responsibilities.

There remain shortcomings in competence. Over the last decade the Department of Agriculture has lost to private competitors its position of preeminence as an analyst of supply and demand in markets for major agricultural products. Commerce, never accomplished at industry studies, has fallen further behind. On the other hand, the new Federal Energy Administration has become the leading source of information and estimates about energy markets. If the government is to stay at least as well equipped with data and analytic skill as the private sector, the key departments must build and retain the necessary staffs. The establishment of a substantial staff of microeconomic analysts in the Council of Economic Advisors or the OMB may also prove necessary.

Finally, for every issue area in which policy is revised,

---

* For example, in 1950 the Foreign Agricultural Service had a budget of $690,000 and employed 163 people; the comparable figures for 1975 were $31.8 million and 892 permanent employees. Commerce's Bureau of Foreign Commerce had a budget of $4.1 million in 1954, while the international programs of the Domestic and International Business Administration (its successor) were budgeted for $37.8 million in 1975. Similarly, the budget of the Office of International Labor Affairs grew from $126,000 to $2.7 million between 1950 and 1975. See *Budget of the U.S. Government* and *Appendices*, FYs 1952, 1956, 1976.

lower-level changes in structures and processes may be required. Implementation remains the work of lower-level bureaus and offices in numerous departments—offices with values, perspectives, and procedures that do not change automatically with shifts in high policy. The recent history of East-West trade makes the point forcefully.[5] The Export Administration Act of 1969 officially abandoned the "economic warfare" objective that had previously restricted U.S. exports to Communist countries. According to the new act, an export license can be denied only if a product will contribute significantly to a potential enemy's military capability, and then only if a comparable product cannot be obtained from a foreign supplier. But the offices in Defense, CIA, and Commerce administering the new policy are the same ones that for twenty years enforced its predecessor. Not surprisingly, their judgments about "foreign availability" and "military significance" have systematically underestimated the first and overstated the second, placing far tighter limits on U.S. exports than the act envisaged. The effect appears in U.S. trade figures: while the United States accounts for 16 percent of the West's total manufactured exports, it provides only 4 percent of Western exports to Communist countries.[6] The lesson is clear: policy made without attention to its implementation is likely to prove futile. We therefore propose that once a new policy is established, one of the ad hoc task forces discussed above should be required to propose and oversee whatever changes in structure, procedures, or staffing are required to implement it. The group's White House member should then monitor those changes.

Relating Government and the Private Sector. Of course, most of the decisions that affect the U.S. economy are not made by the government. Though influenced by governmental monetary and fiscal policy and by assorted official inducements and regulations, decisions about growing soybeans, mining ocean nodules, investing abroad, or loading ships with wheat purchased by the Soviet Union are made by private parties:

farmers, corporations, bankers, unions. Successful handling of many issues of foreign economic policy thus hinges on actions in the private sector. For important decisions, therefore, private representatives of affected interests should be directly (often jointly) consulted. They will not only be assured thereby that their views have been heard, but their views may moderate under the heat of competing interests. At the very least, such consultation would perform an educational function useful over the longer term. Cabinet members—perhaps with White House staff participation—should take the initiative in establishing such consultative groups, taking care, however, that they consult and not direct. Secretary of Labor Dunlop's convening of a number of such groups in 1975 and 1976 provides an attractive model.

Strengthening International Institutions. The tightening economic interdependence of nations poses an extraordinarily difficult dilemma for the last quarter of this century, and perhaps for the century to come. The benefits of interdependence are purchased at some price in national autonomy, yet the nation persists as the unit of political accountability. For the United States, the internationalization of economic activity means on the one hand that Americans enjoy more wealth, a wider selection of consumer goods, and larger markets than they could otherwise. But it also means that Americans' pocketbooks are vulnerable to direct short-run effects of economic events in Germany or Japan or OPEC. Attempts to achieve U.S. domestic economic objectives by manipulating traditional instruments of monetary and fiscal policy can be frustrated by developments in foreign economies that pull short-term money to foreign markets, or increase worldwide demand. Indeed, the degree of economic interdependence among OECD countries in 1976 is greater than that among the thirteen colonies in the year of our Revolution. Over the decades ahead, therefore, the most fundamental challenge of international economic relations will be to create and strengthen international rules, processes, and institutions capable of managing the conditions of interdependence, promoting cooperative problem-solving among nations, and restraining beggar-thy-neighbor practices. In short, the challenge will be to "make the world safe for interdependence"—while most elements of sovereignty continue to reside in the national state.

New institutions will probably be needed to manage the "commons" of mankind, especially the oceans; to control international terrorism; and to regulate foreign direct investment and multinational enterprises.[7] Many existing institutions will need strengthening—the General Agreement on Tariffs and Trade to assure access to supplies as well as to markets, for example, and the International Monetary Fund to assure stability in a system of multiple reserve assets. The performance of postwar international institutions makes clear, moreover, that the most effective international institutions are not multipurpose general assemblies but functionally specific organizations—like the World Health Organization and the International Bank for Reconstruction and Development, whose membership is limited to nations with real stakes in the issues and whose voting rights are distributed in some rough relation to the real influence of their members.

How Might These Arrangements Work?

The actual operation of any arrangements for high-level policy making will obviously depend on the larger context in which issues arise, and on the personal characteristics of the President and other key officials. Nonetheless, a speculative replay of several of the cases discussed above may suggest how the changes we have proposed might importantly affect the information and perspectives brought to bear on the issues, and alter the weights accorded to them.

Consider first August 1971. It had been clear for several years that the U.S. dollar was overvalued relative to other currencies and that this could not be long sustained. Under the organizational arrangements we have proposed, an interagency task force would likely have been established well before summer 1971 to consider alternatives. Operating before a crisis had developed, the group would almost surely have produced a map of the issue that not only identified alternative courses of action but assessed the probable impact of each on the international economic system and on U.S. relations with key allies. Even if early action had not followed and the August crisis had occurred, deliberation of the U.S. response in ExCab would have involved both Secretary Rogers and Presidential Assistant Kissinger. Even assuming no change in the personal interest or economic competence of either, Rogers would nonetheless have been backed by a well-staffed Undersecretary of State for Economic Affairs, for whom the issue would clearly have been first-order business, and Kissinger by a professionally competent deputy for foreign economics. Under these circumstances, it is hard to imagine that one or both would not have strongly advanced the arguments championed by Arthur Burns. Given Secretary Connally's forcefulness and the fact that he was telling the President what he wanted to hear, Connally might still have prevailed. Yet such strong support for the Burns position would have forced sharper recognition of the ultimate costs of the Connally proposal and might well have produced a less heavy-handed strategy for achieving the basic objectives. At a minimum it would have ensured that allies were consulted in advance of unilateral U.S. action.

In the soybean case the probable influence of an organizational difference appears even clearer. A decision to impose an embargo affecting a major ally would surely have come to ExCab, brought there at the initiative of the Department of State or by a presidential assistant if not by the Cost of Living Council. In ExCab the proposal to resort to an embargo as a measure for stabilizing domestic prices would have run squarely into competing objectives and additional evidence. The Secretary of Agriculture would surely have argued that the asserted shortage of soybeans was ephemeral, and that an embargo would violate assurances given American farmers and jeopardize overseas markets. The Secretary of State would surely have made the case, prepared both by his Undersecretary for Economics and by the Assistant Secretary for East Asia, that, following the series of prior American shocks, such an embargo would damage U.S.-Japanese relations, lead the Japanese to seek alternative suppliers, and provide a poor precedent for other trading partners. A presidential decision to impose that embargo, following such a discussion, is hard to imagine.

The energy case discussed in Chapter 1 is more complex, substantively and politically. Even so, it seems likely that the arrangements proposed would have made a substantial difference. Even had no action been taken following the Presidential Task Force report in early 1970, an ad hoc subcabinet group or a White House staff member would likely have been made responsible for monitoring the danger signals identified by the Task Force—particularly the level of U.S. dependence on imported oil. Either would have brought to presidential attention the marked subsequent increase in U.S. oil imports, and probably have presented proposals to insure against possible shortages. Even if no action had been taken to deter or blunt an embargo, and the country had been no better prepared for the OPEC's actions of 1973, the price increases and embargo would have precipitated both intensive discussions in ExCab and a series of interagency studies.

At a minimum, the studies would have developed a common body of data and analysis and delineated more clearly the real shape of the problem and the small set of feasible responses. They would have noted, for example, the necessity for significant conservation measures. The views expressed in ExCab would still have been sharply conflicting, and the President would have faced difficult choices. Given the peculiar circumstances of Watergate, it is unclear whether any system of government could have induced the depth of presidential attention necessary to wise choice and effective action. But that singular circumstance aside, ExCab deliberations would almost certainly have led to more informed choice among more realistic alternatives. They would have produced a package of proposals whose center would surely not have been so hollow as "Project Independence." The Cabinet members who had participated in the design of the program could have been expected—with varying degrees of enthusiasm—to support and advance it before the Congress and the country. And prior consultation with key congressional figures should have enlarged the chances for favorable congressional action.

Chapter 8

Providing for the Common Defense

> Lord Acton's dictum that power tends to corrupt has, to be sure, an abiding relevance for the actions of individual men and of institutions. Yet, in the larger context of the affairs of nations, it is readily misapplied, for it neglects an equally important truth . . . Weakness also corrupts—and can do so fatally.
>
> James R. Schlesinger (1976)

THE defense establishment commands attention because it consumes a quarter of the federal budget—over $100 billion— and accounts for six out of every ten federal employees, some 3 million servicemen and civilians. But it is crucial for what is at stake: the security, independence and potentially the lives of tens of millions of Americans and others. When nuclear war among superpowers can mean the destruction of modern society, the overriding purpose of foreign policy must be the prevention of war and maintenance of a just peace. The preceding pages have stressed the crowding of the traditional foreign policy agenda by new issues arising from the tightening economic relationships among nations. But recognition of those issues cannot obscure the paramount importance of national defense in foreign policy making. In President John F.

Kennedy's oft-quoted words: "Domestic policy can only defeat us; foreign policy can kill us."[1] No structure of the U.S. government can be judged adequate unless it provides every assistance that organization can to the wise management of defense and security issues.

The purposes of American military strength are clear. They are: (1) to deter potential adversaries from using or threatening force against the U.S. or its allies; (2) to defeat opponents if called upon to do so; and (3) to project American power in support of other national interests. But these objectives must be served subject to two important constraints. The size, shape, and deployment of U.S. forces must conform to larger American foreign policy objectives—of collective security through arms limitation, and of stable political relations with close allies, for example. And those forces must be acquired and maintained economically, the scale of defense expenditures reflecting a national judgment about the relative priority of military strength and other national needs, and the composition of the budget reflecting informed judgment about the most effective forces that can be acquired and supported within that total. The defense establishment must, in short, be integrated into the larger framework of U.S. priorities, an integration that has thus far been only imperfectly achieved.[2]

The size of the Defense Department, for one thing, makes integration difficult. In comparison to the other agencies with which it shares responsibility for national security policy, the Department of Defense appears simply overwhelming. For every employee of the Department of State and the Arms Control and Disarmament Agency (ACDA) combined, Defense employs one hundred; among civilian employees the ratio is one to thirty. On every issue addressed by the seventy-man Politico-Military Bureau (PM) of the Department of State, Defense deploys five staffs—one in each service, one serving the joint chiefs, one in the Office of the Secretary of Defense (OSD)—and each of the five is several times larger and technically more expert than PM. But the larger advantage of Defense's great size is political. For every dollar spent by State and ACDA combined, Defense spends $150. The influence of the Defense Department is inevitably reinforced by awareness in both the executive and the Congress that one of every ten American workers is employed in a defense-related industry, that military bases and defense contracts figure importantly in the economy of most congressional districts and all states, and that a department in charge of the common defense evokes strong loyalties. No other foreign affairs agency has similar political heft. As a result, while many perspectives on national security issues have organizational voice—in State, ACDA, Treasury, OMB—the voices are not equally persuasive. The identification of "threats" to the nation's security, the nature of the information available about them, the range of alternative responses considered, the pressures felt by decision makers in choosing among them, the control of the actions chosen—all reflect that inequality.

A second source of difficulty arises from the nature of the military services themselves. U.S. armed services, like those of every other major power, are marked by professionalism, conservatism, and inertia. Professionalism is essential to all large organizations that operate complex equipment, and especially to those that ask their members to risk or sacrifice their lives on command. And conservatism is a natural concomitant of the military mission: responsible for the security and ultimately the survival of the nation, the services are necessarily unwilling to risk underestimating the contingencies for which the nation should prepare or the forces required to meet them. (Recall the navy's oil reserves.) Yet contrary to popular caricature of the military as "warmongers," the armed services are historically more hesitant than their civilian chiefs to initiate warfare. Once the decision for war is made, however, the same caution leads them to seek the use of all force available. And as is true of most professionals who deal in risky activities, proven and familiar procedures are accorded great weight. Training, weapons, and plans adapt only slowly to shifting threats.

Three Kinds of Failure

These defining characteristics of the defense establishment constitute not only its strengths but its weaknesses. Characteristic failures of recent U.S. defense policy were illustrated in two of the cases sketched earlier in the book. Recall the discussion of the Vietnam War. In deciding on an attrition rather than an enclave strategy for the war in the South, or continued escalation of an ineffective bombing campaign against North Vietnam, and on the steady expansion of chemical warfare, the American war effort was driven largely by the incentives, operating procedures, and perspectives of the military services. The results served neither national nor military needs. The point of the nuclear options story is similar but more disturbing: declarations of policy made by four Presidents over fifteen years, supported by five Secretaries of Defense, and unopposed in the Congress have not yet succeeded in altering the actual plans or capabilities of the armed services for executing the single most important order that political authority can give its military commanders—the order to employ strategic nuclear weapons.

An equally characteristic shortcoming in defense performance is captured in a parable told by former Assistant Secretary of Defense Alain Enthoven.

Picture if you will a man who has spent his entire adult life in the Air Force, flying bombers and leading bomber forces. Bombers are his professional commitment and his expertise. His chances for promotion, public recognition and success, and those of the officers serving under him are largely tied to the continued importance of bombers. He believes strongly in what he is doing; that is one of the main reasons he does it well. Now suppose—as happened in the late 1950s and early 1960s—that the development of the intercontinental ballistic missile (ICBM) makes bombers highly vulnerable and less useful as the nation's chief means of deterrence. The nation's needs shift from bombers to missiles. The Polaris missile-firing submarine is developed, and the nation's needs further shift from the Air Force to the Navy. It is no reflection on the honor, patriotism, or dedication of such a man to say that it is unreasonable to expect him to be objective about the shift of the strategic mission from bomber to missiles and from the Air Force to the Navy.

The traditional approach to dealing with this problem has been to say that this man must be made to compromise and reach agreement with another man who has spent a similar career in aircraft carriers. Not surprisingly, the easiest thing for them to agree on is *more* bombers and *more* carriers, and this, more often than not, is what happens. So this approach, rather than solving the problem, simply builds the pressures for more and more spending and creates another problem: that of spiraling and unmet military requirements. . . . There is no reason to suppose that, faced with this financial limit, the "bomber general" and the "carrier admiral" will agree to cut back their preferred weapons to make room for Polaris submarines. Their tendency will be to agree on bombers and carriers, especially to the extent that the matter depends on "judgment" rather than on explicit criteria of national need. Powerful institutional forces push them in that direction. And Polaris, being new, is not likely to be represented at the bargaining table. . . . This problem is not unique to bombers or carriers. It pervades the Defense decision-making process.*

Finally, the history of U.S. military bases in Spain shows how military efforts to advance security objectives can shape rather than be shaped by the broader goals of foreign policy. In 1953, as part of a program to establish a world-wide network of forward bases, the U.S. military services reached an agreement with the government of Spain for construction of several air force bases on Spanish territory—bases then required by the limited ranges of U.S. bombers, which could not reach Soviet targets from the continental United States. Later, facilities for Polaris submarines and for the U.S. Sixth Fleet were added, and the air bases became important transit

---

* And not merely that process. As Enthoven went on to observe:

"The same thing happens in universities. Does anyone expect the classics professor to be objective about a cut in his departmental budget in response to a shift in student interest from classics to physics? . . . The institutional factors working against the national interest in the Defense establishment have their counterparts in all walks of life."[3]

and refueling stops between the United States and the Mideast. Agreements governing the bases have cost the U.S. several billion dollars, mostly in military aid. But a larger cost was for many years less evident. Although successive administrations publicly denied it, the bases constituted an implicit U.S. commitment to defend Spain. As General Earle Wheeler, chairman of the Joint Chiefs of Staff, put it in a secret 1968 memorandum to the Spanish government: "By the presence of U.S. forces in Spain, the United States gives Spain a far more visible and credible security guarantee than any written document."[4] Similarly, during the 1969 negotiations leading to the renewal of the base agreement, the chief U.S. negotiator, Major General David Burchinal, signed a joint minute with his Spanish counterpart declaring that the United States was committed to defend Western Europe, "of which Spain is an integral part."[5] The Burchinal minute was disavowed by the Nixon administration when it came to public attention, but the fact remained: the United States maintained a de facto alliance with Spain based on secret agreements negotiated by the military. Neither the terms of these agreements nor the existence of such a security guarantee were known to the public; nor had they been ratified by the Senate.

These examples highlight three serious and recurring inadequacies in recent U.S. defense performance. First, and most surprising is that, for 15 years, *when the U.S. has resorted to military force, it has failed to achieve its objectives.* The army's costly and unavailing strategy in Vietnam, the futile bombing of North Vietnam, the airdrop to free U.S. prisoners from a deserted camp in the North, the invasion of Cambodia to capture a nonexistent Viet Cong headquarters, the blanket Christmas bombing of Hanoi to force a "peace with honor," and most recently the *Mayaguez* incident, in which thirty-eight Americans were lost to rescue thirty-nine whose release, it turned out, was already in progress—these are not isolated incidents. Sadly, they constitute the bulk of the recent record. That record raises hard questions about the useability of our military forces. It encourages little confidence in plans, doctrines, or capabilities; in the adequacy of military advice to the President; in the reliability or assessments of military operations; or in the capacity to control or alter operations in motion. By overriding good fortune, the nation has faced no nuclear showdown since the Cuban missile crisis. The nuclear options history suggests, however, that if such an ultimate confrontation were again to occur, the President, in Richard Nixon's words, would still "be left with the single option of ordering the mass destruction of enemy civilians, in the face of the certainty that it would be followed by the mass slaughter of Americans."[6]

Second, the *linkage between U.S. military forces and the nation's foreign policy objectives is typically loose and occasionally broken.* In theory, the size and character of our military forces flows from American interests and commitments, and from the threats to those interests and commitments. In practice, however, our forces are related to national perceptions of threat and responsibility only tenuously. Their size, shape, and deployment are primarily a residue of recent history, reflecting mainly the structure and positions of the services immediately after World War II, and their incentives to maintain and expand assigned roles and missions. The gap between objectives and forces thus appears most conspicuous where policy has shifted recently. Rising nationalism, the increasing diffusion of sophisticated arms, and domestic opposition to military involvement abroad have made U.S. military intervention less feasible and less likely, except where vital national interests are at stake. U.S. reactions to crises in Lebanon record the change: in 1958, President Eisenhower sent 15,000 U.S. troops ashore to stabilize the situation; in 1976 President Ford could only warn other countries (unavailingly) not to follow that example. But if "sending in the marines" has become a far less probable course, the size and shape of the corps do not suggest so. The Marine Corps is still composed of three lightly armed amphibious divisions useful only against opposition that is vulnerable to small-scale attack from the sea. The corps has resisted efforts to provide it with the heavy equipment that could make some units useful in the more probable and more important contingency of a European war.[7] Similar questions arise about the structure of the U.S. Army. U.S. commitments in Asia have been sharply scaled down and concern over the growing strength of Soviet forces in Europe has risen. Yet five of the army's sixteen divisions remain earmarked for Asian use; like the marine divisions, they are too lightly equipped for European service.[8]

The 1971 scale-down of our contingency requirements furnishes a more vivid illustration of the gap between objectives and resources. In that year the longstanding requirement that U.S. forces be sufficient to fight "2½ wars" simultaneously (one in Europe and one in Asia, together with a smaller conflict in the Western Hemisphere) was formally replaced by President Nixon's "1½ war" requirement. But this 40 percent reduction in demand caused no scaling down of supply: the next year's Defense budget called for essentially the same numbers of divisions, ships, planes, and dollars.

Indeed, not only do foreign policy considerations fail to control force posture, the opposite is often the case. Military forces have a weight and dynamic of their own: their size and character, their need for exercise, and their search for advantageous bases powerfully influence the foreign policy they are meant to serve. The history of U.S. bases in Spain, of the Panama Canal, and of German offsets amply demonstrates that when U.S. military forces are present in foreign countries, the terms and conditions of their presence there may dominate our relations with those countries. In fact, the dispute between the United States and Panama over the canal now colors U.S. relations with all of Latin America.

Third and finally: *recent defense policy has failed to seriously seek economy*. It is now widely accepted that domestic social problems cannot be solved by "throwing money at them." The same caution applies to military spending. Indeed, a "money is no object" attitude toward defense spending can harm U.S. security by encouraging wasteful and inefficient use of human and material resources. At a time of increasing skepticism about government programs that cannot demonstrate their value, really critical defense appropriations may hinge on the evident effectiveness with which defense budgets are used. Yet neither manpower nor weapons expenditure can now meet such a test.

Soaring manpower costs now consume nearly 60 percent of the entire defense budget.[9] In part this results from a top-heavy manpower system that supports more generals and admirals than during World War II when the services were six times their current size. In part it reflects excessive numbers of civilians and support personnel: military manpower is down 40 percent since 1968, but civilian employment has declined only 23 percent. Moreover, while military pay scales have become competitive with those of private industry, an expensive hodgepodge of fringe benefits, subsidies, bonuses, and other special compensations persists. Finally, the proportion of the defense budget absorbed by military pensions has tripled.[10]

Inefficiency in the use of labor can be offset by the efficient use of capital. In fact, however, if any private business followed the Department of Defense's pattern in its capital purchases, it would soon go bankrupt. As former Deputy Defense Secretary David Packard told the Armed Forces Management Association, "Frankly gentlemen, in defense procurement we have a real mess on our hands."[11] New technologies that lack organizational champions or threaten favorite missions are often resisted by the services—as Polaris submarines were in the early 1960s, and as "smart bombs" were in Vietnam—while familiar technologies that serve such missions are typically pressed to their limits, at great cost. The dramatic escalation in fighter aircraft prices tells the tale: the navy has replaced the F-4 with the F-14, a somewhat more capable aircraft costing five times as much. Such disregard of costs cannot be sustained indefinitely. If, for example, the air force budget for fighter aircraft were to increase only at the rate of general inflation but the unit costs of new generations of fighters were to increase at the rates of the past decades, the air force would be able to purchase only ten planes in the year 2000, and only one in the year 2020. Nor is this merely an air force problem. The new Trident missile-launching submarines bear price tags of more than $1 billion each; the most recently authorized nuclear carrier, together with its aircraft, is estimated at more than $5 billion. The military determination to acquire the absolutely finest conceivable weapons whatever their cost threatens, as one Defense official has remarked, to price the United States out of the war-fighting business.[12]

This peculiar form of unilateral disarmament through unsustainable unit costs is exacerbated by the propensity of the services to preserve, within the limits of their overall budgets, the largest possible force structure—divisions, air wings, carrier task forces, and the like. They manage this by cutting expenditure on ammunition, training, maintenance, and manning of units. The result is lower levels of readiness. The traditional congressional response to escalating costs further saps useable strength. As Barry Blechman and Edward Fried have put it:

> Being unwilling either to permit defense budgets to rise beyond inflation or to challenge fundamental military policies, the Congress has temporized. It seeks short-term economies by reducing the numbers of weapons purchased in a single year, without changing the total number in the program. Or it slows down development programs without killing the proposed new weapons altogether. Or it reduces operating budgets without cutting manpower significantly, thus causing longer queues of equipment waiting for over-haul, smaller stockpiles, and other reductions in readiness.[13]

The Future Compounds Present Problems

Probable trends in the decade ahead make recent levels of defense performance more dangerous and less acceptable. The growth of Soviet military strength, in particular, bodes ill for American defense. In the past decade the Soviet Union has emerged as a global military power rivaling and, in some capabilities surpassing, the United States. Static estimates of the U.S.-Soviet military balance are ambiguous and misleading—classic apples-and-oranges comparisons of differing weapons systems, strategic objectives, and geographical situations. But dynamic trends are clear: in real terms, Soviet military expenditure has increased over the last decade while America's has been falling. The Soviets have both enlarged and improved their forces, and have deployed them more widely. Soviet naval operations, for example, have expanded dramatically in the Mediterranean Sea, in the Indian Ocean, and in the Atlantic simultaneously.[14]

Improved Soviet offensive capabilities match these wider deployments. In the first decades after World War II, the Soviet Union maintained essentially defensive forces. Its fighter aircraft were short ranged, designed to intercept American bombers. Its navy was primarily intended to prevent American carriers from launching nuclear-armed aircraft against the Soviet homeland. But current Soviet aircraft have extended range, payload, and ground attack capabilities, and the Soviet navy has substantial offensive capabilities worldwide.[15] During most of the period since World War II, shortcomings in American military performance could be offset by the preponderance of American military power. Outside Europe the United States was not likely to encounter major ground forces armed with modern weapons, or any significant opposition in the air or on the sea. Those conditions no longer hold. Moreover, perhaps as important as the potential military consequences of the growth of Soviet capabilities are the potential psychological and political ones. Within the Soviet Union, the perception of Soviet military superiority could induce the undertaking of military moves that would otherwise be foregone. Outside the Soviet Union, the conspicuous flexing of Soviet military muscle, if unchecked by the U.S., could eventually result in the "Finlandization" of Western Europe.

Future U.S. defense policy will be further complicated by

forms of pressure and violence that may threaten the United States in the next decades: most frighteningly, by the prospect of small nations or even terrorist or criminal groups wielding weapons of mass destruction. U.S. armed forces might best be thought of as an insurance policy against many possible dangers. The policy cannot be written to cover all contingencies, but the emergence of substantial new threats clearly requires rethinking of the amounts and types of coverage needed. The possible proliferation of nuclear weapons may require special types of military force and new kinds of intelligence capabilities. It may also make prudent a basic reevaluation of U.S. reliance on nuclear weapons and plans for nuclear first use. We might be well advised, for example, to try to make nuclear attack as unthinkable as the use of the much more accessible chemical and biological weapons is now. Such a reevaluation might also make clear the necessity for a network of international agreements governing the conditions under which reactors can be sold and operated and the nuclear fuel cycle controlled.* Indeed, the most effective way to meet many novel or extreme threats is likely to be international agreement to forego particular weapons or actions, just as U.S. security against chemical and biological attacks now relies on mutual adherence to the Geneva Agreement.† Similarly, price gouging by commodity cartels like OPEC, or uncompensated expropriations like that of IPC in Peru may be prevented more effectively by clear international agreements—backed perhaps by stockpiles and the threat of economic retaliation—than by gunboats or marines.

* Despite the clear relationship between "peaceful" nuclear technology and its military applications, the behavior of the Defense Department reflects no sensitivity to threats to U.S. security posed by the spread of nuclear power plants. The department makes no effort, for example, to participate in decisions of the Nuclear Regulatory Commission on the licensing of American exports of nuclear facilities or fuel.
† Interestingly, the U.S. Navy in 1975 strongly opposed congressional initiatives to unilaterally extend U.S. jurisdiction over adjacent seabeds. The navy feared that if the United States acted unilaterally, other nations might respond with extensions of their own territorial waters, thus limiting U.S. freedom on the high seas. But military services rarely argue the national security advantages of foregoing unilateral action.

Future defense policy will also have to take into account public weariness and skepticism about further foreign involvement. Whether the United States ever aspired to the role of "world policeman," no President could now repeat Kennedy's inaugural promise that Americans would "pay any price, bear any burden, meet any hardship, support any friend, oppose any foe . . ." The Nixon doctrine signaled to allies outside Europe and Japan that they could not count on U.S. troops to defend them. The "Pacific Doctrine," as President Ford relabeled it, reflects deep-seated public preferences and a widespread perception that Communist regimes in Vietnam or Thailand do not affect our vital interests. These shifts in U.S. perceptions and their impact on policy, especially regarding the Third and Fourth Worlds, make the reassessment of plans for military involvement in those worlds imperative. Forces, basing requirements, and contingency plans developed under former assumptions will all need revision. And if former Secretary of Defense Schlesinger is right in judging that the American people will not support protracted conflict even where U.S. interests are stronger, the strategies and forces designed for such conflict need review. The size and composition of much of our current navy, for example, are based on its responsibility for keeping sea lanes open during an extended nonnuclear war in Europe or Northeast Asia.

Finally, new technologies present new problems and new opportunities. The risks entailed in any use of force in the nuclear age have impelled all Presidents since Kennedy to reach out for personal control of local military activities. And steadily improving communications allow the President to give direct orders to local commanders anywhere: Presidents gave such orders, for example, in the naval quarantine of Cuba, the bombing of North Vietnam, and the seizure of the *Mayaguez*. White House efforts to manage future military engagements are likely to be even more intense. Yet Presidents do not ordinarily have access to military advice broad enough and accurate enough to support wise tactical choice. Vietnam and the *Mayaguez*, in different ways, are again examples. Procedures for providing the President with realistic military advice, and where appropriate, with the differing views of various commanders, remain to be developed.

Other technical innovations raise questions about doctrine and weapons. The new "precision guided munitions" (PGMs), for example, make it possible to destroy almost any surface target with conventional explosives. Late in the Vietnam War, four aircraft armed with such munitions achieved what the U.S. Air Force had been unable to accomplish in more than three years of conventional bombing—to destroy the bridge complex at Thanh Hoa. They did so, moreover, without the collateral damage that normally accompanied U.S. raids.* Exploiting the United States' current advantage in these technologies, and accounting for our eventual vulnerability to comparable weapons in the hands of others, will require uncomfortable changes in service doctrines, procurement policies, even roles and missions—changes that, if left to themselves, the services are likely to accomplish slowly or not at all. As Admiral Rickover has asserted repeatedly, today's weapons acquisition process requires ten times as many layers of bureaucratic approval at each step as the successful Polaris program did.

What Is to Be Done?

The three principal inadequacies in the performance of the U.S. defense establishment—each likely to be made more severe or more dangerous by the circumstances of the near future—

* The "smart bombs" used in the Thanh Hoa attack had been available for several years. The reluctance of the air force to employ them in a war in which targets were limited is traced by some observers to fear of technological unemployment. (See Frederic A. Morris, "Smart Bombs," in the Murphy Commission Report, Appendix K: "Adequacy of Current Organization: Defense and Arms Control," App. vol. 4, [Washington, D.C.: U.S. Government Printing Office, 1975], pp. 191–98.)

set the agenda for organizational reform. Changes in structures, processes, and staffing within the Defense Department and outside it are needed to ensure that when called into action, U.S. military forces can successfully perform assigned tasks; that the nation's foreign policy objectives more effectively shape the size and deployment of its military forces; and that forces sufficient to our needs be procured at costs the nation can sustain.

Toward Useable Strength. Military operations are by their nature difficult and uncertain; no type or extent of military strength can guarantee success. But forces must be designed to maximize the chances of success. Achieving that design requires attention to the way organization affects all stages of force development: acquisition of weapons, training of troops, initiating and directing military actions (and assessing their results and prospects).

One set of needed reforms seeks to increase the likelihood that the weapons procured will provide effective and needed capabilities. The story of the bomber general and the carrier admiral illuminates some of the disincentives within the services to rational procurement. The painful story of the F-111 reveals others.[16] The F-111 was the ultimate product of Secretary McNamara's efforts to force procurement of a single bi-service tactical fighter. But to preserve its role in a nuclear war and its status within the air force, the Tactical Air Command established specifications for the plane which actually called for a long-range aircraft capable of delivering nuclear weapons against the Soviet Union. The navy, meanwhile, wanted a plane of its own. What emerged from this shotgun marriage was a technically fascinating and enormously expensive light strategic bomber, ineffective for limited war missions and subsequently rejected by the navy (with assistance from its congressional allies).

Half of the lesson of Polaris and the F-111 (and of many other weapons procurements) is that without external pressure and control, the services will tend to procure weapons that better serve the doctrines and ambitions of dominant service commands than they serve the nation. The other half of the lesson is that while the perspectives of appointed civilian officials are likely to be less parochial, their technical understanding is limited and their ability to foresee the difficulties that reluctant services can discover or create is weaker still.

Over the longer run, it may be desirable to make a major attempt to broaden perspectives within the military services —by shifting the power to promote officers to flag rank from the services to Secretary of Defense, for example, or by terminating the separate services entirely at the flag level and making all senior officers nonservice generalists, much as senior business executives are. But for the immediate future an alternative course seems far more feasible; it is to improve the technical understanding of appointive civilian officials and to strengthen their capacity to circumvent implementation problems. We therefore propose the rebuilding of a strong systems analytic staff within the OSD and extending its jurisdiction to include all stages of the acquisition of major weapons systems, including their design specification. A related OSD staff for "implementation analysis" should also be established, and charged with identifying likely obstacles to all important changes proposed for the military services, including the introduction of new weapons systems. The far better-informed civilian review of major weapons decisions that could then be undertaken within the Department of Defense should, finally, be back-stopped by a subcommittee of ExCab, a National Security Subcommittee. Such a committee, discussed more fully below, would not be concerned principally with weaponry but would review the needs, policy implications, and costs of such major new systems as Trident or the B-1 against the larger backdrop of long-term projections of threat, of competing and countertechnologies, and of U.S. purposes.

Contingency planning, long the jealously guarded preserve of individual services, must also be greatly improved. The record of Vietnam and Cambodia demonstrates the costs of insular, ill-informed, and unresponsive planning for conventional operations; the nuclear options case suggests how disastrous comparable performances in the preparation of strategic plans might prove. Monitoring and improving contingency plans drawn up by the services will require professional competence outside the services. This might take the form of a military operations analysis staff either within the OSD or reporting to the single chief military officer proposed below. The staff would periodically review both nuclear and conventional contingency plans to identify those outdated by political or technological change or inconsistent with national policy. Plans requiring interservice coordination—land-based air cover for navy carriers, for examples—would merit special attention, since such plans have typically been sketchy or nonexistent, and have often broken down in practice.[17]

Improving the quality of military advice to the President will require breaking down the system that now typically confronts a President with the unanimous judgment of his service chiefs. In fact, most such unanimity results from interservice bargaining rather than from a concurrence of professional military judgments. Such bargaining is almost impossible to avoid so long as the President's chief military advisers are simultaneously the commanders, and advocates, of particular services. We therefore endorse the recommendations of the 1970 Fitzhugh Report[18] to remove the three service chiefs from the operational chain of command, and to link the President, through his Secretary of Defense, to a single chief military officer (the chairman of the Joint Chiefs of Staff or his retitled successor), and through him to field commanders.* Assisted by his own operations staff, this military chief would

* The 1958 amendments to the National Security Act were intended to accomplish the same reform. They explicitly excluded the service chiefs from the chain of operational command. But under intense pressure, the Secretary of Defense directed that the JCS should act as his only staff for operations. Thus the service chiefs, supported both by the Joint Staff and by staffs in their own services, regained their place in the chain.

be responsible directly to the President. The President might solicit the views of the service chiefs as well, and of course, he would be free to do so. But he would consult them individually, as sources of independent and competitive advice.

To reinforce the effect of such change in the lines of command, the White House should develop regular procedures, perhaps similar to those of the NSSM process, for identifying significant differences of opinions among the services, State, the CIA* and the proposed operations analysis staff. This recommendation derives directly from a lesson of Vietnam. During the war, the National Intelligence Estimates that routinely evaluated progress typically compromised interagency differences to produce agreed-upon conclusions. Independent and controversial opinions were thus submerged in guarded but generally hopeful pictures of the war's progress. On coming into office in January 1969, President Nixon reached behind those pictures, ordering a full review of the war under quite different ground rules.[19] The various agencies were directed to respond separately to a set of pointed and specific questions. Their responses revealed wide divergences of opinion, thus giving the White House for the first time solid grounds for independent judgments.

Conforming Strength to Policy. Tightening the connection between military posture and the nation's foreign policy objectives is a still larger task. It is a job that needs doing at many levels, and most clearly at the top. If there is to be a connection between the nation's ambitions in the world and the means it maintains to achieve them, and if the resources devoted to defense, and the kinds of forces those resources support, are to be commensurate with U.S. policies and commitments, then the President and the Congress must assure that connection. Only they have the power to adjust ambitions to resources, or vice versa.

But that has not been the pattern of the recent past. Over

---

* Or its successor agency, as proposed in the following chapter.

the last decade, the proportions of both the federal budget and of the GNP devoted to defense have declined markedly— from 45 percent of the budget in 1968 to 25 percent in 1976; from 9.7 percent of the GNP in 1968 to 6 percent in 1976.[20] But the shift has been motivated mainly by public demand for "reordered priorities"; it has not been based on informed conclusions about either the nation's defense needs or the relative effectiveness of marginal expenditures on defense as against domestic programs. Nor have the procedures for formulating the defense budget made it easy to reach such conclusions. Instead, the Defense Department has normally proposed to the President a budget it presents as a bare-bones minimum; OMB and the President have made marginal adjustments, and Congress has imposed minor reductions based on little more than the certainty that there must be some fat in anything so large. At no point have the purposes U.S. forces are intended to serve been freshly considered. At the same time, since the main official assessments of external threats are presented in the context of Defense's justification of its budget, Soviet military strength has generally been exaggerated, while American capabilities have been understated.

While organizational change cannot guarantee more penetrating review of defense budgets, it can certainly stimulate more enlightening debate. As a first step, comparison of the marginal $10 billion in the defense budget and in selected domestic programs should become annual ExCab business. To insure genuinely useful staff work on the subject and to promote informative debate, a defense subcommittee of ExCab should be established, chaired by a principal Assistant to the President, supported by a small staff of its own, and comprised of deputy secretaries from each of the concerned departments, together with appropriate intelligence and budget officials. This subcommittee would serve as the principal forum for reviewing defense policy issues against the background of overall foreign policy, and would advise ExCab and the President accordingly. The jurisdiction of the subcommittee would extend to defining the threats and contingencies the United States should be prepared to meet, assessing the force levels necessary to meet them, and reviewing related strategies, deployments, and contingency plans.

The process outlined above will require—in addition to high quality staff work—stronger performance from a number of departments and agencies, especially the Department of State. We have already made specific recommendations for augmenting State's capacity to analyze military issues and for focusing responsibility for politico-military affairs within the department. Without those changes, State's perspectives would be poorly represented in the ExCab subcommittee, and the Secretary of State would be ill supported in the ExCab discussions preceding Presidential choice. The Arms Control and Disarmament Agency should similarly be strengthened. Operating with a professional staff of fewer than a hundred, ACDA has managed to develop a technical expertise on strategic weapons that is unmatched outside of the Pentagon and the CIA. But its capacity to deal with less central arms control issues, such as U.S. military sales of conventional weapons and their effect on regional strategic balances, is far less adequate. A modest strengthening of the ACDA's staff and a substantial increase in its miniscule research budget could improve those capabilities, at the same time providing a useful symbol of presidential interest in an important and organizationally underweighted perspective. Finally, the discussions in ExCab and in its defense subcommittee of the linkage between defense posture and the nation's larger objectives abroad should be backed by an enlarged role for the Office of Management and Budget. In addition to reviewing the cost effectiveness of particular defense programs, as it does now, the OMB should undertake two functions now neglected. It should assess the full defense budget in the light of the nation's broad national security goals, and analyze the marginal effects of shifts in the balance of national expenditures between defense and domestic programs.

The Department of Defense itself is also in need of change, and in particular in need of a tough-minded and managerially capable Secretary, backed by a deputy and assistant secretaries of his own choosing. The Secretary must be able to articulate in ExCab debate coherent and solidly grounded assessments of the forces necessary to meet the nation's security objectives and of the resources required to sustain those forces. Both the President and the Congress will be tempted to fudge; to cling to ambitious conceptions of the nation's role but to shrink from their full costs; to support units but not readiness, or defense employment but not military effectiveness. In these deliberations the Secretary of Defense will be principally responsible for insisting upon a rough consistency between the nation's avowed policies and the military strength the nation actually supports. Within the department, the Secretary will have the reciprocal responsibility of ensuring that day-to-day operations serve the larger objectives the President and Congress have established. In meeting that responsibility, the Secretary will need the support not only of the staffs and subordinates referred to above, but of a rebuilt office of International Security Affairs (ISA). Recent insensitivity to the linkage between defense and broader foreign policy objectives appears largely attributable to a decline in the quality of Defense's "little State Department," which has primary responsibility for monitoring that linkage. The recent elevation of ISA's chief from assistant secretary to deputy secretary status should be matched by a commensurate rebuilding of its staff.

Using Resources Effectively. The United States can afford virtually any level of military strength it believes it requires. But it will not long sustain grossly wasteful expenditures on defense. Over the long run, and especially in periods of relative peace, the maintenance of adequate forces will depend on the use of defense dollars for programs that demonstrably merit public confidence and support.

That is clearly not the case today. Most obviously deficient, despite recent efforts, is the weapons acquisition process.

"Fly-before-buy," "design-to-cost," and "high/low mix"—these phrases from the current jargon all reflect a recognition within Defense that the exponential climb of unit costs must be ended. Yet the incentives in the services and in Congress to seek ever more complex and expensive equipment still lead to oversophistication and extravagance, and, at times, to the creation of artificial "needs" for new arms. The Nixon administration, for example, began building Trident submarines long before the existing Polaris/Poseidon fleet needed replacement. At great cost, for little improvement in the capability of U.S. nuclear forces, it thereby locked the United States into a system embodying the technology of the early 1970s that will remain the backbone of American deterrence until the year 2000.[21]

A number of other reforms should supplement the revisions in procurement processes suggested above. In particular, weapons acquisition procedures should be revised so as to routinely require competing prototypes; to distinguish more sharply between advanced development of potential weapons and the decision to procure such weapons in large numbers; and to require independent review of the services' operational testing.* Creation of an independent defense test agency with overall responsibility for monitoring all weapons testing and evaluation might also be required. The new "weapons impact statement," requirements which oblige the President to submit to Congress an assessment of each major weapon, spelling out its costs, performance, and arms control implications, may provide yet another handle on the problem.

But though major weapons systems provoke—and deserve —the strongest expressions of fiscal outrage, they are not the

---

* The mid-1976 decision making the Pentagon's chief of Research and Development also the chief procurement officer moves in exactly the wrong direction. Instead, there should be a clearer separation between those responsible for researching and developing new weapons (the Directorate of Defense Research and Engineering) and those responsible for deciding which of the many new weapons reaching the stage of advanced development are sufficiently cost-effective to justify acquisition.

major source of possible defense savings. Manpower costs take 60 cents from every defense dollar, and military pay and benefit plans are long overdue for reform. The nonsystem of basic pay, bonuses, and fringe benefits that comprises military compensation should be simplified and its expensive anomalies removed. Many benefits and hidden subsidies (like free cosmetic surgery for officers' wives, for example) were established when the basic salaries of servicemen were far below civilian norms. Now that military pay scales have caught up with (and in some respects surpassed) those of the private sector, fringes should be sharply trimmed.

Retirement plans are similarly ripe for reform. Blechman and Fried have estimated that if the military retirement system could be made to conform with the federal civilian retirement system (itself often criticized for excessive generosity), an annual saving of $1 billion dollars could be realized in fifteen years, with larger annual savings thereafter.[22]

Carving out such savings will be neither glamorous nor popular work. Service and contractor resistance will be felt within Defense, in the press and in the Congress. But fat in the Defense budget is not merely inefficient; it also reduces public confidence in the necessity for substantial defense expenditures in general and tempts the press, public, and Congress to continue arguing defense issues in the dead-end terms of "vital needs" vs. "profligate waste," rather than against the essential criteria of national needs and the capabilities necessary to attain them.

Chapter 9

Intelligence: Seizing the Opportunity

> The operations of Secret Services must remain secret, but the principles by which Secret Services can best be directed and controlled should be considered carefully, discussed and understood by those at government level who are responsible for controlling Secret Services. It is the constant failure to understand these principles that has brought about the ironic situation whereby the majority of Secret Services handicap rather than help the governments they are supposed to serve.
> John Bruce Lockhart* (November 1973)

RECENT revelations of repugnant and illegal activities by U.S. intelligence agencies created a rare and important opportunity, the first since the CIA was established in 1947, to rethink the purpose of foreign intelligence, and to reorient the intelligence community accordingly. But the events that created the opportunity also obscured it. They focused public attention on a secondary function of intelligence—covert action—rather than on the central one—informing decision makers; they confused faults of intelligence with errors of

* Formerly high-ranking official in the British Secret Service.

policy, and they precipitated partial reforms that have appeased the demand for change but leave many basic problems untouched. Determining what still needs to be done, and how, requires starting at the beginning.

What Do We Want of Intelligence?

Foreign intelligence agencies are principally intended to provide information and analyses useful to decision makers. This function is essential; effective foreign policy must be rooted in a detailed understanding of political, economic, and military developments abroad. Secondarily, these agencies enable direct but hidden intervention in events abroad—covert action. Covert action is rarely essential; indeed, a respectable case can be made for forswearing it entirely. (We discuss that position below and, on balance, reject it.) Both these functions of intelligence must be subjected to two constraints: that the methods used remain consistent with fundamental rights and values of our society, and that their costs be commensurate with their benefits.

Achieving these purposes has been particularly difficult over the past decade, for reasons that will persist. The shifting nature of the foreign policy agenda—the growing importance of economic issues, for example—calls for novel kinds of information and unfamiliar methods of analysis. The emergence of new forms of threat—organized terrorism, for example—creates new needs for covert capabilities just as public attention is being drawn to the risks that clandestine activity may pose to constitutional rights and basic values. And the erosion of cold war certainties about U.S. purposes and the means legitimate to advance them leaves vulnerable a community whose objectives, size, and operating methods were formed by the cold war and still largely assume those certainties.

The "Community"

How are we now organized to meet those demands and observe those constraints? A thumbnail sketch of the still unfamiliar "intelligence community" may be in order.[1]

The community is made up of some eleven agencies differing sharply in their functions, responsibilities and lines of command, staffed by more than 100,000 persons, and expending at least $6 billion annually (counting about $2 billion devoted by the military services to "tactical" intelligence).

The Central Intelligence Agency. At the center of the community is the diversified conglomerate, the CIA. An independent agency in the Executive Office of the President, reporting to the National Security Council, the CIA was established in 1947 principally to ensure that all foreign intelligence possessed by the government would be assembled and evaluated as a whole, and made available to all who might need it. The intention was to avoid repetition of the prewar practices—responsible in part for the surprise at Pearl Harbor—by which the separate intelligence arms of the military services jealously hoarded their own information. It soon became clear that another virtue of an intelligence agency separate from the departments of State and Defense and independent of the armed services was that it could provide the President and other policy makers estimates and analyses undistorted by the policy preferences and operational responsibilities that tended to color the conclusions of other agencies. The CIA was also mandated to perform "services of common concern"; to recommend methods for intelligence coordination; and to perform "such other functions and duties related to intelligence affecting the national security as the NSC may from time to time direct." That final ambiguous clause, apparently intended only to authorize clandestine collection of information, has been treated for a quarter century as authority for covert action. The agency was specifically denied any "police, subpoena, law enforcement, or internal security functions."

The CIA employs roughly 15,000 persons and expends some $750 million annually. Roughly half that sum supports an extensive network of clandestine agents and operations. Approximately a third is devoted to the interpretation of data and the preparation of analyses and estimates. Most of the remainder supports a resourceful technical design and engineering arm. Each of the career intelligence officers to have headed the agency—Dulles, Helms, Colby—has previously directed clandestine operations.

In addition to serving as the nation's chief substantive intelligence officer (his briefings provide the customary opening of NSC meetings) the director of Central Intelligence (DCI), has two distinct responsibilities. He commands the CIA; and he is responsible, under the NSC, for coordinating the activities of the entire community. Predictably, DCIs have had far greater success at the first of those duties. As to the CIA, their authority is clear and unchallenged; they control budgets, promotions, and assignments. As to the wider community, however, their authority is tenuous and disputed. Roughly 85 percent of the community lies within the Defense Department, and the Secretary of Defense is a statutory member of the body—the NSC—to which the DCI reports. As a result the community has never effectively been centrally managed.

The National Security Agency. In terms of number of people employed, the community's largest component is the National Security Agency. Established by Executive Order in 1952 and lodged in the Defense Department, the NSA monitors and attempts to decode or analyze a wide range of foreign communications and other electronic signals. It is also responsible for the security of U.S. codes and communications. Operating more than 2000 monitoring stations positioned around the globe, the NSA collects raw data in warehouse quantities.

The National Reconnaissance Office. The community's most expensive agency is also its least known, the National Reconnaissance Office, also lodged in Defense. The NRO operates numerous "overhead" (principally satellite) reconnaissance programs, working largely through the U.S. Air Force. Its products are medium-resolution photographs of wide areas and high-resolution pictures of selected points; these are essential to military and arms control analysts, and useful to economic and other analysts.

Army, Navy and Air Force Intelligence. Each of the armed services maintains its own substantial intelligence organization; their combined staffs total some 50,000 people, largely overseas. Especially concerned with "tactical intelligence"—the capabilities and disposition of their counterpart forces in other countries—service staffs also participate in the production of National Intelligence Estimates and maintain their own cryptological and communications security arms.

The Defense Intelligence Agency. The Defense Intelligence Agency reports to the Joint Chiefs of Staff and the Secretary of Defense. It was established in 1961, principally to reduce interservice duplication and disagreement by performing centrally much of the work then conducted separately by the service intelligence branches. Though it expends roughly $100 million annually, its success in that mission has been limited; the service intelligence branches are now each larger than they were in 1961. The DIA collects little information, but publishes various intelligence digests, performs analyses on a wide range of subjects, and represents the JCS in the drafting of community-wide analyses and estimates. Its performance is constrained by a difficulty it shares with the service arms: intelligence assignments have little promotion value in service careers, and are therefore avoided by the most promising officers.

The Bureau of Intelligence and Research. The State Department's Bureau of Intelligence and Research is the smallest by far of the foreign intelligence agencies; its budget is roughly one one-thousandth of the community's. Engaging in no collection, but able to draw Foreign Service reporting from posts abroad—the largest and often the most important single source of information on foreign political and economic developments —INR provides analyses to State's principal officials and contributes to the national estimates made jointly by the intelligence community. Like the service intelligence arms, INR is not viewed by its department's professionals as a mainline assignment.

Other Agencies. The intelligence units of the FBI, the Treasury Department, and the Energy Research and Development Administration contribute evidence and analysis on matters within their special jurisdiction.

The direction and oversight of the community, reshuffled by President Ford in early 1976, now falls to five committees. The National Security Council remains responsible for "policy control," and has also been given the new task of conducting semiannual reviews of the community's performance. The new Committee on Foreign Intelligence (CFI), chaired by the DCI, with the Deputy Secretary of Defense for Intelligence and the President's Deputy Assistant for National Security Affairs as its other members, is assigned "management and resources control"; the committee is another in the long series of measures that have sought, with limited success, to strengthen the DCI's influence over the community as a whole. The Operations Advisory Group, succeeding the so-called 40 Committee, is responsible for reviewing and advising the President on covert operations and "certain sensitive foreign intelligence collection missions." It is chaired by the Assistant to the President for National Security Affairs, with the Secretaries of State and Defense, and the DCI and chairman of the JCS as its other members, the Attorney General and OMB director being "observers." The new Intelligence Oversight Board (IOB), whose three members are appointed by the President from private life, is charged with assisting the President, the NSC and the Attorney General oversee the propriety and legality of the community's operations. Finally, the President's Foreign Intelligence Advisory Board (PFIAB), expanded by the addition of the IOB's members to its own ranks of prominent citizens, is to continue its exercise of a broad but vague oversight charter. Not influential in recent years, PFIAB has largely limited itself to suggesting new techniques of collection and possible targets for intelligence.

Recent Performance

No assessment of so diverse and shrouded a community can be complete, or completely balanced. But enough is known to justify a number of conclusions.

Inadequate Analysis. The community's capability for collecting information by electronic and photographic means is remarkably good, almost magical. Reportedly, photographs taken from satellites a hundred miles above the earth can distinguish insignia on a military uniform.[2] As a result, analysts—principally in the CIA—are able to assess the numbers and characteristics of foreign military forces, and especially of strategic forces, with considerable confidence. Though the intelligence services still occasionally disagree in their assessments, the disagreements are confined to much narrower ranges than formerly, and U.S. decision makers can rely on technical judgments that are largely agreed and are as accurate as can be reasonably expected. This is a substantial improvement over the time when senior officials were faced with sharply differing and largely self-serving but equally plausible judgments, pressed on them by the competing military services. When the questions are more subtle and the evidence less conclusive, however—as is true for most political and economic questions and for problems of motivation and intentions—the community begins to show serious cracks.

It is a law of bureaucratic behavior that agencies with operational responsibilities produce analyses that support their operating programs. The cause is not dishonesty—indeed, the process may be barely conscious—but the tendency is universal. John Bruce Lockhart's fable describes the process:

> Ruritania is being threatened by Transylvania, and Transylvania believes itself to be threatened by Ruritania. The Ruritanian Chief of Air Staff is convinced that in the interests of Ruritanian security another 20 fighter squadrons are essential. Being a strong and shrewd man, he realises that his only chance of obtaining these extra fighters is to scare the pants off the politicians by stressing the real threat posed by the Transylvania bomber force. As happens in many countries, he controls the collecting and collating of intelligence on the Transylvanian bomber force. He is an honourable man, but as every good intelligence officer knows, the ultimate conclusion in a complex intelligence problem consists of a logical progression on a large number of variants. By exaggerating each variant just a little—"Better be on the safe side, Herr Commandant" —the true figure of 50 Transylvanian bomber squadrons can be made up to 75, with hardly a dishonest or reprehensible step by any of the intelligence officers involved. It is just an accumulation of mild wishful thinking at every stage of the collation process.[3]

The principal virtue of an independent CIA is precisely its presumed ability to counterbalance such tendencies, and indeed the CIA has proven the most reliable single source of U.S. intelligence judgments. But intelligence estimates have still reflected biases of several kinds. National Intelligence Estimates (NIE's), the most formal assessments offered to high-level policy makers, are in form the responsibility of the DCI, but they are also expected to reflect the judgments of the entire intelligence community. A forceful DCI can reject the positions of other agencies, relegating their expression to dissenting footnotes, but the political and bureaucratic pressures to compromise differences are strong. As a result, estimates of enemy strength, for example, tend to reflect the frequently exaggerated views of the Armed Services, and estimates inconsistent with announced positions of Secretaries of State or Defense may be suppressed. As John Huizenga, former chairman of the Board of National Estimates, testified before the Senate Select Committee on Intelligence,

The truth is that the DCI, since his authority over the intelligence process is at least ambiguous, had an uphill struggle to make a sophisticated appreciation of a certain range of issues prevail in the national intelligence product over and against the parochial views and interests of departments, and especially the military departments.[4]

A subtler distortion in judgment arises from the fact that agencies in the business of collecting information have an interest in collecting more; they tend to overestimate future capability to monitor important developments—Soviet adherence to arms control agreements, for example—provided only that additional collection activities are funded.

But the CIA's judgments have probably been most seriously distorted by its involvement in field operations. The story of the U.S. bombing campaign over North Vietnam, sketched in Chapter 2, is a notable case in point. The long, costly, and ultimately unsuccessful U.S. air war against North Vietnam was continuously evaluated by several agencies. Not surprisingly, the agencies responsible for the bombing—the JCS, the air force, and the navy—accounted it effective, and blamed its evident failure to prevent Hanoi from supporting the war in the South on restrictions imposed by U.S. political leadership. Civilian analysts, particularly those from the CIA, took a more critical view. In June 1965, three months after initiation of a bombing campaign that was to continue for more than three years, an estimate asserted that "the odds are against the postulated U.S. attacks leading the DRV to make conciliatory gestures to secure a respite from the bombing; rather we believe that the DRV would persevere in supporting the insurgency in the South."[5] In May 1967 a CIA review of the bombing's effects criticized the campaign sharply: "Twenty-seven months of U.S. bombing of North Vietnam have had remarkably little effect on Hanoi's over-all strategy in prosecuting the war, on its confident view of long-term Communist prospects, and on its political tactics regarding negotiations." Moreover, the report went on, the losses inflicted by the bombing "have not meaningfully degraded North Vietnam's material ability to continue the war in South Vietnam."[6] Later that month, another CIA estimate held out little prospect that further escalation would dissuade Hanoi from its course: "Short of a major invasion or nuclear attack, there is probably no level of air or naval actions against North Vietnam which Hanoi has determined in advance would be so intolerable that the war had to be stopped."[7] As it turned out, those CIA judgments were correct. By January 1969 all the concerned departments, including the JCS, were willing to agree that

> there is no evidence to suggest that these hardships [caused by the bombing] reduced to a critical level NVN's willingness or resolve to continue the conflict. On the contrary, the bombing actually may have hardened the attitude of the people and rallied them behind the Government's program.
>
> While the exact magnitude of [these] supply flows and requirements are all subject to uncertainty, the basic conclusion seems clear. The bombing failed to reduce support below required levels, even at the increased activity rates of 1968.[8]

Yet the bombing had continued and expanded from 1965 through 1968. Why? President Johnson was unwilling to alienate either the military or the influential segments of public and congressional opinion that supported the bombing; that, clearly, was an important reason. But another factor was the undertow of contrary reports from the CIA itself. A number of far more optimistic statements—often at crucial junctures of the war—cut across the CIA's formal contributions to national estimates on the bombing. In April of 1965, while President Johnson pondered whether to commit U.S. ground troops into regular combat, retiring CIA Director John McCone urged heavier air strikes if that course were chosen. "It is my judgment," he argued in a memo for Johnson's principal advisers on the war, "that if we are to change the mission of the ground forces, we must also change the ground rules of the strikes against North Vietnam. We must hit them harder, more frequently, and inflict greater damage."[9] Similarly, while the administration was considering an escalation of the bombing to include the North's petroleum storage facilities, a special CIA report of March 1966 took the unusual step of explicitly favoring the proposed attacks, blaming the prior ineffectiveness of the campaign on its "highly restrictive ground rules." According to the *Pentagon Papers*, "The March CIA report, with obvious bid to turn the attacks into a punitive bombing campaign and its nearly obvious promise of real payoff, strengthened JCS proposals to intensify the bombing."[10] And in October of 1966, after Secretary McNamara had lost confidence in the bombing, the DCI circulated a rebuttal to McNamara's views, arguing that ". . . a bombing program directed both against closing the port of Haiphong and continuously cutting the rail lines to China could have significant impact."[11]

What accounted for the CIA's schizophrenia? Principally, a deep rift between the agency's analysts—generally skeptical of the likely outcome of U.S. efforts in Vietnam—and its clandestine agents, who, like their military colleagues, were deeply engaged in that effort and determined to do what was necessary to win. The CIA's clandestine activities had become large operating programs. In Vietnam and Laos the agency was providing leadership and support for hill tribe armies and managing the systematic effort to identify and kill Vietcong leaders. As a result the DCI was being pulled in opposite directions. The judgments of his intelligence directorate were as skeptical and pessimistic as the reports of his operations directorate were hopeful and affirmative.

Bias is not the only source of inadequate analysis. Another is simple irrelevance. Consumers of intelligence, especially at high levels, are often too busy and sometimes too secretive to identify clearly the issues on which analysis might be most helpful. The Nixon administration established an NSC Intelligence Committee to force high-level specification of intelligence priorities, but it rarely met and has now been abolished —and no mechanism has taken its place. Yet like all bureaucracies, intelligence agencies are governed largely by the laws of inertia. A decade of the OPEC, terrorism, devaluation, threats to the ozone layer, openings to China and wheat deals with the Soviets has demonstrated that both threats and opportunities can take novel forms. Making intelligence consistently useful requires the clear and early communication of revised priorities from levels of the government high enough to force response.

Finally, even where appropriate questions are addressed and biases are absent, the intellectual quality of analyses and estimates—especially those attempting to predict political or bureaucratic behavior—is often low. Poor information, the absence of rigorous analytic methods, and the necessity to compromise the views of various agencies tend to produce political analyses so waffled or Delphic in their conclusions, and so reticent about the bases for them, as to stymie their readers. Accordingly, many policy-level officials now do not bother to read these estimates. Perfection is not the appropriate standard—assessments of complex situations must often be hedged, and will often be mistaken. But more useful analyses are clearly needed and clearly possible.

Unacceptable Means. However accurate its information or prophetic its estimates, the intelligence community must conform to acceptable standards of conduct. It obviously has not done so. It is now clear that virtually all U.S. foreign intelligence agencies have been involved in the surveillance in the United States of persons having no relation to any foreign power, or in monitoring the mail or telephone and telegraph communications of large numbers of U.S. citizens, or worse. The CIA plotted—and perhaps effected—the death of national leaders with whose countries the United States was not at war. The results have been a blurring of the moral standards that should distinguish the behavior of an open society, an erosion of prohibitions that protect all societies—especially open ones—and a hemorrhage of confidence in agencies previously held in general respect. The ugliest truth is that these

200 REMAKING FOREIGN POLICY

were not the acts of a rogue bureaucracy. Few were unauthorized; indeed, most were sanctioned by Presidents.

Identifying villains and punishing them may be necessary, but it will not be sufficient. Three roots of the problem remain: neither law nor tradition has established clear rules of behavior; the enforcement of such rules as exist has been left to interested parties (parties doubly insulated, moreover, by the secrecy and designed "deniability" of much covert behavior); and the ultimate check on such activities, the Congress, has shown until recently a decided preference for ignorance over implication.

Waste. The third problem is less critical. In recent years the White House and at least two DCIs have worked to limit the costs of intelligence and to allocate the community's resources in accordance with an integrated sense of national requirements. The result has been a substantial cutback in intelligence personnel (chiefly from NSA) and a leveling of the intelligence budget. Moreover, some waste is tolerable, since in an uncertain world, too large an intelligence effort is preferable to one too small.

Still, important economies can be made. The community's many agencies, funded through separate budgets, pursue partially overlapping assignments. They are tempted to large investments in exotic hardware by rapid advances in photographic, electronic, and data-processing technologies, and they give little consideration to the marginal value of additional information. As a result, analytic work (which is cheap) is underfinanced, while collection (which is expensive but glamorous, intellectually easy, or technically challenging) is performed prodigally. Of the $4 billion expended by the community on "national" intelligence, probably half a billion could be saved, and the gains would be not merely monetary. Large and activist intelligence services inevitably press against the behavioral constraints of an open society. The ready availability of funds—some unvouchered—compounds the problem, and also relaxes the pressure to distinguish the high priority problems from trivial ones. Tighter budget control would do much both to discipline behavior and to focus attention on the most important concerns.

What Is to Be Done?

Intelligence reforms must serve a number of partially competing objectives. They must ensure that the community (1) provides "eyes and ears" of the highest capacity; (2) develops a "mind" capable of using the eyes and ears to the fullest and of drawing penetrating inferences about future developments; (3) maintains independence and objectivity in analyses and estimates; (4) has access to the President and to the Congress and is heard in the process of decision; (5) observes constitutional rights and basic social values; and (6) absorbs only the resources its tasks require.

Many proposed reforms attend to some of these objectives, without regard for others. The steps taken by President Ford in February 1976 for example, relate only to the final two objectives.[12] The recommendations of the Senate Select Committee, while far broader, largely ignore the first three objectives. We propose here the outlines of more comprehensive change.

Splitting the CIA. The need to insure the neutrality and independence of advice to the President provides the main reason for having a Central Intelligency Agency. Unlike the military services and the Department of State, CIA was intended to be free of operational and policy responsibilities and hence exempt from the commitments and loyalties those responsibilities engender. The central analysts were to share an organization with clandestine operators, but these were engaged principally in the collection of intelligence, and the advantages of cohabitation seemed substantial: collectors would keep analysts abreast of what was known, analysts would keep collectors aware of what was needed.

Experience has proven otherwise. Differences in style, temperament, lines of command, and requirements of secrecy have divided the two functions and limited communication between them. Much detailed information held by operators is unknown to analysts; some has been denied even when specifically requested. While the advantages have thus been slight, the disadvantages have been great. As noted above, the director of CIA has owed his allegiance largely to the clandestine side of the agency, and clandestine work has involved substantial programs. The result has been a partial compromise of the agency's freedom from institutional bias, and hence of a principal reason for its existence.[13]

The surest way to avoid such compromise is to divide the CIA, placing the analysts in a separate and autonomous organization. Taken alone, the insulation of analysts from the biases inherent in program responsibilities might not justify such radical surgery. But it does not stand alone. Benefits of at least four other kinds would flow from the separation of analytic and estimating staffs from clandestine collection and covert operations. First, in the study of many questions affecting our foreign relations, and in the development of improved analytic methods, the most advanced work goes on not in intelligence agencies or anywhere in the government, but in the academic community and in "think tanks." During World War II and in the early years of the cold war, the intelligence agencies drew effectively on these intellectual resources, but as the agencies became increasingly associated with disputed policies and large-scale covert activities, their university connections weakened and broke. They need to be restored, a goal the clear separation of analysts from operators would facilitate. Second, the splitting of the CIA, following revelations of clear misconduct, would help ensure future sensitivity in all U.S. clandestine services to the importance of observing more demanding standards of behavior. Third, the disappearance of the CIA would relieve the nation of a name and organization that will otherwise remain a target of derision, suspicion, and perhaps attack. But most important, assigning the central analytic function to an organization focused wholly on producing assessments and estimates of the highest quality would encourage recruitment and training practices more likely to develop superior analysts, and promotion policies more likely to retain them. It would also secure the undivided attention of the nation's chief intelligence officer to the crucial analytic function rather than to the supervision of delicate clandestine work or the management of a complex community.[14]

Establishing a Foreign Assessment Agency. The analytic and estimative tasks of the CIA would be assigned to a new entity organized and staffed solely to produce analyses and estimates as accurate as the state of the art permits. An appropriate title might be the Foreign Assessment Agency. The agency would assume most of the functions and personnel of the CIA's Directorate of Intelligence, including its interpreters of photography and other technically derived data, but would not be engaged in any collection. It would select, pay, and promote its analysts principally for their expertise, skill in analysis, and effectiveness in presentation. Able analysts would be encouraged to enter the agency at middle and senior levels as well as at junior ones. (The current practices of the CIA's Directorate of Intelligence are quite different: most recruitment is at the bottom levels, lateral entry is rare, and most senior positions are reserved for administrators.) The agency would seek strong working relations with university research centers and think tanks, and should sponsor one or more RAND-like institutes specifically devoted to the development of more dependable techniques of analysis and forecasting. The Foreign Assessment Agency would contain a Board of National Estimates charged with producing its best assessments of important issues. Where the views of other intelligence agencies were significantly different, the disagreements would be explicitly set out, together with full exposition of their nature and source.

The director of the Foreign Assessment Agency would rank as the community's senior "producer" of analyses and estimates, inheriting the DCI's current role as intelligence adviser to the President. He would have no responsibility for clandestine collection or covert action, and would not attempt to manage or direct the community as a whole. Instead, in intellect and temperament the director should embody the highest aspirations of his agency: analytic discipline and depth, a compulsion to follow the evidence wherever it leads, the assumption of personal responsibility for the reliability of his judgments, and a capacity to present them with force and cogency.

There is a substantial argument against such an agency. In calling shots as it saw them it would make few friends, and without clandestine programs of its own or supervisory responsibility for the rest of the community, it might become a bureaucratic lightweight, readily elbowed aside. On balance, we think this risk worth running. The record of the CIA demonstrates that an agency which does operate programs of its own, and does claim authority over the community as a whole, can still be deflected in its judgments by external pressure. The same record demonstrates also that when responsibilities for community coordination, for analysis, for covert collection, and for covert action are lodged in a single agency, the hardest and most important of those functions, the first and second, are slighted. An agency of this kind should be able to produce analysis and estimates of far more consistently authoritative quality. Its analytic skill would be backed by its special capabilities for interpreting aerial photographic and electronic data. Over time, its record of having been more consistently right than any other source of advice should make such an agency dangerous to ignore. And its role might be further strengthened by statutory provisions requiring that Foreign Assessment Agency views be considered prior to specified kinds of decisions, and by the responsibility of the Foreign Assessment Agency director to submit requested analyses to the Joint

Intelligence Committee of the Congress proposed below, a committee responsible for confirming his appointment to office.

Additional Analytic Staffs. The Foreign Assessment Agency could not meet all day-to-day needs of senior officials for analyses utilizing intelligence data. But it need not. Responsibility for the production of analyses and estimates, now highly centralized, can readily be diffused. The collection of information is frequently complicated, expensive, and therefore important not to duplicate. But the analysis of most information requires relatively few people and little machinery, and improves with duplication. Nothing raises the quality of analytic work so powerfully as the existence of competing sources of analysis. Small analytic and estimating staffs, like the Net Assessments group that reports to the Secretary of Defense, should therefore be created for all key intelligence consumers who want them. The additional costs of such staffs would be trivial, but their benefits should be substantial. They would give policy-level officials an opportunity to pose and repose questions whose answers would be most helpful to their own work, and to receive these answers from analysts whose performance they were able to reward or penalize. The associated danger— that analysts so situated would tend to produce the responses their bosses found most congenial—would be largely offset by the existence of competing staffs elsewhere, and by the retention of an authoritative and well-insulated central analytic agency.

Creation of a Special Services Agency. The case can be made that the United States should abolish its clandestine agencies, abandon espionage, and deny itself a capability for covert action. That argument stresses the declining benefits of human agents as technical means of collection become more sophisticated, and it points to the risks created by failures or disclosures of covert actions. It also points to the evidence that such agencies tend to infringe constitutional rights and may again engage in actions, like assassinations, that affront the most basic standards of international behavior in peacetime.

Those arguments have weight; the risks involved in maintaining covert capabilities are real. But we believe that the dangers of forswearing them entirely are larger. Recall, for example, the rapid growth in the world supply of plutonium, coupled with the relative accessibility of the technology for manufacturing crude nuclear weapons. As was noted in Chapter 1, the problem is not confined to the possible behavior of unstable states or irrational rulers; a nuclear device in the hands of political terrorists (or simple criminals) is not grossly improbable, over time. Supplementing the formal systems responsible for keeping track of fissionable material should be given high priority by the information-gathering arms of U.S. intelligence; it would be folly to deny the nation a capacity to act, if clearly necessary, on what the intelligence disclosed.

The question "Clandestine services, yes or no?" therefore seems to us the wrong one. The appropriate questions are how to assure that a clandestine service treats the collection of intelligence and not the conduct of covert operations as its principal function, and how to guarantee that covert actions, when undertaken, are controlled as tightly as their dubious nature requires. In dealing with these questions the Ford reforms of 1976 were a useful start. They appear to ensure that the extraordinarily casual processes by which the old 40 Committee approved covert actions and thereafter failed to review them will be ended. To those reforms we would propose only two additions: that covert actions be authorized only to support policy which has been publicly acknowledged—a principal violated by U.S. intervention in Chile, for example—and that the most sensitive covert actions be undertaken only after written presidential authorization which must become part of the administration's permanent historical record.

Important problems of scale of covert operations, and of the internal incentives of a covert agency remain. We would meet them by assigning clandestine collection of intelligence and covert action to a new, small, and specialized agency. It would incorporate elements of the CIA's present Directorates for

Operations, Science and Technology, and Administration. The reduced size of the agency would signal the diminished importance of its functions, and its pay and promotion practices should provide clear incentives to treat reportage as its preferred mission. A name like "Special Services" would emphasize the relatively narrow nature of its tasks.

The proper location of such an agency is debatable, and in fact any placement has important defects. But since it must be kept sensitive to the foreign policy implications of its action, and also given some insulation from direct political-level control, we would favor making the SSA an independent agency, reporting to the President through the Secretary of State as the Arms Control and Disarmament Agency (ACDA) does now. The director of the SSA should be held by statute to a limited term, perhaps six years.

Making Community Management a Presidential Responsibility. To ensure that collection and analysis focus on priority concerns, and that the intelligence community's resources are effectively deployed, someone must serve as the community's central manager. The DCI is presently assigned that responsibility, but no DCI yet has been able to handle it—for a number of reasons. First, they have lacked the necessary authority. The great preponderance of the community falls under the jurisdiction of the Secretary of Defense, while the DCI, its nominal head, is subordinate to the NSC, a body on which the Secretary of Defense sits as a statutory member. That is an awkward position from which to attempt leverage. Second, the DCI is evidently biased. He is viewed in the community as necessarily partial to the interests and perspectives of the particular organization he heads, the CIA.[15] His position is comparable to that of a Secretary of, say, the navy, who attempted simultaneously to serve as the Secretary of Defense. He must attempt to command services with which his own competes.

The many efforts to make the DCI responsible for community-wide direction have not only failed, but have exacted a high price: the DCI's devotion to producing analyses and estimates of the highest possible quality—the key responsibility of his own agency—has inevitably been diluted. Quite independently of our proposals for splitting CIA, therefore, we believe that continuing to assign responsibility for directing the community to the DCI is a mistake.

Who then should perform the task? We believe it can only be performed in the Executive Office of the President, since the President is the only official to whom all agencies in that disparate community report. Establishing consumer priorities, assessing producer performance, developing budgets that allocate resources across the community in accordance with the national importance of the functions being performed—such functions can be effectively carried out only by someone who speaks in the President's name. Probably that official should be titled Assistant to the President for Intelligence, chosen for strong managerial competence and located, together with a small staff, in the Executive Office Building. A relationship of mutual support between the Foreign Assessment Agency director and this Assistant will be essential. In addition to eliciting from the principal consumers of intelligence better specifications of intelligence priorities and sharper evaluations of intelligence performance, the Assistant for Intelligence would develop and defend a comprehensive community-wide foreign intelligence budget. The budget would be used to enforce clearer divisions of responsibility among the various agencies and would be authorized by the Joint Committee of the Congress on Intelligence proposed below.

Setting Boundaries to Behavior. The intelligence community's surveillance of U.S. citizens not connected with foreign powers, its links with organized crime, its involvement in attempted assassinations make it imperative that more demanding standards of behavior be set and enforced. That will require dealing with the three main sources of past failure: neither law nor tradition had established clear rules of behavior; monitoring the observance of such rules as existed was left to interested parties; and Congress, the ultimate guarantor of oversight, defaulted.

The Ford reforms begin to address the first two problems by imposing public restrictions on potentially abusive intelligence activities, prohibiting assassination, and by giving the Intelligence Oversight Board (IOB) clear responsibility for monitoring potentially illegal or improper activities and for reporting on them to the President and the Attorney General. What is lacking, however, is a role for the Congress. One way to stimulate greater congressional involvement would be to establish an independent Inspector General of Intelligence who, unlike members of the IOB, would be confirmed by the Senate and mandated to report any discovered violation of statute or Executive Order to both the President and the Congress. But congressional oversight of intelligence should obviously be far broader.

Active Congressional Oversight. The new rules and procedures covering clandestine and covert activities will begin to construct barriers against the abuse of power, but standing alone they can all be circumvented. In the end, the most reliable check against executive abuse is the same for intelligence as it is for other policy areas: an informed Congress imposing effective oversight. We have never had such oversight, for a variety of reasons: the real and imagined exigencies of the cold war; deference to the President as Commander-in-Chief; the location of main congressional responsibility for intelligence in the Armed Services committees; and the desire of most members of those committees—and of the Congress generally—to maintain a state of innocence by avoiding knowledge of the seamy details. But the costs of congressional passivity are now clear. Effective congressional oversight of intelligence requires a standing committee specifically concerned with intelligence, capable of viewing the purposes of the community broadly and assessing its performance critically. If such a body is to receive, as it should, all relevant information, its membership must be limited and its procedures capable of fully safeguarding genuinely sensitive material. Those needs point toward a single joint committee rather than committees of each House. Its membership should be drawn from the

Foreign Relations, Armed Services, Judiciary, and Economic Policy committees of each House. To keep the committee representative and avoid its capture by the community, its membership should rotate.*

The committee should exercise jurisdiction over all intelligence agencies, and over the intelligence activities of all departments, proposing statutory charters for the agencies, reviewing their internal regulations and monitoring performance. It should confirm the appointments of directors of the Foreign Assessment and Special Services agencies and of the Inspector General of Intelligence. It should be empowered to receive and staffed to review all requested estimates, analyses, or information (except policy advice to the President), and should be regularly briefed on all major issues of intelligence policy. It might be empowered to designate particularly sensitive activities for which it could require advance notice. But it must bear the associated responsibility of adopting rules of procedure capable of protecting the confidentiality of the information it receives. Finally, the joint committee should review and authorize the comprehensive community-wide intelligence budget prepared by the Assistant for Intelligence.

This is a formidable list of reforms. But it is prompted by the nation's first opportunity in a quarter century to rethink what it needs from intelligence and how to get it. Absent further scandals or disasters, no additional such opportunity is likely to arise in this century. This is the time, therefore, to ensure that U.S. intelligence not only observes defensible rules of behavior, but that it perform its hardest, least glamorous, and most important task to higher standards.

---

* Replacing the current requirement that six committees receive notice of covert activities with the larger jurisdiction of such a single body of congressional trustees of intelligence incurs some risks. They are well conveyed by Senator Hollins' characterization of the behavior of the Armed Services Subcommittee on Intelligence: "They told them and they told them and they told them, and what did they do? They just squatted on it." Broader composition and rotation of membership, together with the changed congressional attitudes that have followed recent revelations, should minimize those risks.

Chapter 10

Meeting the Challenge

WE began this book with the commonplace observation that the U.S. government's recent performance in foreign affairs leaves much to be desired. The chapters above present our answer to the question why. We acknowledge that the problems of foreign policy making are extraordinarily difficult (and likely to become more so); that human beings are fallible (and unlikely to become less so); and that a host of other intractable factors have contributed to the unhappy record of the recent past. But there is one factor that seems both critical to that record and amenable to change: the disorganization of the U.S. government for the conduct of foreign policy. It is a major theme of this book that organization matters—decisively in some instances, importantly in almost all—and that, unless substantial reforms are undertaken, the nation will continue to find the gears of foreign policy machinery failing to mesh with the problems the external world presents.

In our view, current organizational arrangements embody three principal defects. First, they are *out of balance*. They favor immediate results over long-range objectives, policy making over policy implementation, maintenance of the status quo over management of change, and narrow military and economic concerns over broader foreign policy considerations. Second, they bring *too little competence* to bear on complex issues: likely foreign developments are poorly assessed, obstacles in implementation are neglected, and insufficient technical expertise is devoted to the advancement of general foreign policy perspectives. Perhaps most fatally, current arrangements make almost inevitable the *disintegration* of policy: they neglect the many-sidedness of issues like oil or nuclear energy, fail to assure careful assessments of costs and benefits on all dimensions, and lack the capacity to insure that the decentralized actions of diverse agencies bear some consistent relation to each other, and cumulatively serve the nation's interests. We have not presented the full record of the recent past, but have tried to illustrate these inadequacies with examples from recent events. We have also proposed a large number of organizational reforms aimed at these deficiencies. It remains to consider whether our prescriptions fit the diagnosis, and to what extent they are feasible.

Virtually all of our principal proposals address in varying ways the crucial problem of integration—of drawing national policy from a system of broadly dispersed power. In general, these proposals seek to enlarge the forums in which issues are analyzed and decisions justified, without further diffusing the power to take action. This is the underlying principle of ExCab, of the integrated White House staff, of the Interdependence Committees of the Congress, and of the various proposals for earlier, closer and more continuous interaction between the Executive and the Legislature. While the particular proposals have only been sketched out here, and thus may well be inadequate or incomplete, the goal toward which they reach seems to us clearly right. They would substantially enlarge the likelihood that centers of authority throughout the government understood the links between their own concerns and the larger needs and purposes of the nation. And they would improve the ability of the President and Congress to appreciate the diverse interests affected by foreign policy making as well as to view those interests against larger national objectives.

To fill the gaps in competence in policy making, we have urged that the President invest the effort and the political capital to recruit and appoint as Secretaries of ExCab departments persons of genuine distinction, competence, and strength —capable of both counseling a President and of managing large departments—and that those officials be given the mandate and the freedom to make appointments of comparable quality at lower levels. Specific competences—those of foreign assessment and economic and political-military analysis in the Department of State, for example—would be strengthened by particular reforms while a number of changes should diminish the most deepseated impediments to competent decision making: the quiet civil war between the appointive and permanent governments.

Imbalances in decision making would be mitigated in part by the measures addressed mainly to better integration: wider forums in the Executive and Congress would in themselves clarify the relative importance of the various interests affected by major decisions. Further improvement would result from the adoption by the Department of State of the advocacy role we have proposed. A vigorous department, bringing to U.S. policy debate a sharper sense of likely developments abroad and their long-run implications for the U.S., would remedy the largest single imbalance in current decision making, the tendency to slight the importance of developments beyond our shores.

Such reforms will not be easy to accomplish. Yet they should prove far more feasible than others that might have comparable effect. The proposals we have made are largely informal. They require little statutory change, few transfers of authority, no revolutions in motivation or denials of self-interest. Many could be accomplished by a determined President acting alone.* A President committed to linking key Cabinet officers to himself and to each other could find worthy individuals and appoint them. A President who wanted to shrink the size and limit the functions of the White House staff and to integrate now separate presidential staffs would find such changes manageable. A President who wished to engage congressional leaders in steady informal consultation (especially if they were of the same party) would find this opportunity ready to be seized. Redefining the functions of the State Department and mobilizing the competence to fit those functions will be more difficult, but it is a change long overdue and one for which the department is partially ready. Rebuilding effective relations between the appointive and permanent governments will be far harder, requiring steady, patient effort for a decade. But it will certainly prove easier over the long run than the continued attempt to govern without the government. Other changes—Interdependence committees in the Congress, further reform in the Intelligence community, attention to problems of implementation—will also be difficult. But none are impossible and public frustration with government is likely to support far more ambitious change. The time, in short, is ripe.

---

* The President's authority to reorganize executive departments subject to Congressional veto within 60 days lapsed in 1973, a victim of Watergate. It should be restored.[1]

Notes

Preface

1. *New York Times*, 1 February 1976.

Chapter 1: The Argument: Organization Matters

1. See Forrest R. Frank, "CBW: 1962–67; 1967–68; 1969–72," in *Report of the Commission on the Organization of the Government for the Conduct of Foreign Policy* (hereinafter cited as Murphy Commission Report), Appendix K: "Adequacy of Current Organization: Defense and Arms Control," app. vol. 4 (Washington, D.C.: U.S. Govt. Printing Office, 1975), pp. 305–24.

2. U.S. Cabinet Task Force on Oil Import Control, *The Oil Import Question* (Washington, D.C.: U.S. Govt. Printing Office, 1970), pp. 128, 33.

3. Ibid., p. 69.

4. Ibid., p. 129.

5. William O. Doub and Joseph M. Dukert, "Making Nuclear Energy Safe and Secure," *Foreign Affairs* 53, no. 4 (July 1975): 756.

6. John S. Foster, "Nuclear Weapons," *Encyclopedia Americana* (New York: Americana Corp., 1973), 20: 520; quoted in Mason Willrich and Theodore Taylor, *Nuclear Theft: Risks and Safeguards* (Cambridge, Mass.: Ballinger, 1974), p. 7.

7. See "How Israel Got the Bomb," *Time*, 12 April 1976.

8. Quoted in *New York Times*, 5 January 1976.

9. For a fuller discussion of the nuclear power/nuclear proliferation problem, see Committee on Economic Development, "Nuclear Energy and National Security" (forthcoming).

10. For additional discussions of the extent to which organization shapes policy, see Morton H. Halperin, *Bureaucratic Politics and Foreign Policy* (Washington, D.C.: Brookings Institution, 1974), and Henry Kissinger, "Domestic Structure and Foreign Policy," *Daedalus* 95 (Spring 1966): 503–529; for a contrary view, see Stephen A. Krasner, "Are Bureaucracies Important?" *Foreign Policy* 7 (Summer 1972): 159–179; and Robert Art, "Bureaucratic Politics and American Foreign Policy: A Critique," *Policy Sciences* 4, no. 4 (December 1973): 467–90.

Our definition of organization is not, of course, the only one. But it is worthwhile to note that explicit definitions are often avoided in discussions of the subject. The classic work in the field of organization theory, March and Simon's *Organizations*, opens with a refusal to define the term: ". . . we need not trouble ourselves about the precise lines to be drawn around an organization or the exact distinction between an 'organization' and a 'nonorganization.' We are dealing with empirical phenomena, and the world has an uncomfortable way of not permitting itself to be fitted into clean classifications." See James G. March and Herbert A. Simon, *Organizations* (New York: John Wiley and Sons, 1958), p. 1.

11. Edward K. Hamilton, "Summary Report: Principal Lessons of the Past Decade and Thoughts on the Next," in Murphy Commission Report, Appendix H: "Case Studies on U.S. Foreign Economic Policy: 1965–74," app. vol. 3 (Washington, D.C.: U.S. Govt. Printing Office, 1975), pp. 7–8.

Chapter 2: The Problems: Recent Cases

1. Perhaps the most telling critique of the broad lines of American foreign policy to 1968 is Henry Kissinger's "Central Choices in American Foreign Policy" in Kermit Gordon, ed., *Agenda for the Nation* (Washington, D.C.: Brookings Institution, 1968); a related commentary on problems of alliance policy is Francis M. Bator's "Alliance Politics: the U.S. and Western Europe" in the same volume. Critiques of more recent economic policy include C. Fred Bergsten, *Toward a New International Economic Order: Selected Papers of C. Fred Bergsten, 1972–1974* (Lexington, Mass.: Lexington Books, 1975); Edward F. Fried, "Foreign Economic Policy: The Search for a Strategy," in Henry Owen, ed., *The Next Phase in Foreign Policy* (Washington: Brookings Institution, 1973); Paul C. Warnke, "Apes on a Treadmill," *Foreign Policy* 18 (Spring 1975): 12–29; Barry M. Blechman, "Toward a New Consensus in U.S. Defense Policy," in Henry Owen and Charles Schultze, eds., *Agenda for the Decade Ahead* (Washington: Brookings Institution, 1976); George W. Ball, *Diplomacy for a Crowded World* (Boston: Little, Brown, 1976); Stanley Hoffman, "Weighing the Balance of Power," *Foreign Affairs* 50, no. 4 (July 1972): 618–43; Stanley Hoffman, "Will the Balance Balance at Home?" *Foreign Policy* 7 (Summer 1972): 60–87; Stanley Hoffman, "The Elusiveness of Modern Power," *International Journal*, Spring 1975; Zbigniew Brzezinski, "America in a Hostile World," *Foreign Policy* 23 (Summer 1976): 65–96; Zbigniew Brzezinski, "The Deceptive Structure of Peace," *Foreign Policy* 14 (Spring 1974): 35–56; Zbigniew Brzezinski, "The Balance of Power Delusion," *Foreign Policy* 7 (Summer 1972): 54–59; Zbigniew Brzezinski, "U.S. Foreign Policy: The Search for a Focus," *Foreign Affairs* 51, no. 4 (July 1973): 708–27.

2. See Gregory F. Treverton, "'Offsets' and American Force Levels in Germany: 1966, 1967, 1969," in Murphy Commission Report, Appendix K: "Adequacy of Current Organization: Defense and Arms Control," app. vol. 4 (Washington, D.C.: U.S. Govt. Printing Office, 1975), pp. 240–51.

3. Quoted in Stephen S. Rosenfeld, "The Panama Negotiations—A Close-Run Thing," *Foreign Affairs* 54, no. 1 (October 1975): 1.

4. Ibid., p. 2; also Thomas M. Franck and Edward Weisband, "Panama Paralysis," *Foreign Policy* 21, Winter 1975–76, p. 185.

5. U.S. Congress, Senate, Resolution no. 301, 93rd Cong., 2nd sess., 29 March 1974.

6. U.S., Congress, House, 94th Cong., 1st sess. October 2, 1975, H. Rept. 94–527.

7. Quoted in Franck and Weisband, "Panama Paralysis," p. 169.

8. See Linda S. Braebner, "The New Economic Policy, 1971," in Murphy Commission Report, Appendix H: "Case Studies on U.S. Foreign Economic Policy: 1965–74," app. vol. 3 (Washington, D.C.: U.S. Govt. Printing Office, 1975), pp. 160–84.

9. U.S. Bureau of the Census, *Statistical Abstracts of the United States 1975* (Washington, D.C.: U.S. Govt. Printing Office, 1975), p. 799.

10. See Henry S. Rowen, "Formulating Strategic Doctrine," in Murphy Commission Report, Appendix K: "Adequacy of Current Organization: Defense and Arms Control," app. vol. 4 (Washington, D.C.: U.S. Govt. Printing Office, 1975), pp. 217–34.

11. *New York Times*, 11 January 1974.

12. *U.S. Foreign Policy for the Seventies*, 18 February 1970 (Washington, D.C.: U.S. Govt. Printing Office), p. 122.

13. See Gregory F. Treverton, "United States Policy-Making Toward Peru: The IPC Affair," in Murphy Commission Report, Appendix I: "Conduct of Routine Relations," app. vol. 3 (Washington, D.C.: U.S. Govt. Printing Office, 1975), pp. 205–11.

14. See Anne Karalekas, "Fighting in South Vietnam" and "Bombing North Vietnam," in Murphy Commission Report, Appendix K: "Adequacy of Current Organization: Defense and Arms Control," app. vol. 4, (Washington, D.C.: U.S. Govt. Printing Office, 1975), pp. 383–416.

15. Robert W. Komer, *Bureaucracy Does Its Thing: Institutional Constraints on U.S.-GVN Performance in Vietnam*, Defense Advanced Research Projects Agency Report no. R-967-ARPA (Santa Monica, Calif.: RAND Corporation, 1972).

16. Quoted in Robert L. Galluchi, *Neither Peace Nor Honor: The Politics of American Military Policy in Vietnam* (Baltimore: Johns Hopkins University Press, 1975), p. 84.

17. U.S. Congress, Senate, Committee on Foreign Relations, *The Geneva Protocol of 1925*, Hearings, 91st Cong., 1st sess. (1971), p. 186.

18. For further evidence on this point, see Adam Yarmolinsky, "The Military Establishment (or How Political Problems Become Military Problems," *Foreign Policy* 1 (Winter 1970–71: 78–97; and *The Military Establishment: Its Impacts on American Society* (New York: Harper and Row, 1971); Morton H. Halperin, "The Good, the Bad, and the Wasteful," *Foreign Policy* 6 (Spring 1972): 69–83; and Graham T. Allison, "Overview of Findings and Recommendations from Defense and Arms Control Cases," Murphy Commission Report, Appendix K: "Adequacy of Current Organization: Defense and Arms Control," app. vol. 4 (Washington, D.C.: U.S. Govt. Printing Office, 1975), p. 23f.

19. For broader discussions of problems of implementation in various governmental settings, see Anthony Downs, *Inside Bureaucracy* (Boston: Little, Brown, 1967); Graham T. Allison, *Essence of Decision: Explaining the Cuban Missile Crisis* (Boston: Little, Brown, 1971), p. 89f.; I. M. Destler, *Presidents, Bureaucrats, and Foreign Policy* (Princeton, N.J.: Princeton University Press, 1972); Morton Halperin, *Bureaucratic*

Politics and Foreign Policy (Washington, D.C.: Brookings Institution, 1974), ch. 13; and Jeffrey L. Pressman and Aaron Wildavsky, *Implementation: How Great Expectations in Washington are Dashed in Oakland* (Berkeley: University of California Press, 1973).

20. Before entering the government, Henry Kissinger commented extensively on this problem of bureaucratic inertia: "The purpose of bureaucracy is to devise a standard operating procedure which can cope effectively with most problems. . . . Bureaucracy becomes an obstacle when what it defines as routine does not address the most significant range of issues or when its prescribed mode of action proves irrelevant to the problem." See "Domestic Structure and Foreign Policy," *Daedalus* 95 (Spring 1966): 507.

21. For similar views on the necessity of integrating the various strands of foreign policy, see Stanley Hoffman, *Gulliver's Troubles, or the Setting of American Foreign Policy* (New York: McGraw-Hill, 1968); John F. Campbell, *The Foreign Affairs Fudge Factory* (New York: Basic Books, 1971); and Charles Yost, *The Conduct and Misconduct of Foreign Affairs* (New York: Random House, 1972). Other observers, particularly in the wake of the Presidential abuses of power over the past decade, have argued that too much coordination is even more to be feared than not enough. See Robert L. Rothstein, *Planning, Prediction, and Policy Making in Foreign Affairs: Theory and Practice* (Boston: Little, Brown, 1972); Stanley Hoffman, "Choices," *Foreign Policy* 12, (Fall 1973), pp. 3–42; and Lloyd and Suzanne Rudolph, "Summary Report," in Murphy Commission Report, Appendix V, "Coordination in Complex Settings," app. vol. 7 (Washington, D.C.: U.S. Govt. Printing Office, 1975), p. 111f.

Chapter 3:   The Future Will Be Harder

1. For broadly similar views of the future, see, for example, Zbigniew Brzezinski, "The International Community in the Next Two Decades," and Robert R. Bowie, "The Tasks Ahead for U.S. Foreign Policy," both appearing in Murphy Commission Report, Appendix A: "Foreign Policy for the Future," app. vol. 1 (Washington, D.C.: U.S. Govt. Printing Office, 1975), pp. 11–19 and 20–31. For an excellent brief exploration of the organizational implications of the future foreign policy agenda, see Adam Yarmolinsky, "Organizing for Interdependence: The Role of Government," paper prepared for the National Commission on Coping with Interdependence, Aspen Institute, Aspen, Colorado, January 1976.

2. Economic Statistics Bureau of Washington, D.C., *The Handbook of Basic Economic Statistics*, January 1976, pp. 198, 199, 225; and *Monthly Supplement*, March 1976, p. 16.

3. Joseph S. Nye, "Multinational Corporations in World Politics," *Foreign Affairs* 53, no. 1 (October 1974): 160.

4. Statement of C. Fred Bergsten before U.S. Senate Committee on Banking, Housing, and Urban Affairs, Subcommittee on International Finance, 94th Cong., 2nd sess., 16 June 1975.

5. For more on the problems of economic interdependence and their implications for the U.S. government, see C. Fred Bergsten, *Toward a*

New International Economic Order: Selected Papers of C. Fred Bergsten,
1972–1974 (Lexington, Mass.: Lexington Books, 1975); C. Fred Bergsten
and Lawrence B. Krause, eds., World Politics and International Economics (Washington, D.C.: Brookings Institution, 1975); Richard N.
Cooper, The Economics of Interdependence (New York: McGraw-Hill,
1968); and Cooper, ed., A Reordered World: Emerging International
Economic Problems (Washington, D.C.: Potomac Associates, 1973); and
Edward F. Fried, "Foreign Economic Policy: The Search for a Strategy,"
in Henry Owen, ed., The Next Phase in Foreign Policy (Washington,
D.C.: Brookings Institution, 1973).

6. For an excellent review of the implications of world physical interdependence, see Robert O. Keohane and Joseph S. Nye, "Organizing for
Global Environmental and Resource Interdependence," in Murphy Commission Report, Appendix B, "The Management of Global Issues," app.
vol. 1 (Washington, D.C.: U.S. Govt. Printing Office, 1975), pp. 46–64.
On the world food problem, and the U.S. government's response to it,
see Lester L. Brown, By Bread Alone (New York: Praeger, 1974); Jean
Mayer, "Coping With Famine," Foreign Affairs 53, no. 1 (October
1974): 98–120; and Emma Rothschild, "Food Politics," Foreign Affairs
54, no. 2 (January 1976): 285–307. On the world ecological situation,
see Barry Commoner, The Closing Circle: Nature, Man and Technology
(New York: Knopf, 1971).

7. Marina v.N. Whitman, "Leadership without Hegemony," Foreign
Policy 20 (Fall 1975).

8. Statement of C. Fred Bergsten before Subcommittee on International Finance.

9. This data was supplied by the Office of International Conferences,
Department of State.

10. For a review of the implications of multilateralism for U.S. foreign policy, see Murphy Commission Report, Appendix C, "Multilateral
Diplomacy," app. vol. 1 (Washington, D.C.: U.S. Govt. Printing Office,
1975), pp. 262, 295, esp. paper by Harlan Cleveland, "The Management
of Multilaternalism." Also see Stanley Hoffman, "Weighing the Balance
of Power," Foreign Affairs 50, no. 4 (July 1972): 618–43; and "Choices,"
Stanley Hoffman, Gulliver's Troubles, or the Setting of American Foreign
Policy (New York: McGraw-Hill, 1968); Foreign Policy 12, (Fall 1973).

11. For more on this point, see Hoffman, Gulliver's Troubles, op. cit.,
and Louis J. Halle, "Does War Have A Future?" Foreign Affairs 52, no.
1 (October 1973): 20–34.

12. John E. Rielly, ed., "American Public Opinion and U.S. Foreign
Policy 1975" (Chicago Council on Foreign Relations, February 1975).

13. Patrick H. Caddell and Albert C. Pierce, "Alienation and Politics:
What Is the Electorate Telling Us?" (Cambridge Research Institute,
1975), p. 9.

14. On the problem of restoring confidence and trust in the U.S.
government, see esp. Bayless Manning, The Conduct of United States
Foreign Policy in the Nation's Third Century (Claremont, Calif.: Clare-
mont College, 1975), and "Goals, Ideology and Foreign Policy," Foreign
Affairs 54, no. 2 (January 1976): 271–84. See also Anthony Lake,
"Lying Around Washington," Foreign Policy 2 (Spring 1971): 91–113;
Simon Serfaty, "No More Dissent," Foreign Policy 11 (Summer 1973):
144–158; Nicholas deB. Katzenbach, "Foreign Policy, Public Opinion,

and Secrecy," *Foreign Affairs* 53, no. 1 (October 1973): 1–19; and McGeorge Bundy, "Towards an Open Foreign Policy," in Murphy Commission Report, Appendix A: "Foreign Policy for the Future," app. vol. 1 (Washington, D.C.: U.S. Govt. Printing Office, 1975), pp. 32–39.

Chapter 4:   The President's Tasks

1.   Richard E. Neustadt, *Presidential Power*, 3rd ed. (New York: John Wiley and Sons, 1976), p. 280.
2.   Among the most useful discussions of the organization of the Presidency are Neustadt's, *Presidential Power*, Keith C. Clark and Laurence J. Legere, eds., *The President and the Management of National Security* (New York: Praeger, 1969); I. M. Destler, *Presidents, Bureaucrats, and Foreign Policy: The Politics of Organizational Reform* (Princeton, N.J.: Princeton University Press, 1972); Arthur M. Schlesinger, Jr., *The Imperial Presidency* (Boston: Houghton-Mifflin, 1973); Emmet John Hughes, *The Living Presidency* (New York: Coward, McCann and Geoghegan, 1973); and Joseph A. Califano, Jr., *A Presidential Nation* (New York: Norton, 1975).
3.   The figures for 1947–50 are drawn from *Statistical Abstracts of the United States 1952*, pp. 10, 345; for 1955–70 from *Statistical Abstracts 1975*, pp. 5, 242; and for 1975–76 from US Civil Service Comm., *Monthly Release of Federal Civilian Manpower Statistics*, May 1976, pp. 5, 12, and US Bureau of the Census, "Estimates of the Population of the United States to April 1, 1976," *Population Estimates and Projections*, May 1976.

Year	Exec. Branch employment (1,000s)	US population (1,000s)	Exec. Branch employment per 1,000 pop.
1947	2,143	143,375	15.0
1950	2,069	151,240	13.7
1955	2,376	165,931	14.3
1960	2,403	180,671	13.1
1965	2,507	194,303	12.8
1970	2,891	204,878	14.1
1975	2,816	213,135	13.2
1976	2,808	214,850	13.1

4.   Neustadt, *Presidential Power*, p. 77.
5.   Testimony of Francis M. Bator before U.S. Congress, House, Committee on Foreign Affairs, Subcommittee on Foreign Economic Policy, *U.S. Foreign Economic Policy: Implications for the Organization of the Executive Branch*, 92nd Cong., 2nd sess., 1972, pp. 109–10. The definition of the problem of executive organization as the issue of central coordination of decentralized operation is Bator's.
6.   *Life*, 17 January 1969, p. 62B; quoted in Destler, *Presidents, Bureaucrats, and Foreign Policy*, p. 90.
7.   Readers interested in descriptions of these systems and a more extended analysis of their characteristic performance are referred to

Graham Allison, "Overview of Findings and Recommendations from Defense and Arms Control Cases," Murphy Commission Report, Appendix K: "Adequacy of Current Organization: Defense and Arms Control," vol. 4 (Washington, D.C.: U.S. Govt. Printing Office, 1975), pp. 35ff.

8. Bator testimony in U.S. Foreign Economic Policy, p. 114.

9. For an elaboration of this point, see Destler, *Presidents, Bureaucrats and Foreign Policy*, 1974 ed., pp. 301 ff.

10. Pub. L. 80–253, 61 Stat. 495.

11. Quoted in Hughes, *The Living Presidency*, p. 335. For a fuller discussion of the Cabinet, see Richard F. Fenno, Jr., *The President's Cabinet* (Cambridge, Mass.: Harvard University Press, 1963).

12. Quoted in Neustadt, *Presidential Power*, p. 107.

13. A similar body was proposed by former chairman of the Joint Chiefs of Staff Maxwell D. Taylor in "The Exposed Flank of National Security," *Orbis* 18, no. 4 (Winter 1975): 1011 ff.

14. See David K. Hall, "The 'Custodian-Manager' of the Policymaking Process," in Murphy Commission Report, Appendix D: "The Use of Information," app. vol. 2 (Washington, D.C.: U.S. Govt. Printing Office, 1975), pp. 100–19.

15. U.S. Congress, Senate, Committee on the Judiciary, Subcommittee on the Separation of Powers, *Executive Privilege: The Withholding of Information by the Executive*, Hearings, 92nd Cong., 1st sess., 1971, p. 17.

16. For example, see President Nixon's proposal of February 1971, "The Federal Executive Service," reprinted in *Public Administration Review*, March/April 1971, pp. 235–52.

17. Myers vs. United States, 272 U.S. 52, 293 (1926).

18. Quoted in Robert A. Pastor, "Coping with Congress's Foreign Policy," *Foreign Service Journal*, December 1975, p. 16.

19. Neustadt, *Presidential Power*, pp. 115–122.

Chapter 5:   The Role of Congress

1. Richard E. Neustadt, *Presidential Power*, 3rd ed. (New York: John Wiley & Sons, 1976), p. 77. For recent discussions of Congress' role in foreign policy making, see Alton Frye, *A Responsible Congress: The Politics of National Security* (New York: McGraw-Hill, 1975). Also see Louis Fisher, *The President and Congress* (New York: The Free Press, 1972), esp. Chs. 6 and 7; David B. Truman, ed., *The Congress and America's Future*, 2nd ed. (Englewood Cliffs, N.J.: Prentice-Hall, 1973); and Committee for Economic Development, "Congressional Decision Making for National Security," Sept. 1974.

2. In *The Complete Jefferson*, ed. S. K. Padover (New York: Duell, Sloan, and Pearce, 1943), p. 138. Cited in Arthur M. Schlesinger, *The Imperial Presidency* (Boston: Houghton-Mifflin, 1973), p. 14.

3. See esp. *The Federalist*, no. 64 (Jay).

4. Schlesinger, *The Imperial Presidency*, p. 14.

5. See David Halberstam, *The Best and the Brightest* (New York: Random House, 1972), pp. 146, 528–29; see also Adam Yarmolinsky,

The Military Establishment: Its Impact on American Security (New York: Harper & Row, 1971), p. 130.

6. Allen Schick, "The Supply and Demand for Analysis on Capitol Hill" (Congressional Research Service, 1975), p. 14.

7. *The Federalist*, no. 75.

8. Les Aspin, "The Defense Budget and Foreign Policy: The Role of Congress," in *Daedalus*, Summer 1975, p. 163.

9. Walter F. Mondale, *The Accountability of Power: Toward A Responsible Presidency* (New York: David McKay & Co., 1975).

10. Clem Miller, *Member of the House*, John Baker, ed. (New York: Scribner's, 1962), p. 110.

11. Quoted in Robert Sherrill, *Why They Call It Politics* (New York: Harcourt, Brace, Jovanovich, 1972), pp. 104–105.

12. Aspin, "The Defense Budget and Foreign Policy," pp. 164–65.

13. Ibid., p. 167.

14. *Congressional Record*, 31 July 1967, Senate, 90th Cong., 1st sess., p. S10488. Quoted in Schlesinger, *The Imperial Presidency*, pp. 327–28.

15. James Bryce, *Modern Democracies* (New York, 1921), vol. 2, chap. 61. Quoted in Schlesinger, *The Imperial Presidency*, p. 282.

16. Woodrow Wilson, *Congressional Government* (New York: Meridian Books, 1956), pp. 195, 198.

17. Mondale, *The Accountability of Power*, p. 100.

18. We are indebted for the outlines of these proposals to Morton H. Halperin and Daniel Hoffman; see their forthcoming book on secrecy and national security policy.

19. Robert O. Keohane and Joseph S. Nye, "Organizing for Global Environmental and Resource Interdependence," in Murphy Commission Report, Appendix B: "The Management of Global Issues," app. vol. 1 (Washington, D.C.: Govt. Printing Office, 1975).

20. Committee for Economic Development, "Congressional Decision Making for National Security," pp. 23–24.

Chapter 6: *A Function for State*

1. Quoted in Arthur Schlesinger, Jr., *A Thousand Days* (Boston: Houghton-Mifflin, 1965), p. 431.

2. Among the more important official studies of the structure and performance of the State Department are: Hoover Commission, *Task Force Report on Foreign Affairs* (Washington, D.C.: U.S. Govt. Printing Office, 1949); William Y. Elliott et al., *United States Foreign Policy: Its Organization and Control* (New York: Columbia University Press, 1952); H. Field Haviland, Jr., et al., *The Formulation and Administration of United States Foreign Policy*, a report for the Committee on Foreign Relations, U.S. Senate, Committee on Government Operations, Subcommittee on National Policy Machinery; *Organizing for National Security*, 3 vols. (Washington, D.C.: U.S. Govt. Printing Office, 1961); Herter Committee, *Personnel for the New Diplomacy* (Washington: Carnegie Endowment, 1962); and American Foreign Service Association (AFSA), Committee on Career Principles, *Toward a Modern Diplomacy* (Washington: AFSA, 1968). Other noteworthy studies include: Stanley Hoff-

man, *Gulliver's Troubles, or the Setting of American Foreign Policy* (New York: McGraw-Hill, 1968); John Harr, *Professional Diplomat* (Princeton, N.J.: Princeton University Press, 1969); John F. Campbell, *The Foreign Affairs Fudge Factory* (New York: Basic Books, 1971); Charles W. Yost, "The Instruments of American Foreign Policy," *Foreign Affairs* 50, no. 1 (October 1971): 59–68; William Macomber, *The Angels' Game: A Handbook of Modern Diplomacy* (New York: Stein and Day, 1975); and Donald P. Warwick, *A Theory of Public Bureaucracy: Politics, Personality, and Organization in the State Department* (Cambridge, Mass.: Harvard University Press, 1975).

3. Statement of the Honorable George F. Kennan before the Commission on the Organization of the Government for the Conduct of Foreign Policy, 24 September 1974.

4. President Johnson's Cabinet-level Task Force on Government Organization (the Heineman Commission), for example, recommended in 1967 a reorganization of State to make it "preeminently the director and coordinator, for and on behalf of the President, of all U.S. foreign and national security policy." Its conclusion accorded with those of virtually all previous official commissions and study groups. Among individual commentators, I. M. Destler, Charles Yost, and John F. Campbell have argued for a "State-centered" organizational strategy. See Destler, *Presidents, Bureaucrats, and Foreign Policy* (Princeton, N.J.: Princeton Univ. Press, 1972); Campbell, *The Foreign Affairs Fudge Factory*; and Yost, "The Instruments of American Foreign Policy."

5. Destler, *Presidents, Bureaucrats, and Foreign Policy*, 1974 ed., p. 161.

6. Lawrence E. Fouraker and John M. Stopford, "Organizational Structure and the Multinational Strategy," *Administrative Science Quarterly* 13, no. 1 (June 1968): 47–64.

7. See Richard E. Neustadt and Jay Urwitz, "The Skybolt Affair, 1962," in Murphy Commission Report, Appendix K: "Adequacy of Current Organization: Defense and Arms Control," app. vol. 4 (Washington, D.C.: U.S. Govt. Printing Office, 1975), pp. 259–65.

8. Ibid., p. 271. A study performed for the Murphy Commission found among the more general deficiencies of Foreign Service reporting: inadequate feedback and direction from Washington to the field, poor analytical quality, and excessive quantity. See William D. Coplin, et al., "Towards the Improvement of Foreign Service Field Reporting," Murphy Commission Report, Appendix E, app. vol. 2 (Washington, D.C.: U.S. Govt. Printing Office, 1975), pp. 137–208. For a more detailed analysis of the organizational roots of shortcomings in foreign assessment, see Susan Irving, "Of Mice, Cages, and Cheese: Foreign Assessment and the Foreign Service Personnel System," Ph.D. Thesis, John F. Kennedy School of Government, Harvard University, January 1976.

9. See Lloyd I. Rudolph and Suzanne H. Rudolph, "The Coordination of Complexity in South Asia," in Murphy Commission Report, Appendix V: "Coordination in Complex Settings," app. vol. 7 (Washington, D.C.: U.S. Govt. Printing Office, 1975), p. 143.

10. Quoted in Robert A. Pastor, "Congress' Impact on Latin America: Is There a Madness in the Method?" in Murphy Commission Report, Appendix I: "Conduct of Routine Relations," app. vol. 3 (Washington, D.C.: U.S. Govt. Printing Office, 1975), p. 170.

Chapter 7: "Foreign" Economics

1. Quoted in Richard N. Cooper, "Introduction," to Cooper, ed., *A Reordered World: Emerging International Economic Problems* (Washington, D.C.: Potomac Associates, 1973), p. xxiv.

2. For the most useful general discussion of the organizational dimensions of foreign economic policy problems, see the testimony of Francis M. Bator before the U.S. Congress, House, Committee on Foreign Affairs, Subcommittee on Foreign Economic Policy, *U.S. Foreign Economic Policy: Implications for the Organization of the Executive Branch*, Hearings, 92nd Congress, 2nd session (1972), p. 107f. Also see Edward K. Hamilton, ed., "Case Studies on a Decade of U.S. Foreign Economic Policy: 1965–1974," Murphy Commission Report Appendix H; and Murphy Commission Report Appendix J: "Foreign Economic Policy," both contained in app. vol. 3 (Washington, D.C.: U.S. Govt. Printing Office, 1975) pp. 1–196 and 297–344.

Excellent more general studies include, Francis M. Bator, "The Political Economics of International Money," *Foreign Affairs* 48; no. 1 (October 1968) pp. 51–67; C. Fred Bergsten, "Reforming the Dollar: An International Monetary Policy for the U.S.," Council on Foreign Relations Occasional Paper No. 2, September 1972; and *Toward a New International Economic Order: Selected Papers of C. Fred Bergsten 1972–1974* (Lexington, Mass.: Lexington Books, 1975), esp. Chapter 34: "Organizing for Foreign Economic Policy," and Chapter 35: "Organizing for a World of Resource Shortages." See also C. Fred Bergsten and Lawrence B. Krause, eds., *World Politics and International Economics* (Washington, D.C.: Brookings Institution, 1975), esp. chapter by Bergsten, Robert O. Keohane, and Joseph S. Nye, Jr., "International Economics and International Politics: A Framework for Analysis"; Richard N. Cooper, *The Economics of Interdependence* (New York: McGraw-Hill, 1968), and Cooper, ed., *A Reordered World*. Also see Edward R. Fried, "Foreign Economic Policy: The Search for a Strategy," in Henry Owen, ed., *The Next Phase in Foreign Policy* (Washington, D.C.: Brookings Institution, 1973); and Anthony M. Solomon, "Administration of a Multi-Purpose Diplomacy," *Public Administration Review* November/December 1969.

3. William Safire, *Before the Fall: An Insider's View of the Pre-Watergate White House* (Garden City, N.Y.: Doubleday, 1975) pp. 513–514.

4. See Edward F. Graziano, "Commodity Export Controls: The Soybean Case, 1973," in Murphy Commission Report, Appendix H: "Case Studies on a Decade of U.S. Foreign Economic Policy."

5. See Richard Huff and Robert E. Klitgaard, "Limiting Exports on National Security Grounds," in Murphy Commission Report, Appendix K: "Adequacy of Current Organization: Defense and Arms Control," app. vol. 4 (Washington, D.C.: U.S. Govt. Printing Office, 1975).

6. Rogers Morton, "The United States' Role in East-West Trade: Problems and Prospects" (U.S. Department of Commerce, August 1975) p. 6.

7. See C. Fred Bergsten, "Interdependence and the Reform of International Institutions," *International Organization* 30; no. 2 (Spring 1976) pp. 361–372; Miriam Camps, "The Management of Interdependence: A Preliminary View," a Council on Foreign Relations paper, 1974; and Adam Yarmolinsky, "Organizing for Interdependence: The Role of Government" (Aspen, Colo.: Aspen Institute for Humanistic Studies, 1976).

Chapter 8:   Providing for the Common Defense

1. Quoted in Arthur M. Schlesinger, Jr., *The Imperial Presidency*, (Boston: Houghton-Mifflin, 1973), p. 401.

2. For a detailed review of recent performance, see Graham T. Allison, ed., "Adequacy of Current Organization: Defense and Arms Control," Murphy Commission Report Appendix K, app. vol. 4 (Washington, D.C.: U.S. Govt. Printing Office, 1975). Other important studies of the defense establishment include: Paul Y. Hammond, *Organizing for Defense* (Princeton, N.J.: Princeton Univ. Press, 1961); Samuel P. Huntington, *The Common Defense: Strategic Problems in National Defense* (New York: Columbia Univ. Press, 1961); Keith C. Clark and Laurence J. Legere, eds., *The President and the Management of National Security* (New York: Praeger, 1969); Blue Ribbon Defense Panel ("Fitzhugh Report"), *Report to the President and the Secretary of Defense on the Department of Defense* (Washington, D.C.: U.S. Govt. Printing Office, 1970); Alain C. Enthoven and K. Wayne Smith, *How Much Is Enough?* (New York: Harper and Row, 1971); Adam Yarmolinsky, *The Military Establishment: Its Impacts on American Society* (New York: Harper and Row, 1971); and Morton H. Halperin, *Bureaucratic Politics and Foreign Policy* (Washington, D.C.: Brookings Institution, 1974).

3. Enthoven and Smith, *How Much Is Enough?* pp. 5–6.

4. Quoted in U.S. Congress, Senate, Committee on Foreign Relations, *United States Security Agreements and Committments Abroad*, Hearings, 91st Cong., 1st sess., 1969, 2: 2360.

5. Flora Lewis, "State, Pentagon Split on Commitments to Spain," *Washington Post*, 25 February 1969.

6. *U.S. Foreign Policy for the 1970s*, 18 February 1970, p. 122.

7. For a fuller discussion of the future of the marines, see Martin Binkin and Jeffrey Record, *Where Does the Marine Corps Go From Here?* (Washington, D.C.: Brookings Institution, 1976).

8. See Barry M. Blechman and Edward R. Fried, "Controlling the Defense Budget," *Foreign Affairs* 54; no. 2 (January 1976) 240, 244.

9. Ibid., p. 246.

10. See Martin Binkin, *The Military Pay Muddle* (Washington, D.C.: Brookings Institution, 1975).

11. *Aviation Week and Space Technology*, 31 August 1970, p. 7.

12. For more on the process of weapons acquisition, see J. A. Stockfisch, *Ploughshares into Swords: Managing the American Defense Establishment* (New York: Mason and Lipscomb, 1973); J. Ronald Fox, *Arming America: How the U.S. Buys Weapons* (Cambridge: Harvard Business School, 1974); and Frederic A. Morris, ed., "Acquiring Weap-

ons," in Murphy Commission Report, Appendix K: "Adequacy of Current Organization: Defense and Arms Control."

13. Blechman and Fried, "Controlling the Defense Budget," p. 240.

14. See Barry M. Blechman, *The Changing Soviet Navy* (Washington, D.C.: Brookings Institution, 1973); also see Michael T. Klare, "Superpower Rivalry At Sea," *Foreign Policy* 21 (Winter 1975–76) pp. 88–89.

15. Donald H. Rumsfeld, *Annual Defense Department Report, FY 1977* pp. 126–129.

16. See Robert F. Coulam, "The F-111," in Murphy Commission Report, Appendix K: "Adequacy of Current Organization: Defense and Arms Control," pp. 118–138.

17. Enthoven and Smith, *How Much Is Enough?*, pp. 307, 314. Also see Anne Karalekas, "Conducting Military Operations," in Murphy Commission Report, Appendix K: "Adequacy of Current Organization: Defense and Arms Control," pp. 437–440.

18. Blue Ribbon Defense Panel, *Report to the President and the Secretary of Defense.*

19. See Edwin A. Deagle, Jr., "NSSM-1," in Murphy Commission Report, Appendix K: "Adequacy of Current Organization: Defense and Arms Control," pp. 417–436.

20. U.S. Department of Commerce, Bureau of the Census, *Statistical Abstracts of the United States, 1975*, pp. 225, 316.

21. See Barry E. Carter and John D. Steinbruner, "Trident," in Murphy Commission Report, Appendix K: "Adequacy of Current Organization: Defense and Arms Control," pp. 175–182.

22. Binkin, *The Military Pay Muddle*, pp. 46–66; Blechman and Fried, "Controlling the Defense Budget," p. 247.

Chapter 9: Intelligence: Seizing the Opportunity

1. Among the most useful sources of background on the community are Harry Howe Ransom, *The Intelligence Establishment* (Cambridge, Mass.: Harvard University Press, 1970); Victor Marchetti and John D. Marks, *The CIA and the Cult of Intelligence* (New York: Alfred A. Knopf, 1974); and *Foreign and Military Intelligence*, Book 1 of the Final Report of the Select Committee to Study Governmental Operations with respect to Intelligence Activities, United States Senate (Washington, D.C.: U.S. Govt. Printing Office, 1976) [94th Congress, 2nd sess.].

2. See Patrick J. McGarvey, *CIA: The Myth and the Madness* (New York: Saturday Review Press, 1972), p. 40.

3. Lecture by John B. Lockhart, Esq., "The Relationship Between Secret Services and Government in a Modern State," Royal United Services Institute, 21 November 1973, p. 1.

4. Book 1, Final Report of the Select Committee cited, p. 76. For discussion of problems of intelligence bias generally, see pp. 73–83.

5. *Pentagon Papers*, Senator Gravel ed. (Boston: Beacon Press, 1971) 3: 295.

6. Ibid., 4: 168–69.

7. Ibid., p. 180.

8. Reprinted in U.S., Congress, *Congressional Record*, 10 May 1972, "Extensions of Remarks," pp. E5063–64. 92nd Cong., 2nd sess.
9. *Pentagon Papers*, 3: 353.
10. Ibid., 4: 71–74.
11. Ibid., p. 129.
12. Executive Order of February 18, 1976, "United States Foreign Intelligence Activities."
13. Book 1, Final Report, pp. 423–509.
14. John McCone was the first DCI to attempt to play a community management role. A former member of his staff has estimated that despite that effort, 90 percent of McCone's time was spent on issues relating to clandestine operations. What was left for the care, management and improvement of estimates? See Book 1, Final Report, p. 117.
15. See statement of former DCI James R. Schlesinger at pp. 94–95, Book 1, Final Report.

Chapter 10

1. Under the Reorganization Act of 1949 (63 Stat 203), reorganization plans became law 60 days after the President submitted them unless either chamber of Congress passed a resolution of disapproval. Congress had no opportunity to amend a plan after the President submitted it. Most executive reorganization in recent years proceeded under this authority. The Reorganization Act as amended in 1971 (85 Stat 574) expired on April 1, 1973.

Index

Index